CLAIRE CLAIRMONT

BY THE SAME AUTHOR

MARY SHELLEY
(OXFORD UNIVERSITY PRESS, 1938)

BYRON AND ALLEGRA

*From the original water-colour sketch
by H. Corbould.*

CLAIRE CLAIRMONT

Mother of Byron's Allegra

by

R. GLYNN GRYLLS

＊

JOHN MURRAY
ALBEMARLE STREET
LONDON

First Edition . . . 1939

Made and Printed in Great Britain by Butler & Tanner Ltd., Frome and London

CONTENTS

*The Author's acknowledgments will be found at the end of the book.
They are printed there because of their length and their necessary connection
with the sources of Bibliography.*

137486

LIST OF ILLUSTRATIONS

List of Illustrations

GENEALOGICAL TABLE

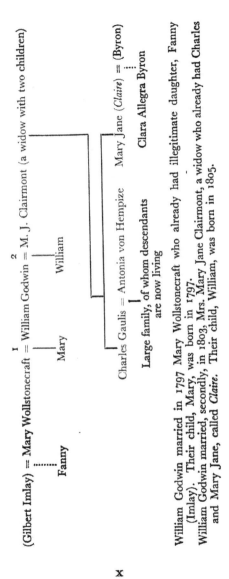

(Gilbert Imlay) = Mary Wollstonecraft = William Godwin = M. J. Clairmont (a widow with two children)
           1   2

Fanny   Mary   William

Charles Gaulis = Antonia von Hempize Mary Jane (*Claire*) = (Byron)

Large family, of whom descendants   Clara Allegra Byron
are now living

William Godwin married in 1797 Mary Wollstonecraft who already had illegitimate daughter, Fanny
(Imlay). Their child, Mary, was born in 1797.
William Godwin married, secondly, in 1803, Mrs. Mary Jane Clairmont, a widow who already had Charles
and Mary Jane, called *Claire*. Their child, William, was born in 1805.

x

PREFACE

THERE is always a temptation to be patronizing in biography ; the patronage of the dead by the quick.

> remember what you have
> no ghost ever had immured in his hall.

But that may be our only superiority. The Romantic of the 1820's is no more ridiculous than the Highbrow of the 1930's who has substituted the Oppression of the Capitalist Classes for the Tyranny of Kings, the " red steppes of freedom " for the resurgent Isles of Greece, or indignation at Italian occupation of the Tyrol for Austrian occupation of the Venetian Republic.

Other values remain ; Shelley's practical goodness that was never outrun by his principles, the redeeming last Act of Byron's shoddy pageant, the courage of the " romantic " Claire, for whom emotional adventure had not been shorn of risks. Our friends are still,

> . . . exultations, agonies,
> And love, and man's unconquerable mind.

* Explanatory comments and sources
are collected in the Notes at the end
with page references to the text.

Part One

THE GIRL

Maidens, like moths, are ever caught by glare.
BYRON, *Childe Harold*, I, 9.

I

SHE was happy when she could sing ; her voice rising over the chimneys and roof-tops of the dingy street, the words her own when they were strung together with any meaning at all, and the melody making up in joyousness what it lacked in form. For that was how she liked to sing ; crouching by the attic window with a book in her hand and no one to set her exercises or correct her time. She could look out across the tops of the houses opposite to the heights of Hampstead beyond and imagine herself far away from the school-room where the French lessons lay unfinished on the table and the piano reproached her for not practising. She could dream of what she would do if she were free from the tyranny of her home and living in a rural solitude with only books about her and the beauties of Nature ; waited on hand and foot by devoted servants and one day meeting a poet, a 'man of loneliness and mystery,' who would be consumed by a hopeless passion for her and write verses that she could sing. Her name would no longer be Mary Jane, but Constantia or Claire, and she would be gracious and beautiful, a Spanish ' dark-glancing daughter '—for not even in imagination could she see herself the pale fragile beauty of her ideals.

But " Jane, Jane," her mother would call up the stairs to set her to something useful, and she would have to slip her book away, for it was usually Lord Byron's *Corsair* that she read and Mamma did not like poetry. She had a prejudice against it and against philosophy since the literary marriage which had not come up to her expectations. She had thought that Godwin's fame would have gone with better circumstances and had not realized that a philosopher could be so improvident in his practical affairs.

But if she blamed herself for not having done better for her children, it did not improve her temper with them nor make her less hard put to it to keep up an appearance of impartiality between them and the other members of the family; and when she saw Jane's eyes grow sullen that could be so glowing when she was pleased, it rankled that she had to make her share the household work with Fanny. Fanny, she considered, was lucky to have a roof over her head at all, though she dared not say so, for Godwin had kept himself sufficiently aloof from his second wife to make her respect him while he exasperated her.

She had tried to reform him when they first married; tried to put some order in his affairs and tried to limit the visits of friends who, she considered, wasted his time with their talking and arguing. But now those who were rich had stopped coming of their own accord, and the poor ones, who had never appreciated what she was doing for him, pushed past her through the shop downstairs and hurried up to the library where he sat all day with his books, the dust piling up on his papers and over the glass on the portraits; over Opie's picture of Mary Wollstonecraft that hung over the mantelpiece, and the portraits of Godwin himself by Opie and by Lawrence. There

4

they talked and talked, so that she heard them late into the night when she went to bed alone, and the girls heard the echo of it too. Mary, when she was at home, expected to be allowed to sit up listening to all hours, and Fanny had shown signs of wanting to join her, a thing she would never have suggested alone. Jane at least spared her that nonsense, though as a child at The Polygon she had hidden one night with the others behind the sofa to hear Mr. Coleridge read *The Ancient Mariner*. None of them would ever forget him ; a short man with a large head and bulging eyes, he had made their hair stand on end and sent thrills up and down their spines, then taken them on his knee and petted them, talking, talking, so that they never wanted to do anything in the world again but listen to him. He never came now, and when his name was mentioned Papa and Mr. Lamb shook their heads. Mr. Lamb talked too, but not in the way the children liked. He was small and wizened and they couldn't forget how he had frightened them by telling them sharply not to stare at his sister ; they had heard there was something odd about her and they wanted to see what it was.

Other men came whose names were well known in the outside world : Mr. Basil Montague, and Dr. Raine who was headmaster of Charterhouse, and Mr. Marshall who wrote for Papa in a big bold hand for hours on end : but they were all old and not poets. Jane had never seen a poet, not a real one who looked the part, like Lord Byron. She often wished that he might call. But it was no use crying for the moon— and Byron was sun and stars and the whole firmament of heaven !

5

Skinner Street was no place for day-dreaming. There were lessons to be prepared and Fanny to be helped and William to be kept amused when he came in from school, for he must not disturb Godwin and Mamma dared not be too severe with him in case he ran away again as he had two years ago and thoroughly frightened them all for a whole day and night.

Mamma was a tyrant, but once Jane had settled down to help prepare the supper or to play chess with her half-brother, she did not sulk for long. She soon forgot her fancies, for she was only fifteen and of a pliable enough disposition to enjoy doing anything to which she gave her mind. It was a good deal better being at home, even in unromantic Skinner Street, than at the boarding school in Walham Green, talking French all day and having to help the younger girls with their lessons because she was not as well off as the others. And next week there was something to look forward to, for Mary was coming home from Dundee.

II

Summer, 1814.

If the head of the household at 41 Skinner Street had considered the assortment of human beings under his roof he might have been a little disconcerted at the responsibility in which they involved him, but, like other experts in abstruse thought, he was not given to speculation that might be personally uncomfortable. In home affairs William Godwin lived by faith ; money would turn up from somewhere, just as a wife had been provided in his need to look after the children left upon his hands. Some admirers, like the talented Mrs. Inchbald, might have sneered when he first abandoned his free love principles and married Mary Wollstonecraft, but friends who had welcomed the union had been right, for happy it had been and would have continued to be, if his wife had not died after giving birth to his first child, Mary.

Left with her and Mary Wollstonecraft's other daughter, Fanny, he had taken a woman cousin into the house to help him, but her expectations of regular money supplies and regular meal times led him to seek for less exaction in a new wife. Refused by Mrs. Maria Reveley, and by the joint authoress of *The Canterbury Tales*, Miss Sophia Lee (whom he rated soundly for her lack of judgment), he was not involuntarily taken in marriage by the widow, Mary Jane Clairmont who had come to live next door in The Polygon. She made her first appearance as much like a *dea ex machinâ* as possible by exclaiming from her balcony, " Is it possible that I behold the immortal Godwin ? "

Her hopes of the culture and protection that she was securing for herself and her two children were soon disappointed. Godwin's high thinking went with much lower living than she had bargained for, and domestic economy left little time for improving the mind. Her attempt in early married life to fan his ardour as a lover and reform his habits as a husband was met with a rational discouragement that dispelled all such tender whims for the future. When she threatened to leave him, he wrote :

' . . . The separation will be a source of great

misery to me ; but I can make up my resolution to encounter it, and I cannot but wish that you should have the opportunity of comparing it with the happiness which is completely within your reach, but which you are eager to throw away.

As to the ground of your resentment, I owe it to myself to re-state it, with all the additions with which you in your remarks have furnished me. Mr. Curran promised to dine with me on Tuesday, the 18th inst., and again on Wednesday the 26th. Yesterday he promised to come to me at twelve o'clock and spend the day with me. On each of the first days I provided a dinner for him and was disappointed. Yesterday you provided a dinner, contrary to my order to the servant, since his promise, *which I gave you in writing*, showed that if I did not see him by twelve or one (coming from breakfast at Lord Hutchinson's), I had no right to expect him at four. A woman of any humanity would have endeavoured to console me under these repeated disappointments. . . .

You part from the best of husbands, the most anxious to console you, the best qualified to bear and be patient towards one of the worst of tempers. I have every qualification and every wish to make you happy, but cannot without your own.

October 28, 1803.'

The birth of William in 1803 increased Mrs. Godwin's anxiety for some larger source of income than was provided by the Wollstonecraft rents and her own work at translation, and she decided to capitalize Godwin's literary talent by opening a publishing business and a book-shop in Hanway Street. The first success of this encouraged her to move, in 1807, to larger premises in Skinner Street where the family could be accommodated over the shop ; but though newly built and central enough (it ran between Newgate Street and Holborn) the district somehow never attracted prosperity. Its amenities, either for business or sensibility, were not increased by the derelict warehouse burnt out in 1810, the animals driven over the cobbles in the early morning with shouts and blows to Smithfield, or prisoners continually passing to Newgate from the Giltspur Compter. On the day of an execution, it was impossible to pass along the street for the rabble that collected and regaled themselves with ices or ginger-pop according to the season supplied by Italian merchants from brightly painted barrows. In 1817 a man was hanged outside a gunsmith's that he had robbed at No. 58, on the literal principle of bringing the crime home to the culprit. Unfortunately there are not recorded the reflections of the author of *Political Justice.*

No. 41 was on the Snow Hill corner, and over the door had an artificial stone head of Æsop relating his fables to children. The long front window was low down to the ground, so that quite small urchins could press their noses against it and gaze at the books and coloured prints displayed inside. Beyond the shop there was a counting house where clerks and a porter were employed, and Mrs. Godwin claimed that she worked from nine in the morning till nine at night.

' The inglorious transaction below-stairs,' Godwin wrote when engaged on his *Answer to Malthus,*

ST. SEPULCHRE'S, SKINNER STREET

The church is all that now remains of Skinner Street, which ran between Newgate Street and Holborn but although central enough somehow never attracted prosperity. Its amenities in 1814 were not increased by the derelict warehouse burnt out four years earlier or by the daily sight of the animals driven with shouts and blows to Smithfield and the rabble that collected round Newgate.

HOLBORN CROWDS AT AN EXECUTION

. . . the crowds watching prisoners passing to execution at Newgate from the Giltspur Compter regaled themselves with ices and ginger-pop supplied by Italian merchants from painted barrows.

'furnishes me with food, clothing and habitation and enables me to proceed.'

But however inglorious and, in the event, doomed to failure the transaction might be, it was a gallant attempt to provide for the household. This, in 1814, comprised William Godwin, aged eleven, at school at the Charterhouse ; the Clairmonts, children of Mrs. Godwin's first marriage, Charles, aged twenty, and Jane, aged fifteen ; Mary Wollstonecraft Godwin, a few months older than Jane ; and Fanny, aged twenty-one, who went by the name of Godwin, but was really Mary Wollstonecraft's illegitimate daughter by Gilbert Imlay.

Fanny had deep blue eyes and her mother's rich auburn hair and would, like her mother, have achieved beauty if anyone had been at pains to discover it. She was docile and conscientious, intelligent, with a good memory, but with no boldness of imagination— in every way unlike the traditional love-child of romance, which was a rôle much better suited to Jane, the perfectly legitimate daughter of the practical Mrs. Godwin and her Swiss merchant husband. Both Jane and her brother had a foreign air, for they were exceptionally dark and talked and moved with vivacity. Charles was under the average height and not strictly handsome, but when he was animated his features lit up, like his sister's, and made him seem better looking than he was. He was at this time in Edinburgh where Godwin had found him a situation in Constable's printing house, but as he was erratic and more given to hare-brained schemes for fortune-making than hard work the Godwins were prepared for his return home at any time.

11

Mary was also in Scotland, living in Dundee at " Craigtay," the home of a rich merchant friend of Godwin's, William Baxter, whose daughters, Isabel and Christy, were to pay an occasional visit to London in exchange. The situation of the house with its terraced garden overlooking the estuary and only separated by a steep wooded lane from an ancient churchyard provided ideal sustenance for her romantic imagination, and in Isabel she thought she had found a Celia to her Rosalind, but it was probably in its orderliness and stability that the Baxter household exercised an influence over her for the rest of her life, stronger than she knew.

At sixteen Mary seemed grown up beside the more impulsive and forthcoming Jane, for she had a reserved manner that hid the warmth of her emotions as her fair gentleness belied the determination of her character. ' Singularly bold, somewhat imperious and active of mind,' her father called her, and Mrs. Godwin would have said " obstinate."

Her return from Dundee was not likely to be altogether welcome to her stepmother, but to Jane it was something exciting to look forward to—and she lived on things that were exciting to look forward to. And although Mary had been a little arrogant as well as reserved when she was at home before, often calling Jane stupid because she was not so quick to learn, the younger girl bore her no resentment : she admired her far too much, for she was pale and interesting-looking, as she would like to have been herself ; a Genevra who could be a heroine of romance :—

Jane's Admiration for Mary

Thine eyes' blue tenderness, thy long fair hair,
And the wan lustre of thy features—caught
From contemplation—where, serenely wrought,
Seems Sorrow's softness charm'd from its despair—

Fanny was always too busy for confidences and
William was only a school-boy, very often teasing and
troublesome ; Charles when he was at home was
sympathetic enough and enjoyed making up adventures with her, but she was always afraid he might
laugh if she confided to him those secrets that only
another girl of her own age could understand.   When
Mary came they would talk and read together and show
each other their private writings, and Jane would
guard jealously any confidences that Mary made to
her, for she was determined to be worthy of her real
friendship.

I I I

Summer, 1814.

When Mary did arrive, Jane admired her more
than ever and envied the tartan dress she had bought
at Dundee.   She tried to do her hair in the same way,
flat on the head with rows of curls at the side, but it
was too thick and wiry for that and would keep
breaking loose.   Mary was still reserved, but occasionally she would come out of her shell, and when they
discussed poetry, particularly the dazzling poetry of
Lord Byron, their two young voices rose to a crescendo
of enthusiasm.   But if Mamma came after them to
give them something useful to do Mary would be
quietly obedient, and then silent for the rest of the

day. Jane took her part vehemently and called Mamma a cruel tyrant to prevent Mary sitting with her father and his friends when they came to drink tea with him upstairs in the evening. It was no wonder that more and more she went out alone, stealing away from the house with books under her arm and refusing to say where she was going.

But on the evening of May 5th everyone was in a good humour, for Mr. Shelley was coming to supper ; Papa had said something about post-obits and Mrs. Godwin promised Jane a new dress. Even Fanny was excited ; for he was a poet, and she had been in correspondence with him since he came a year ago with his beautiful wife who had been dressed in a purple satin frock in the height of fashion. They had a little girl called Ianthe, and sometimes when they called they had brought with them Mrs. Shelley's sister, Eliza Westbrook ; and once there had come a Miss Hitchener from Sussex who was very clever indeed. Now Mr. Shelley was to come without Harriet, for she was at Binfield and not very well. He would be particularly interested to meet Mary, Fanny assured them, for he worshipped the memory of Mary Wollstonecraft.

It was on May 5th that Shelley came to Skinner Street and first saw Mary ; talked to her of her mother, of poetry, of revolution, and arranged to come and read Italian with her and Jane in the school-room and to join their walks. ' We both used to walk with him,' wrote Jane years after, ' in the Wilderness of the Charterhouse and also to Mary Wollstonecraft's tomb—they always sent me to walk some distance from them, alleging that they wished to talk on philosophical subjects and that I did not like or know anything about those subjects—I willingly left. I did not hear what they talked about.'

Their talk was to move quickly from philosophy to matters nearer the heart. He confided to her Harriet's inability to understand him, her frivolity and coldness, and the tyranny of her sister who lived with them and had made their home miserable. And in return he heard that Mary was unhappy too, persecuted by Mrs. Godwin and kept away from the father to whom she was devoted, her only solace the hours that she spent with her books in St. Pancras Churchyard beside her mother's tomb.

But when he suggested that they should break through their bondage and find happiness together, Mary would not hear of it. He pressed his arguments and began to have long letters delivered to her by the shop porter, but Mary was determined to be resigned, and when Godwin, warned by somebody more perspicacious than himself, questioned her, she was able to assure him that his fears of their relationship were unfounded.

Only to the fly-leaves of her copy of *Queen Mab* did she confide her real thoughts : ' This book is sacred to me and as no other creature shall ever look into it, I may write what I please. Yet what shall I write ? That I love the author beyond all power of expression and that I am parted from him. Dearest and only love, by that love we have promised to each other, although I may not be yours, I can never be another's.'

After Godwin's protest there was no more walking ahead in the Charterhouse wilderness for Jane, and she had to watch Mary growing still more reserved and spending longer and longer hours away from home, and when she was in, sometimes depressed, sometimes strangely gay. (" *Oh, coz, my pretty little coz, if you but knew how many fathoms deep I am in love!* ") Jane longed for her confidence, but she would not seek it ; she tried to be quiet and understanding and ready for it if she was thought deserving . . .

Then on the evening of July 17th everything came out. Mary and Shelley loved each other and could not be separated longer ; they had determined to die together, bought laudanum and poured it out, willing to suffer ' the misery of a fatal cure,' but had hesitated and once more considered their situation. It was not so hopeless. Mary was free from any tie (only her love for her father held her back, but surely the author of *Political Justice* and the husband of Mary Wollstonecraft would understand ?), and Shelley was free ; for Harriet had shown that she no longer loved him and he could not believe that she would wish to hold him by any other bond. Only Mrs. Godwin might interfere, for she had vulgar notions of philosophy and was past enlightenment.

If they were to be together, they must fly the country, and they had now decided to leave for France on the morrow.

Would Jane come with them ? Mary was nervous of the journey and Jane could talk French and help them. There was no time for delay. If Jane would come she must pack her things at once, for in the early morning Shelley was to have a coach ready outside the lodgings he had taken in Hatton Garden.

So began the connection that was not to end until after thirty years, when Mary was a widow and had a married son. " Don't go," she implored her daughter-in-law when Jane was to pay them a visit, " don't leave me with her, she has been the bane of my life since I was three years old."

I V

July 28th, 1814.

As Fanny was away from home Jane had their room to herself and no one to ask why she was so restless in the night. Every hour she woke at the last stroke of the clock on St. Sepulchre's and jumped up to the window to look into the street below, for Shelley was to come for them at 4 o'clock and she had to warn Mary. But over the roof-tops the sky was still dusky without a hint of dawn, and when she looked at the time by the flicker of the watchlight she laughed at her panic and went back to bed. Lying there before she dropped off to sleep again, she heard the heavy tread of the night watchman along the cobbles, and counted the laggard City clocks that struck their quarters after the chiming of Bow Bells.

At last it was three and she decided to get up and dress. The day was warm now with a mist across the Hampstead hills that promised intense heat later on. She crept about the room on bare feet, for the boards creaked at the least pressure on them and an unaccustomed noise so early would be sure to rouse Mamma.

There was a low knock on the door and Mary let herself in already dressed for the journey with a shawl about her black silk dress and a veil ready to tie round her bonnet. She tiptoed to the bed and climbed on to it to look down into the street. She might have been Rapunzel come to life—if only the gauzy golden hair had been longer and the window wide enough to admit anything but a dwarf lover! Jane's eyes glowed as she watched her and she wanted to sing aloud for excitement. Freedom and Adventure were ahead ; Life was beginning.

" He is here ! " But as Mary jumped down from the bed she remembered that the desk with her books and letters was still in her room and there were some important papers that she had omitted to put in. It was tiresome but it would take a few minutes to collect them. Shelley would have to go on alone and they would join him.

Together the two girls carried their portmanteau down the rickety stairs and through the shop to the street door where Shelley greeted them with delight and would have rushed in if they had not stopped him with much frowning and pointing to the upper windows. Mary whispered an explanation about the desk which Shelley agreed could not possibly be left behind and he promised to go off quietly with the luggage if they would join him immediately they could. Waving the two girls back into the shadowy doorway he went down the street, dragging the portmanteau behind him.

About a quarter of an hour later Jane and Mary carefully shut the shop door and, clutching their last minute packages, crept silently to the end of Skinner Street, but, once round the corner into Holborn Hill, they picked up their skirts and ran, and did not stop until they reached Hatton Garden and saw Shelley standing by the horses. He came to them to take the parcels and, laughing with relief and excitement, they all three clambered up into the chaise.

They were a little late in starting and, in order not to be overtaken before reaching Dover, they took two extra horses at Dartford. As the day grew hotter and hotter Mary began to look faint and tired and Jane suggested a sea-bathe while they waited for the packet. But when, at 4 o'clock in the afternoon, they at last arrived they found that it had already gone and unless they could hire a boat they would have to wait for the next day's service. This did not suit Shelley's impatience and in any case the delay was risky as Mrs. Godwin would be quite capable of employing the whole force of the law to prevent the elopement if she overtook them, so, after buying them bread to eat, he went off to make enquiries for a boatman willing to take them across, and the two girls went down to the machines on the shore for a bathe. By six o'clock he had successfully engaged a sailing boat with two sailors, and, having seen customs officials and arranged for the luggage to follow was ready to embark for Calais.

The sailors had promised a two-hour crossing but as the evening wore on the clouds gathered and the wind rose. Mary, worn out by emotion and the journey, slept at the bottom of the boat against Shelley's knees, waking fitfully to ask if they were nearly there and to hear him answer, ' Not quite half-way.' A thunderstorm broke and ' waves rushed into the boat ; even the sailors believed that our situation was perilous,' wrote Shelley in the Journal ; ' I had time in that instant to reflect and even to

19

reason upon death ; it was rather a thing of discomfort and of disappointment than horror to me.
We should never be separated, but in death we might
not know and feel our union as now.'

But Jane proved an excellent sailor and welcomed
the silence of the others that gave her an opportunity
for reflection on all that had happened. She imagined
the to-do in Skinner Street when their absence was
discovered, and for a minute felt a little sorry at
deceiving Mamma ; but that was not at all in keeping,
Mamma must be the tyrant and she and Mary the
victims, the heroines escaping to freedom and romance.
Not that Shelley looked a hero—nor a Corsair either
—for all the open boat and " the breezy freshness of
the deep beneath." His hair, blowing wildly now
about his head, was always indiscriminately brown and
rather untidy and could never be tossed imperiously
from the brow ; not for him,

> a forehead high and pale
> The sable curls in wild profusion veil.

He had fine, delicate features and would have looked
tall if he had heeded how he carried himself and how
he wore his clothes, instead of always walking about
with a book in his hand or scurrying along as if he
had an appointment with the Cosmic Possibility. But
he was great fun to be with ; his bright blue eyes
lighting up when he talked and his voice rising to
a high pitch when he laughed. He made up macabre
stories for them, fantastic and horrible, and then
would unexpectedly say something ludicrous so that
they would shudder and giggle at the same time with
excitement. Now, watching over Mary, he looked

more responsible and much older than his years, as
though a driving spirit were wearing out his youth
and he belonged to those :—

> Those to whom the miseries of the world
> Are misery and will not let them rest.

With the passing of the darkness the wind dropped
and Jane was woken from her day-dreams by Shelley's
voice gently rousing Mary : " Look, the sun rises
over France."

V

July—September, 1814.

Calais might be the outpost of Freedom and Adventure, but there was first of all an inn to be sought where
the exhausted Mary could rest and be refreshed, and
then a carriage and driver to be found who would
take them to Paris as soon as the luggage had come
off the packet. Mary noted the strange dress of the
people : ' . . . the men with earrings ; ladies walking about with high bonnets or *coiffures* lodged on the
top of the head, the hair dragged up underneath,
without any stray curls to decorate the temples or
cheeks. There is, however, something very pleasing
in the manners and appearance of the people of Calais,
that prepossesses you in their favour. A national
reflection might occur, that when Edward III. took
Calais, he turned out the old inhabitants, and peopled
it almost entirely with our own countrymen ; but
unfortunately the manners are not English.'

Mary's disconcertingly imperialistic sentiment was,

no doubt, prompted by conditions at the Inn, for the *table d'hôte* system meant that all the guests had to sit. down together at the same table and accept what food was proffered, generally greasy and ill-prepared, and served with many delays. "*Tout de suite, tout de suite,*" called the waiters, but made not the least effort to hurry, and the *bonnes* took a lot of persuading before they would bring even cold water for a wash. When a towel was insisted upon as well, there would be still more grumbling and many warnings that the meal would be missed by such unnecessary fussing.

Adventure had its seamy side and for the moment even Freedom was in doubt, for the Captain of the packet burst into the room and announced that a fat lady had arrived who declared that Shelley had run away with her daughter.

Jane went with him to her mother, and, perhaps touched by her appeal, or dismayed at the prospect of sleeping in a strange room at the Inn, decided to spend the night with her.

In the morning she went to the Shelleys and told them that she would go back to England with Mrs. Godwin. She felt small as she said it ; was this to what her slavery at home amounted and her fine independence ? She reminded herself of the restrictions at Skinner Street and the alternative of going out as a governess ; thought of what it would be like not to have Mary and to give up Shelley's high enthusiastic talk . . .

' Take an hour to decide,' was Shelley's sober advice.

She went back to her mother and told her that she had changed her mind. Perhaps because out of England she was powerless to interfere, or perhaps because she had found that it was Mary and not her own daughter whose reputation was to be lost, Mrs. Godwin collected her not inconsiderable wits about her and made a dignified exit from a stage where rapture and irresponsibility held the boards. 'Mrs. Godwin departed without saying a word,' records the Shelley Journal.

Their luggage had also arrived by the packet, so the next day, July 30th, they left Calais in a cabriolet appropriately drawn by a Pegasus. 'To persons who had never before seen anything but a spruce English chaise and post-boy,' wrote Mary, 'there was something irresistibly ludicrous in our equipage. . . . The three horses were placed abreast, the tallest in the middle, who was rendered more formidable by the addition of an unintelligible article of harness resembling a pair of wooden wings fastened to his shoulders.'

In Paris they went to the Hôtel de Vienne where, in accordance with the continental custom of the time, they had to rent apartments for a week, 'a bed-chamber, another closet with a bed and an ante-chamber which we used as a sitting room.' In spite of the excessive heat they went enthusiastically sight-seeing, eager to worship at the shrines where the rights of man had been proclaimed and to wonder at the paths where the feet of Napoleon had so recently trod ; feet of clay, alas ! not because of his overthrow by their own countryman and the humiliation of Elba, but because of the inner failure when he accepted a crown, " the Hero sunk into the King."

The French capital had closer ties for Mary ; it was in the Paris of the Terror that her mother had watched the tumbrils from her window and then escaped to Fontainebleau with Gilbert Imlay and when he had to return to the bloody city, had watched for him daily at the barrier with a sweet anguish and uprising at her heart that owed nothing to the course of Revolution. It was here that for the first time in her life Mary Wollstonecraft had been happy ; but for her daughter, twenty years later, life was beginning and happiness was secure ; Shelley still believed that man had only to be freed from his chains to be happy, and Jane dreamt romantically of love with no suspicion of its pangs. They could not pay to the dead tributes beyond their power. They went to call on Helen Maria Williams who had been Mary Wollstonecraft's friend, and read her *Answer to Burke* and *The Letters from Norway* and they visited the Palaces and sat in the gardens of the Tuileries.

Each day Shelley had to call on Tavernier, an agent through whom he was expecting supplies of money without which they could not go on to Switzerland, but they were not over concerned at the delay in its coming. It was much more important to reform the world at large and to begin by educating themselves and arranging what was to be done for Harriet.

This did not present much difficulty ; she was to be invited to join them as a ' dear sister,' with Ianthe and the child whose birth she was now expecting, and they would all live together and found an ideal community, like the Assassins who fled from the siege of Jerusalem. And for education, Jane must read the books that Shelley set her, while he and Mary pored over the old letters she had brought in the desk and those secret writings that Jane had never been allowed to see. They began to keep a Journal together in

24

an exercise-book bought at a Paris stationers, and when Jane wanted one as well, Shelley gave her a note-book that he had been using for quotations. There was a line from Dante and some latin prose in it and a quotation from St. Augustine's Confessions, " *Nondum amabam*, etc. " : the lines that he was to use later for a motto to *Alastor*.

On the last day of the week the money came and they were free to leave. ' After talking over and rejecting many plans, we fixed on one eccentric enough but which, from its romance, was very pleasing to us.' They decided to walk. The excited warnings of *Madame l'hôte* that the ladies would probably be *enlevées* by the disbanded soldiers now roaming the countryside did not deter them. Only they went to the Ass Market to buy a donkey to carry, by turns, Mary and the portmanteau.

Along the dusty white roads of France they set off, the two girls in their black silk dresses reaching to the ground and Shelley in tight trousers and jacket, but with an open shirt from which he had cast away the black necktie. They discussed every subject under the sun and disposed with high intolerance of any opinion that did not fit in with theirs, and, when the problems of the world were exhausted, Jane would sing snatches of songs to them and Shelley make up romances, or " jocosely horrible " stories.

They picnicked in woods or by the roadside, or Shelley would munch a hunk of bread as he walked, for he disapproved of animal food and hated set meals ; he liked to get fresh milk at a cottage or drink cups of tea for which he had an inordinate capacity at any time of the day. Sometimes it was not easy to obtain provisions : the villagers were inclined to be surly and in some places had nothing to sell, for the Cossacks had ravaged the harvest and driven off the cattle. It was a country only recently the field of war, and its people were still too sore to make themselves amiable to the young travellers who, like the English of any other generation, never paused to consider if their patronizing internationalism might not be even more irritating than traditional insularity.

Disappointed by the lack of response to his genuine sympathies, already a little strained by uncomfortable nights at the inns, Shelley wrote from Troyes to Harriet, ' . . . I must remark to you that, dreadful as these calamities are, I can scarcely pity the inhabitants ; they are the most unamiable, inhospitable, and unaccommodating of the human race. . . .'

But the towns were as picturesque as, in a foreign country, they ought to be, and Jane described them every night in her Journal :

' *Monday [August] 15th, 1814*. . . . Reach Langre about eight—Sup at the table d'hôte with a numerous and vulgar set who come to the fair here—This town is extremely old, [as] indeed most of the french towns are—It stands on a hill by the side of the road. On your [right] as you ascend is the Town, and on your left you look down on a lovely valley full of trees between whose verdant foliage you catch glimpses of a sweet stream. The Buildings which are black from age are in the Gothic and Roman style—The Town is narrow and very dirty—Were it not for the grand ruins at its entrance I would have it pulled down and destroyed for I observe that old towns are always dirty——'

They had set out to find romance, so a bright morning—and the elasticity of their youth—made quick work of tiredness and discomfort, and the evenings brought their proper reflections with them :

' *Wednesday*, *August 17th* . . . I read *As You Like It* [and] found the wild and romantic touches of this play very accordant with the scene before me and my feelings. It was indeed a lovely Evening. How much is lost by those who pass their lives in cities. They are never visited by those sweet feelings which to recollect alone is Heaven—It is fortunate for them that they imagine themselves happy—how boundless and terrific would be their surprize if they could suddenly become philosophers and view things in their true and beautiful point of view. We sleep all night by the Kitchen fire—Shelley much disturbed by the creaking door, the screams of a poor smothered child and the *fille* who washes the glasses.'

V I

August, 1814.

The ass which had very soon proved itself less fit to carry than be carried was succeeded by a mule on which Shelley, who had sprained his ankle, rode into Troyes with the two girls following. There the beast was changed for a carriage, ' an open *voiture* on four wheels for five napoleons ' and ' a man with a mule for eight more to convey us to Neufchâtel in six days.'

It was this *voiturier* who was responsible for the night spent by the kitchen fire, for he had begun to lose his head as soon as he quitted his native plains, and, after a mile and a half uphill, driving ahead while his employers walked, he had insisted on stopping at the Inn at Mort. It was a miserable place and they would all have had to share the one bedroom. ' It was of little consequence as we had previously resolved not to enter the beds.'

They started off at three in the morning, hoping to reach Pontarlier and cross over into Switzerland that day, but the driver, hill-scared, had become ' disobliging, sullen and stupid.' He insisted on a wait of two hours at Nouailles, and then, while they were walking leisurely in the woods, drove on alone to Maison Neuve, ' leaving word that he expected to meet us on the road.' The midday sun was strong and Shelley's ankle painful, but they went on by foot only to find at the next *auberge* that the driver had left for Pontarlier, six leagues distant. A short cut along a cross-road to the next inn brought dinner, but no driver, and another message that he was two leagues ahead. The sun was setting by now and they had to go on, but with a two hours forced march still did not overtake him until they procured a rough cart and in this arrived late and exhausted at Pontarlier. ' The voiturier has a thousand excuses, all falsehoods. Shelley's ankle very bad all the way. Go to bed much fatigued.'

They sent the hopeless driver back home ; and by horseback, with a Swiss for guide, reached Les Verrières, the barrier town of France and Switzerland. Here they were prepared to be impressed, for countries have fashions in glamour, and if, in 1815, France was guilty of having betrayed the high hopes of an earlier generation, Switzerland was still the country of the Two Voices. Her people were expected to be as much loftier in mind as her Alps rose above the fells.

'*Friday*, [*August*] *19th, 1814* . . . I should take up volumes if I were to attempt to describe all I saw—at last we reach Les Verrières which is considered as The barri[er] of France and Switzerland—There is an immense chain suspended from a high mountain which is thrown across the valley to the opposite mountain in time of War—The road is most delightful and is cut through the middle of the mountains which close in so closely that there is only room for a clear little rivulet to run. The mountains are covered with immense forests of Pine—now and then a bold rugged and bare rock protrudes itself amidst its green and woody neighbours forming a most sublime contrast. Half way to Neufchâtel the lake is discovered—it is nine miles broad. First you see an indistinct line of hills that seems more like rising and uneven ground and bear no marked or peculiar character, then comes a second line still darker and more rugged and characteristic ; behind these is a third [line] of very high dark hills, rude and broken. Then—oh then come the terrific Alps. I thought they were white flaky clouds [and] what was my surprize when after a long and steady examination I found them really to be the snowy Alps. Yes they were really the Alps—Peaked broken, one jutting forward, another retreating, now the light airy clouds rested a few moments on their aspiring [fr]onts and then fled away that we might better behold the sublimity of the scene. How much more should I have enjoyed the scene if I had been permitted to

29

remain in silence, but at the village where we dined
we had procured a new voiturier and horses, and in
the kindness and freedom of his heart he would talk
to us—he would talk of the Brave Roi de Prusse and
of his own contentment, and where he had travelled
to—all of which at any other time I should have been
delighted to hear but now it was like discord in music
—or like the ringtac [?] scrapings of a tuning fiddler
—besides his associations with the mountains [were]
those of butter and cheese—how good the pasturage
was for the cows—and then the cows yielded good
milk and then the good m[ilk] made good cheese—
and so on from step to step—but however the air of
the mountains seem to have done him some good ;
there was freedom in his countenance, indeed everything seemed to change the moment we passed from
France to Switzerland—The Cottages and people as
if by magic became almost instantaneously clean and
hospitable. The children were rosy and interesting,
no yellow care-worn looks—in France it is almost
impossible to see a woman who looks under fifty—
most of them bear marks of advanced age—their
cottages are in a horrible state—dirt and ruin seem
to have taken up their everlasting abode with them,
but in Switzerland you see cheerful, contented, smiling, healthy faces. Our Voiturier replied in answer
to some observations that I made to him of this kind.
Ah ! it is because we have no king to fear ! when we
have paid our rent to the Siegneur we have nothing
to dread. We need not even take off our hats to him,
we are perfectly free and may sit contentedly with our
children by our fireside. Then we have only four
Seigneurs in all the country and we are not Roman

Catholics and have no priests that eat up our patrimony. We arrived at Neufchâtel about eight ; it is a very clean neat town on the banks of the lake— We slept at the Faucon which is the best inn we have ever yet entered.'

But the more they saw of the scenery, the less was man, even Republican man, Nature's paragon :

' *Thursday*, *August 25th* . . . This would be a most delightful residence if it were not for the amazing populousness of the country. The Mountains are covered with cottages. It is impossible to find a wild and entire solitude. In other countries the Mountains however beautiful are generally deserted, but this being a republic, and the people multiplying exceedingly, no spot is deserted, for no spot in this fertile country is barren, except the very tops of the mountains. The people are rich, contented and happy. A poor beggar is never seen. The people are uninteresting for they are most immoderately stupid and almost ugly to deformity. The children beg the moment they see you, not from poverty but merely from habit which I suppose has descended from their ancestors who originally begged from Poverty . . .'

At Brunnen they decided to settle within sight of the chapel of Wilhelm Tell and rented two rooms in a château for six months. They hired beds and then sat on them to discuss ways and means. The banker at Neufchâtel had advanced Shelley some money, which he had brought home in a sack, and they had laughed and counted out the coins like people in a fairy story, but the number of them had diminished fast. It had cost them £60 to travel from Paris to Neufchâtel and now they had only £28 left. There was little hope of more money coming from London and Harriet was hardly likely to arrive with fresh supplies. She had not answered the letter from Troyes and on consideration they could not perhaps altogether expect her to undertake the journey alone. It might be as well to get back to England as soon and as quickly as possible.

Jane left Shelley and Mary to decide ; money had little meaning for her and coins in a sack seemed untold wealth. She went upstairs to write her Journal:

'*Friday*, *August 26th*. Rainy morning. Project of going back to England pursued. Read Abbé Barruel. Settle to go to London. Go to Bed early.'

VII

They decided as soon as their linen had been retrieved from the washerwoman to go back to England by water, up the Reuss and the Rhine.

'*Saturday*, *August 27th*. Get up at five. Bustle toil and trouble. Most laughable to think of our going to England the second day after we entered a new house for six months. All because the stove don't suit. As we left Dover and England's white cliffs were retiring I said to myself I shall never see these more ; and now I am going to England again—Dear England. After having travelled and viewed the follies of other nations my own country appears the most reasonable and the most enlightened. It is now six o'clock. We shall set off in a moment. What will the Abbé and the Médecin say ? I should like to know

what a Pack Horse is ? Shelley explains the pheno-
nomon [*sic*] at one o'clock in the boat. Set off at seven.
Rainy morning. Very uncomfortable. The clouds
only just above our head. We pass through one.
Stop under a shed for half-an-hour. Mount Pilate
almost hid by thin white clouds. Reach Lucerne
about half after twelve. Go to the Cheval.

Read *King Richard III*, and *King Lear*. Quite
Horrified—I can't describe my feelings for a moment.
When Cornwall tears out the eyes of the Duke of
Gloster. This play is the most melancholy and produced almost stupendous despair on the reader. Such
refinement in wickedness and cruelty—Lear is exactly
what he calls himself—" But I am a fond foolish old
Man ". Jealous and anxious for the display of affection and praise. In most of Shakespeare's Plays there
are generally secondary Plots and Characters which
are rather tiresome than interesting, but in *Lear*
there is not a line that does not teem with vigour and
energy and awakens fresh anxiety and horror. I
think Lear treats Cordelia very ill. " What shall
poor Cordelia do—Love and be silent." Oh [this] is
true. Real Love will never shew itself to the eye
of broad day. It courts the secret glades.

In a fortnight we shall perhaps be in London. How
wild the people will think us. All because the stove
did not burn rightly and there were two many
Cottages.'

The Rhine provided scenery as Gothic as could be
desired ; after Mainz, Claire wrote in her Journal ;

' *Sunday, September 4th.* Rise at six. Walk down
to the Quay. Go in a Boat a league from the town to
where the Diligence for Cologne is stationed. Set off

about seven. The Banks of the Rhine are very beautiful. The River itself is narrow and runs between mountains which though not high are of every different shape and description. Ruined castles are here very numerous and many most romantically situated. Ruins have a fine effect, and henceforth I shall hardly think any scene complete without them. I think we passed no less than twenty Castles and about five Towns—At a small Village there is a ruined Cathedral of a fine brown colour. We dined at Bingen near which is a very strong Castle built on the top of a very high and rock Mountain. Sleep at Braubach . . .

We had a most horrid set on board. Nothing could surpass the Manners that prevailed in the Cabin below. Drinking, smoking, singing and cracking jokes of a disagreeable nature. We sat upon the deck the whole day with one or two tolerable men who smoked it is true but were brought to own it was wrong. Among these two sat talking with us almost the whole day. One was a man that pretended to something and the other an Agriculturist going out to Surinam with no pretensions to anything but an unaffected simplicity and good Nature. We had on board besides a school Master who spoke a little English. The latter and the Man of Pretensions sung many German Airs which I admired very much. As we were just entering the dangerous defile the Man of Pretension turned to us and said—" Allons il faut prier le bon Dieu "—We laughed. He answered—" Eh ! bien donc il faut chanter "—The Schoolmaster immediately began and they sang an animated German song which had a much finer effect when seconded by the breaking of the waves over the Rocks. Sleep at Rens. See the only beautiful girl we have seen since we started from Paris.'

But romantic appreciation was evidently a sustaining mental diet: for, the three of them, "Rousseau Men" as they were, regardless of the company or weather would sit on deck writing, reading their Shakespeare, or listening to *The Letters from Norway* read aloud. They each had a work on hand: Shelley, *The Assassins*; Mary, a novel to be called *Hate*; and Jane a *magnum opus*, the *Ideot*. 'This has been for years a favourite plan of mine. To develope the Workings and Improvements of the mind which by Common people was deemed the mind of an Ideot, because it conformed not to their vulgar and prejudiced views.'

Sometimes they slept under the stars, but more often they had to go to the uncomfortable Inns where fellow travellers were far from agreeable. Only on rare occasions, however, did human nature of 21 and 17 break through, and then the ineffectual angel could be quite effective with his fists. In the *diligence pareau* after Loffenburgh they returned from landing for refreshments to find their seats occupied by some Germans. 'Their brutal rudeness to us, who did not understand their language,' wrote Mary in the *History of a Six Weeks' Tour*, 'provoked S. to knock one of the foremost down; he did not return the blow, but continued his vociferations until the boatman interfered and provided us with other seats.'

Jane's Journal describes a typical day:

'*Monday, September 5th.* Rise at three. Set sail without any milk. Dreadfully cold—so dreadfully that we were reduced by dire necessity to descend into the cabin. Talk with the Man of Düsseldorf and a Merchant a *cher ami* of his. They tell us of their intention to stay at Coblentz and that they can no longer endure the Canaille who snatched the meat out of their plates the Evening before at Supper. Arrived at Coblentz about seven. The Man and the Agriculturist take a most tender farewell. I find it is the custom for men to kiss each other at parting. The Canaille take advantage of this and kiss each other all day which with their horrid leers and slime has a most loathsome effect. Never was a more disgraceful set than the common order of people of Germany. Your soul shrinks back to its inmost recesses when by accident you cast your eye over countenances begrimed with mental and bodily depravity—Stay half an hour at Coblentz—opposite which is a very commanding and rugged rock—The Ruins of a fortress stand upon its top. . . .'

They arrived at Rotterdam in the evening of September 8th and, being unable to pursue the voyage because of a contrary wind, examined the country-side. ' Holland is exactly what may be termed a pretty country,'—' the Dutch are sober and slow. They have no German licentiousness about them. They pay an unbounded respect to everything in the shape of riches and are, I doubt not, a very sordid and interested nation. They dress almost like the English and speak their language very well.' On the 11th they left, and arrived at Gravesend on the 13th, but without enough money to hire a boat to take them up the river :

' *Tuesday*, *September 13th*. Rise late. Find our two Scotchmen gone and Mr. and Mrs. Turner.

Arrive at Gravesend about ten. Custom house officers come on Board. Row to the Custom house Cutter. Meet our Scotchman again then. Get to Gravesend. Great trouble. At last get a Waterman. Delightful Row up the River—Arrive at Blackwall at two. Get into the Stage. Arrive at Leadenhall Street in about an hour. Get into a hackney Coach and drive to Martin and Call's—No money there. Go to Hookham's. Only Edward at home. Stay a long time at the door. Drive then to Voisey's, Pall Mall. Mrs. V. very indignant. Henry Voisey kind. He runs to Chapel Street while we drive there. Shelley meets Voisey and go to Harriet's. Wait there for him two hours. Gets dark. Part with our kind Boatman. Shelley returns. Drive to Stratford Hotel, Oxford Street. Dine and go to Bed.'

VIII

September–November, 1814.

Back in London Freedom was still precious and the lodgings at 56, Margaret Street luxurious because they were not Skinner Street, and, if it was a pity not to be able to astonish Fanny and Charles with the adventures on the Continent, the Godwins' boycott provided a mild form of persecution that was pleasantly stimulating—less pleasant, perhaps, for Fanny who had been deprived of her supper and sent to her room, like a naughty child, for receiving a lock of hair from Mary !

Jane enjoyed the excitement of being the messenger going backwards and forwards to Harriet at her father's

house in Chapel Street with notes from Shelley—notes
in which he could explain with sweet reasonableness
that she was no longer his wife as he was united to
another, and add in a P.P.S. 'I am in want of stockings,
hanks. and Mrs. W.'s posthumous works.' Harriet's
replies were temporizing for, as Mrs. Godwin reported,
she was in good spirits as 'everybody tells her that
love affairs last but a little time and her husband will
be sure to return to her.' To which Mrs. Godwin
added the candid reflection of her own, 'That is
indeed but too true and what a gloomy prospect it
opens to us.'

Mrs. Godwin wrote long letters about the elopement
to Lady Mountcashell, a former pupil of Mary Wollstonecraft's who had kept up with the Godwins and
was now in Italy where Mrs. Godwin thought the girls
might have gone. The letters ring true in many of
the details they relate, but are unreliable in major
facts. She complained, for instance, that Shelley forbade her to see Jane, but the Journal entries both of
the Shelleys and of Jane prove the contrary, as the
following extract shows :

'*Friday, September 16th.* Rise at nine. Breakfast. Read *Rasselas*, and *De l'origine de l'inégalité
des Hommes.* Curious and weak letter from Harriet
with Shelley's books. S. writes to Papa and Charles.
Letter from Turner. Hookham Dines. Just before
dinner about six—Mama and Fanny pass the Window.
Shelley runs out to them. They won't speak. Hookham quits us early. Voisey at tea. He explains De
Gall's System. Departs about half past ten. Mary
retires. Shelley is writing to Papa and I am reading
the notes to *Queen Mab* when we hear stones at the

Window. Look out and there is Charles. Joyful meeting. He stays till three in the Morning. Tells us about their Plan of putting me in a Convent.'

The entry is typical of their days : alarums and excursions alternating with letter-writing and study. They were overworked, thought Mrs. Godwin, when she saw them again, and under-fed, but, if Jane had grown a little pale from the vegetable diet, she was quite happy. ' . . . I asked J. if she liked Mr. Shelley and she answered with her usual enthusiasm that she thought him absolutely perfect . . .'

For his part, Shelley was delighted to have the chance to mould such propitious material and prove that with equal opportunity a woman's intellect was in no way inferior to that of a man—a tenet of Mary Wollstonecraft's faith that Godwin had not troubled to put into much practice with his children. He had left it to his second wife to ' give them an excellent education and many accomplishments.' ' . . . Charles knows Latin, Greek and French, mathematics and draws well. The girls have been taught by Mr. Godwin, Roman, Greek and English History, french and italian from masters—Frances and Mary draw well— Jane could never draw and therefore she had learnt music and singing . . .' But this was not enough for Shelley's ambition ; he wanted Mary and Jane to study metaphysics and learn Greek so that they could join in the discussions that he had with the two friends who came to visit them, Thomas Jefferson Hogg and Thomas Love Peacock.

Not that it was all Greek with them. Hogg was busy in the day, or made out that he was, as he had been newly called to the Bar and could only come in the evenings to talk and play chess ; but Peacock walked over daily from Southampton Buildings and went with them to Hampstead to sail boats on the ' pond past Primrose Hill.' Mary was not really good with her hands but she succeeded in making fire boats for Shelley to sail, to the great delight of the children who crowded round them. He might have been one of them himself, so whole-heartedly did he throw himself into the sport, and have to be brought back to earth—and to dinner—by Peacock.

It was a pity that Peacock was always so matter-of-fact, for Jane considered that he had great possibilities. He had a very good intelligence and was undoubtedly romantic looking in appearance, and would have been more so if he had not been so fond of his dinner and his bottle of wine. His thick black hair fell in disorderly curls over quite a lofty brow and his features were regular, although they lacked pallor ; indeed he had a superfluity of good health and already gave indications of portliness to come. If Shelley could convert him to a vegetable diet he might change, for Shelley was a disciple of Godwin's friend, Mr. Newton, the vegetarian, and had himself written an essay to prove that all the coarseness and corruption of man comes from consuming animal food. But Peacock laughed at them and went on making fun, sometimes rather unfeelingly they thought, of what he called Shelley's " passion for reforming the world."

If Peacock became enlightened, he and Hogg could elope with Shelley's sisters, Elizabeth and Hellen, and then they would all live together in an ideal community, an Association of Philanthropists. It is perhaps not surprising that Shelley was undaunted by a project of Pantisocracy that had tied Coleridge and Southey for life to Sara and Edith Fricker (for we are always going to do better than the generation just before us), but it is a significant comment on Shelley's mentality that it did not occur to him to provide a partner for Jane in the Association. That she was an extremely attractive young woman he never seems to have noticed, although he would probably have troubled less with her if she had not been-; just as he might have been less easily persuaded into an altruistic marriage with a plain Harriet! His indifference to her from this point of view shows his complete lack of sensuality, and makes it the more ironical that the misfortunes which befell him from his relationships with women should have always evoked less pity than blame. If he had been a philanderer and libertine like Byron, the world would have been more ready to condone the mistakes that he made in his youth ; but, as it is, neither the price he paid nor the essential goodness of his nature have ever been allowed to expiate them.

But though Shelley had eyes only for Mary and to Jane was not a major poet, but a lanky young man with a stoop and a high-pitched voice, she still could not refrain from sometimes wishing that he would look upon her with rather more interest. With horror Shelley recorded in his Journal :

'*Friday, October 14th*. Jane's insensibility and incapacity for the slightest degree of friendship. The feelings occasioned by this discovery prevent me from maintaining any measure in security. This highly incorrect ; subversion of the first principles of true philosophy ; characters, particularly those which are unformed, may change. Beware of weakly giving way to trivial sympathies. Content yourself with one great affection—with a single mighty hope ; let the rest of mankind be the subjects of your benevolence, your justice . . .'

Because she wanted attention Jane began to make scenes :

' *Friday, October 14th.* Get up late. Go down in a very ill humour—Quarrel with Shelley—But to know one's faults is to mend them—perhaps this morning though . productive of very painful feelings has in reality been of more essential benefit to me than any I ever yet passed. How hateful it is to quarrel—to say a thousand unkind things—meaning none—things produced by the bitterness of disappointment. I hate those feelings. Walk home through the Regents Park—Leave them and go home by myself. Peacock calls. Laughs at us. Good news of Eliza. Shelley comes into my room and thinks he was to blame—but I don't—how I like good kind explaining people—S and P go to the Pond—Walk out a little by myself. Peacock goes after tea—Read *St. Leon*—Go to bed at nine—About half after ten Shelley comes up and I go down and sleep with Mary because I groan. Go to sleep at half past two.'

" To know one's faults is to mend them "—and very agreeably, in examination of them for hours together, titillating the emotions by remorse and inviting sympathy that would open the way again for more confession, and more remorse . . . and it was agreeable to go for walks alone with Shelley, and return late at night when Mary had gone to bed and they could sit over the fire and talk of ghosts and supernatural

42

wonders until she was too excited to sleep and had to go for comfort to Mary.

Mary was so kind and so strong ; if she was sometimes irritable now it was because she was not well as she was expecting a child in a few months' time, and there was the new worry that Shelley might be committed to prison for debt by Harriet's creditors. He had to keep away from home for days together.

Peacock put him up at night, and by day he had to wander about the City and send Mary messages where to meet him. Kentish Town Fields or St. Paul's Churchyard where they could go into the Cathedral and sit down, were favourite places ; but they were all some way off and Mary often returned home exhausted in the evening. Sometimes she found no supper, for the landlady had become suspicious and refused to send up food until her bill was paid. Then Peacock would come to the rescue and send cakes.

Claire thoroughly enjoyed the excitement.

' *Monday, October 24th.* Rise at eight. Breakfast. Write my journal. M. reads aloud *She stoops to Conquer*—She sets out to see Shelley at eleven. I stay at home and read *Political Justice*—Go about one to Mrs. Peacock's. Mary comes, she has not seen Shelley—She goes home—I return and stay in Fleet St. till 3 o'clock—come back to Peacock's—Maryann there—Go home to Pancras—I find M. set out for London again—suspicious men been in my absence —Set out again for Southampton Buildings—find only poor old Mrs. P. at home—have some grumbling conversation with her—Most luckily M. comes in search of P. She had been to the Coffee House and seen Shelley—I go out to him in Holborn—we go to Harris's the optician, he won't have our microscope—I go to Peacock, fetch him and the microscope—He talks to Shelley a little while in Holborn. S. and I go to Davison's in Skinner Street. We are sent away for half an hour. Walk up and down Chatham Place though we are both so tired we can hardly stand—I am so hungry for I had had nothing since breakfast and it was now six o'clock—Return again to Davison's ; get 5 Pounds for our microscope. In my absence Peacock had gone all the way to Pancras ; we were not at home—He sees the waiter of St. James' Hotel there—much frightened and returns home—Part with S. in Holborn—Send Peacock to him. Have some dinner in Southampton St. Return with M. in a Coach about half past eight—Find that a gentleman (I suppose Charles) had been with a letter from Fanny to me in our absence. But the extraordinary way he had knocked at the door had almost frightened the children into fainting fits. Fanny requests an interview at Marshalls to-morrow—To bed at nine.'

Money from Shelley's pawned microscope was to pacify Mrs. Page, the landlady, and to provide means for a night's lodgings at an Inn where Mary and Shelley could be together.

' *Monday*, *October 31st*. Get up at nine. Breakfast. Read a Canto of *Queen Mab* and Louvet's Memoirs. I am much interested in Louvet—but like all Frenchmen he is so intolerably full of himself and never lets the reader find out the merit he may possess—but praises his own actions in the grossest way —he foresees—he plans—he would direct—but his prognostications are not attended to—his plans are neglected and his directions unobeyed—He then shows how much injury the cause of Republicanism suffered from Condorcet and Brissot's want of his penetration and judgement—Surely this could not have been the case. A man of Condorcet's wonderful genius must have seen deeper into things than Louvet—by whose account Condorcet's weakness was the cause of Robespierre's maintaining his situation and of his numerous massacres—Mrs. Page wants some money—set out in search of Shelley and Mary—Go to Aldersgate St. See Mama in Charlton St, they are not at the Castle and Falcon—Search for them ; call twice at Peacock's— find them at the Cross-Keys, St. John Street. Very detestable situation. Dine with them. Shelley walks home with me as far as Peacock's.—When I get home find a letter from Mary and that Charles has been— Sit up till eleven reading Louvet's Memoirs. I never remember be[ing] more interested in any book. So many fine instances of individual republican spirits displayed—so many generous Women—such constancy in misfortune.'

' *Monday, November 7th.* Rise at nine—Work. Read *Political Justice*—Mary dines at one and goes to Shelley. Read *King Richard the third*—Dine by myself at four—Mary returns at six—Talk with her and read some miscellaneous poetry—Hogg is going to drink tea with Shelley to-night—Shelley had seen Charles and Lambert—the last is playing a double part —but I think we shall not suffer him to deceive us —Lambert is worth £300,000 and he oppresses and insults Godwin for the paltry sum of a hundred and fifty—pretending at the same time to admire his energy and talent—And it is for these people that

45

Godwin has sacrificed his happiness and well being
—that he refuses to see his daughter and Shelley, the
two people he loves best in the world.'

By the 9th November, the danger of arrest was over
and they decided to move to new lodgings. The
relief, however, from Shelley's embarrassment did not
altogether bring back the old good nature to Mary.
She was often irritable, and when news came of the
birth of Harriet's child she even reproached Shelley
for his satisfaction, entering in her Journal that he
was writing ' a number of circular letters of this event,
which ought to be ushered in with ringing of bells,
etc., for it is the son *of his wife* . . .'

Shelley was shocked for a moment at her attitude,
but with his usual understanding ' soon made everything all right.' But he could not stay long in the
house nowadays ; he seemed to have become possessed
by a need for movement since his enforced wandering.
For hours together he would walk quickly and nerv-
ously as if he were being pursued, and, whether he
talked to her or strode ahead in silence, he liked to
have Jane with him for a companion.

Mary had become less resentful of their walks
abroad ; perhaps because it was more peaceful when
Jane was not in the house, perhaps because her vanity
was soothed by Hogg's frequent visits to play chess
with her and talk late into the night.

They were all agreed that Hogg was a disappointing
person ; he had undoubtedly been noble in his self-
sacrifice at Oxford when he had insisted on being sent
down with Shelley, and he was very clever, reading
Greek and Latin as readily as English, but that he was
intelligent made it all the worse that he should hold

such unworthy opinions, as Jane noted sententiously in the Journal :

' *Thursday, November 8th.* Rise at nine—Read through the *Man of Feeling* who would have just suited Fanny for a husband. Mary writes to Isabel. I copy the letter for her—She dines at two and goes to meet Shelley—violent storm of thunder and lightning—one clap was the loudest I ever heard. Read *Political Justice.* Mary returns about six. Shelley had seen Charles in the morning who had taken Morgan the £10—Hogg had been with him the evening before and asked him after his *two wives.* He joked all the time and talked of the Pleasures of Hunting—It fills me with surprize that the Author of *Prince Alexy Haimatoff* should delight in Sporting and Hunting—Human Nature is a composition of contradictions. Read *Paul and Virginia* in the Evening . . .'

Hogg would never do in a Pantisocracy ! Indeed the idea was broached much less often now, for her conduct over the bailiffs had proved Harriet to be quite unsuitable, and, when it came to the point, neither Hogg nor Peacock showed great enthusiasm for carrying off the Shelley sisters. And, although Jane either did not or would not see it, Mary's opinion on an ideal community had settled into the conviction that it should consist of two and no more.

I X

January–May, 1815.

She would not have admitted it, but Jane was beginning to get a little bored. Everything happened to Mary ; nothing happened to her. It was sad, of course, for Mary when her baby was born too soon and died after a week, but at least she had had one, and she still had her lover and would have other children. Jane was seventeen now and felt that Time was passing :

'*Sunday, November 6th.* Rise at nine. Talk all the morning. Read *Prince Alexy Haimatoff* and *King Richard III.* Shelley writes many letters. Dine at four. Mary and Shelley and I sleep all the Evening. S. goes at ten. Very philosophical way of spending the day—to sleep and talk—why, this is merely vegetating.'

She had written that in her Journal in November and now it was the New Year and she was often so wretched that she did not care what she did. She knew that Mary and Shelley wanted to get rid of her and were trying to find her a situation as a governess, for she could not go back to Skinner Street, as Fanny's schoolmistress Aunts were over from Dublin and feared that she would contaminate the niece who was to succeed them in their school. She did not mind not going back to Skinner Street although it would not have been so bad with Charles there for a companion ; she did not mind what she did.

Accidie is the deadly sin that is really deadly to the soul, and it was Jane's worst enemy. She could rise to occasions and show great courage in facing hardship and grief, but to attacks of the most insidious vice she had little resistance. Bored, she became sulky and quarrelsome, so that Mary wrote, ' *November 9th* . . . Jane gloomy ; she is very sullen with Shelley. Well, never mind, my love—we are happy ' ; and ' *March 14th* . . . Shelley and I go upstairs and talk of Clare's going ; the prospect appears to me more dismal than ever ; not the least hope. This is indeed, hard to bear . . .'

The situation seemed to have reached a deadlock, but with one of those sudden decisions that Shelley was not afraid of making when the need was urgent, he had seen her off to Lynmouth by the middle of May. It has been concluded that she made the arrangement herself after winning a lottery prize, but the draw was on April 15th, when Mary's Journal recorded, ' She buys two desks after dinner.' It is not likely that she won another or had enough money left a month later to take a journey and support herself for several months. Besides, on May 6th, Shelley and Mary paid two visits to Mrs. Knapp, a friend of God-win's with whom he was hoping to place Jane as a companion, but were disappointed that she could not take her. It is much the most likely that, as usually happened in the Shelley circle, Shelley paid.

However it may have been, Mary was able to write at the end of the exercise-book in which all the adventures of the year had been recorded :

' With my regeneration I begin a new Journal.'

And she and Shelley packed up and went to travel in Devonshire.

They intended to settle permanently in a country

home near London later in the year, and at the end of July Shelley went to house-hunt while Mary stayed at Clifton. None too trustful of Jane's rural enthusiasm, she wrote to ask if she had joined him. . . . ' I have enquired several times and no letter, but seriously, it would not in the least surprise me, if you had written to her from London, and let her know that you are without me, that she should have taken some such freak.'

But Jane was staying quietly at Lynmouth; whether the novelty of uninterrupted communion with Nature had not had time to pall, or whether her mind was occupied with the plans she was making for the future (*reculer pour mieux sauter*), she was able to write to Fanny with what seems genuine contentment : ' you told me you did not think I should ever be able to live alone. If you knew my constant tranquillity, how cheerful and gay I am, perhaps you would alter your opinion. I am perfectly happy.'

There is no Journal for this period, but the following letter to Fanny shows Jane's charm as a letter writer and its sentiments are typical of the young romantic, the " Rousseau man ", that she was at seventeen.

'*Sunday, May 28, 1815.*

' MY DEAR FANNY,

Mary writes me that you thought me unkind in not letting you know before my departure ; indeed I meant no unkindness, but I was afraid if I told you that it might prevent my putting a plan into execution which I preferred before all the Mrs. Knapps in the world. Here I am at liberty ; there I should have been under a perpetual restraint. Mrs. Knapp is a forward, impertinent, superficial woman. Here there are none such ; a few cottages, with little rosy-faced children, scolding wives, and drunken husbands. I wish I had a more amiable and romantic picture to present to you, such as shepherds and shepherdesses, flocks and madrigals ; but this is the truth, and the truth is best at all times. I live in a little cottage, with jasmine and honey-suckle twining over the window ; a little downhill garden, full of roses, with a sweet arbour.

[Description of two " gentleman's seats."]

You told me you did not think I should ever be able to live alone. If you knew my constant tranquility, how cheerful and gay I am, perhaps you would alter your opinion. I am perfectly happy. After so much discontent, such violent scenes, such a turmoil of passion and hatred, you will hardly believe how enraptured I am with this dear little quiet spot. I am as happy when I go to bed as when I rise. I am never disappointed, for I know the extent of my pleasures ; and let it rain or let it be fair weather, it does not disturb my serene mood. This is happiness ; this is that serene and uninterrupted rest I have long wished for. It is in solitude that the powers concentre round the soul, and teach it the calm, determined path of virtue and wisdom. Did you not find this—did you not find that the majestic and tranquil mountains impressed deep and tranquil thoughts, and that everything conspired to give a sober temperature of mind more truly delightful and satisfying than the gayest ebullitions of mirth ?

Now for a little chatting. I was quite delighted to hear that Papa had at last got £1000. Riches seem to fly from genius. I suppose for a month or two you will be easy—pray be cheerful. I begin to think there is no situation without its advantages. You may learn wisdom and fortitude in adversity, and in prosperity you may relieve and soothe. I feel anxious to be wise ; to be capable of knowing the best ; of following resolutely, however painful, what mature and serious thought may prescribe ; and of acquiring a prompt and vigorous judgment and powers capable of execution. What are you reading ? Tell Charles, with my best love, that I will never forgive him for having disappointed me of Wordsworth, which I miss very much. Ask him, likewise, to lend me his Coleridge's Poems, which I will take great care of. How is dear Willy ? How is every one ? If circumstances get easy, don't you think Papa and Mamma will go down to the seaside, to get up their health a little ? Write me a very long letter and tell me everything. How is your health ? Now, do not be melancholy ; for heaven's sake be cheerful ; " so young in life and so melancholy ! " The moon shines in at my window ; there is a roar of waters and the owls are hooting. How often do I not wish for a curfew " swinging slow with sullen roar " ! Pray write to me. Do, there's a good Fanny.

Affectionately yours,
M. J. CLAIRMONT.'

X

By the spring of 1816 it was time to leave Lynmouth but Jane had no intention of joining Mary and Shelley at Bishopgate. She was quite content to go home to Skinner Street and set about the two projects on which she had made up her mind ; to be called Claire [1] in future, and to get to know Lord Byron.

What manner of letter was it that Claire Clairmont wrote to Byron that induced him to answer ? He was the idol of London society who took his pleasure where he listed. Women of every grade of society wrote letters offering him every grade of love ; they fainted when he came into a room—and recovered to feel affronted if they were not given a chance to fall. He was prodigiously handsome and the infirmity of his lameness only stimulated that eleemosynary principle on which women's emotions work most readily, and he had a reputation as a poet and as a personality which was unparalleled, and has never been outshone.

At the time when Claire wrote to him Byron was on the Board of Management of Drury Lane theatre, but she did not make the excuse of submitting a play, although this was to follow later ; she did not exploit her stepfather's name—for she wrote anonymously ; nor her looks—for there were no photographs to enclose. She wrote two letters to ask for an interview and Byron responded.

The first was signed E. Trefusis and gave an address in Marylebone, probably some bookshop where she

[1] She used " Clare," " Clara," and even " Clary " before settling on this final form.

could pay a box fee ; the second had only a few lines and was delivered by a messenger. As she chose the initials G. C. B. for it, she may have intended Byron to think it had no connection with the earlier letter. These letters and Byron's answering note are given below in full.

(1) ' An utter stranger takes the liberty of addressing you. It is earnestly requested that for one moment you pardon the intrusion, and, laying aside every circumstance of who and what you are, listen with a friendly ear. A moment of passion or an impulse of pride often destroys our own happiness and that of others. If in this case your refusal shall not affect yourself, yet you are not aware how much it may injure another. It is not charity I demand, for of that I stand in no need : I imply by that you should think kindly and gently of this letter, that if I seem impertinent you should pardon it for a while, and that you should wait patiently till I am emboldened by you to disclose myself.

I tremble with fear at the fate of this letter. I cannot blame if it shall be received by you as an impudent imposture. There are cases where virtue may stoop to assume the garb of folly ; it is for the piercing eye of genius to discover her disguise, do you then give me credit for something better than this letter may seem to portend. Mine is a delicate case ; my feet are on the edge of a precipice. Hope flying on forward wings beckons me to follow her, and rather than resign this cherished creature, I jump though at the peril of my Life.

It may seem a strange assertion, but it is not the

less true that I place my happiness in your hands. I wish to give you a suspicion without at first disclosing myself ; because it would be a cruel addition to all I otherwise endure to become the object of your contempt and the ridicule of others.

If you feel your indignation rising, if you feel tempted to read no more, or to cast with levity into the fire, what has been written by me with so much fearful inquietude, check your hand : my folly may be great, but the Creator ought not to destroy his creature. If you shall condescend to answer the following question you will at least be rewarded by the gratitude I shall feel.

If a woman, whose reputation has yet remained unstained, if without either guardian or husband to control she should throw herself upon your mercy, if with a beating heart she should confess the love she has borne you many years, if she should secure to you secrecy and safety, if she should return your kindness with fond affection and unbounded devotion, could you betray her, or would you be silent as the grave ?

I am not given to many words. Either you will or you will not. Do not decide hastily, and yet I must entreat your answer without delay, not only because I hate to be tortured by suspense, but because my departure a short way out of town is unavoidable, and I would know your reply ere I go. Address me, as E. Trefusis, 21, Noley Place, Mary le Bonne.'

(2) ' Lord Byron is requested to state whether seven o'clock this Evening will be convenient to him to receive a lady to communicate with him on business of peculiar importance. She desires to be admitted

alone and with the utmost privacy. If the hour she has mentioned is correct, at that hour she will come ; if not, will his lordship have the goodness to make his own appointment, which shall be readily attended to though it is hoped the interview may not be postponed after this Evening ? G. C. B.'

(3) *Byron to " G. C. B."* ' Ld. B. is not aware of any " importance " which can be attached by any person to an interview with him, and more particularly by one with whom it does not appear that he has the honour of being acquainted. He will however be at home at the hour mentioned.'

Why did Byron consent to see her ? There are few bounds to human curiosity and fewer to human vanity and for Byron everything was acceptable that bolstered up the legend of himself. Among the quantity of fulsome love-letters that he received, Claire's note gave a promise of something a little different which was maintained by the naïve sincerity of those that followed : the nameless girl expected him to find time to read her play and criticize it ! And when she did secure an interview, her good looks were not unhelpful.

Her earnest enthusiasms were such as it most amused Byron to mock. He laughed at those rights of women that she so eagerly championed. ' Sophie,' she had commented in her Journal, when she first read her Rousseau under Shelley's instruction, ' Sophie is the most finished of coquettes. Emile is astonished at her infidelity. " He is sure that as Sophie proved weak, there can be no truth in Woman."

It is indeed partial to judge the whole sex by the conduct of one whose very education tended to fit her for a seraglio than the friend and equal of Man.'

Byron might like Sophies and prefer women " tamed to the cage," but the type of the young blue-stocking was new enough to be interesting and Claire did something to take his mind off Annabella, who was being tiresome with the stories she spread about him from the Milbanke home. Now that hostesses were beginning to retract their invitations, he did not mind whiling away some idle hours with such an ardent—and pretty —admirer and her voice even pleased him enough to prompt the lines beginning, " There be none of Beauty's daughters," for his inspirations were always personal, but when she did not make use of his introductions at Drury Lane, he began to suspect her intentions as a playwright and as an actress, and the too familiar note of tenderness had only to creep into her letters for him to show unmistakable signs of boredom.

This did not make him break the *liaison* ; and if Claire went from asking his advice on a play to asking his advice on an acting career, and from offering her selfless devotion to offering that gift of herself that always rather shocked him, what followed must remain Byron's responsibility. She was young, not yet eighteen, brought up on an ill-compounded mixture of advanced thought and Gothic romance, with no sufficient occupation for an active mind and a pretty body. When he allowed her to persuade him into her first ridiculous scheme for spending a night with him out of London it was too late to go back—too late for Byron, who had all the weakness of a vain man and the cruelty of a sentimentalist. Without the excuse of passion or of pleasure, for the Don Juan *manqué* of Piccadilly Terrace was a half-hearted libertine, he took her, and by April she had become pregnant with his child.

From Claire's point of view, she had scored a success beyond her wildest dreams ; not because she had desired the intimacy for itself, for it is a great mistake to think that the romantic temperament is necessarily passionate, nor for any prospect it might offer of a permanent union, for nothing could be more shocking to emotional sensibility than the monotonous familiarities of marriage, but she had set out to get to know Byron and she had succeeded. When she showed him off to Mary it was a Shelleyan community of spirits that she wanted to claim, not a relationship she shared with a number of casual chambermaids.

But if she was not passionate, Claire was young and inexperienced enough to be susceptible to a physical magnetism that had been the undoing of wiser women. Like Annabella before her, she fell in love with that beautiful face ; she told him so, ' I shall ever remember the gentleness of your manners and the wild originality of your countenance,' and protested that she was too grateful for his kindness to want anything more. But she had overstepped the bounds of her philosophy, as Annabella went beyond the morals of her Sunday school, though she did not know it yet and relished her success (' you betrayed passions I believed no longer alive in your bosom '), indulging in the sighs and sentiments that became a heroine of melodrama, without any presage of agony to come.

Between the lines of her letters, the whole story

tells itself ; the course of Byron's feelings easy to trace in the one-sided correspondence, where the flagging of her reasonableness and her sprightliness alike show her consciousness of his growing indifference. The letters which she could write, so ready and acute, he never saw, for love ties more tongues than it loosens, and Claire was never at ease with her lover. (' Do you know I cannot talk to you when I see you ? I am so awkward and only feel inclined to take a little stool and sit at your feet. This is how I always feel towards the person I love. When I behold them, nothing gives me half so much delight as to kneel down by them and hiding my head, to think about them.')

The letters quoted below are selected from a collection of some dozen that she wrote between their first meeting and his departure for the Continent ; Childe Harold trailing the Pageant of the Bleeding Heart.

(1) ' You bid me write short to you and I have much to say. You also bade me believe that it was a fancy which made me cherish an attachment for you. It cannot be a fancy since you have been for the last year the object upon which every solitary moment led me to muse.

I do not expect you to love me ; I am not worthy of your love. I feel you are superior, yet much to my surprize, more to my happiness, you betrayed passions I had believed no longer alive in your bosom. Shall I also have to ruefully experience the want of happiness ? shall I reject it when it is offered ? I may appear to you imprudent, vicious ; my opinion detestable, my theory depraved ; but one thing, at least, time will show you that I love gently and with affection, that I am incapable of any thing approaching to the feeling of revenge or malice ; I do assure you, your future will shall be mine, and every thing you shall do or say, I shall not question.

The Girl

Have you then any objection to the following plan? On Thursday Evening we may go out of town together by some stage or mail about the distance of ten or twelve miles. There we shall be free and unknown ; we can return early the following morning. I have arranged every thing here so that the slightest suspicion may not be excited. Pray do so with your people.

Will you admit me for two moments to settle with you *where*? Indeed I will not stay an instant after you tell me to go. Only so much may be said and done in a short time by an interview which writing cannot effect. Do what you will, or go where you will, refuse to see me and behave unkindly, I shall never forget you. I shall ever remember the gentleness of your manners and the wild originality of your countenance. Having been once seen, you are not to be forgotten. Perhaps this is the last time I shall ever address you. Once more, then, let me assure you that I am not ungrateful. In all things have you acted most honourably, and I am only provoked that the awkwardness of my manner and something like timidity has hitherto prevented my expressing it to you personally.

CLARA CLAIRMONT.

Will you admit me now as I wait in Hamilton Place for your answer?'

(2) 'Mary has promised to accompany me to-night. Will you be so good as to prepare your servants for the visit, for she is accustomed to be surrounded by her own coterie who treat her with the greatest politeness. I say this because on Monday evening I waited nearly a quarter of an hour in your hall, which though *I* may overlook the disagreeableness, *she* is not in love and would not. I have informed her of your name, so you need not appear in a mask ; she is very curious to see you. She has not the slightest suspicion of our connection. For pity's sake, breathe not a word. Do not mention my name. Talk only on general subjects. . . .

Pardon the abruptness of these sentences, my time is short. Believe that of all human evils none can scarce afflict me except

offending you.   I shall stay a few moments after her departure
to receive your last instructions.'

(3) ' If amidst your bustle you have a moment to give, pray tell
me if I may see you an instant this evening.   I will only stay
one half hour.   I know this is very very selfish of me to teize
you so, but love is always selfish in proportion to its sincerity.
Pray write me a few words, to tell me your address.

Monday morning.'

(4) ' Hour after hour and no news of you !   I do not think this
unkind of you ; poor creature, you are no doubt overwhelmed.
Write me but a few lines—tell me when you go ; I pray give
me some explicit direction, for I shall be at Geneva soon and it
will break my heart if I do not know where you are.   Keep my
messenger as long as you please, so you do but write.   If you
could but know with what palpitating anxiety, what restless
impatience I have been counting these hateful lingering
moments, surely you would write.   Tomorrow I shall wake
and find you gone ; a thousand times I shall question the reality
of all that has passed and feel [undecipherable] wretchedness at
the departure of an object who has of late occupied my ceaseless
thoughts.

A few hours and you will be away—flying from town to town,
resting in no place.   And a few hours more and this peopled
echoing city shall become to me the most desolate and hateful of
places.

In England I shall see you no more.   Blessed and quick be
the time when I shall watch its receding shores.   Think of me
in Switzerland : the land of my ancestors.   Like my native
mountain I am tranquil and [" like " crossed out] as they are
tranquil so is my affection.   One thing tell me ; say that you
go well and somewhat tranquil ; and if you can, say you think
well of me, but not unless you do.   And when you read this
letter say in that most gentle tone of yours, " poor thing ".
Now do not smile complacently and call me a " little fool " when
I tell you I weep at your departure.

Farewell ; you have been kind to me under the most un-

61

favourable circumstances and kindness is so rare to me that I can never, never forget you.   We shall meet again at Geneva ; to me the most beautiful and endearing of words.

Your most grateful
CLARE.

Pray write.   I shall die if you don't write.'

XI

April–August, 1816.

If Claire was determined to follow her lover into exile when the world crashed about his ears, her only way to do it was to persuadé the Shelleys to take her. They were intending in any case to leave England ' to escape,' as Shelley wrote, ' that contempt which we so unjustly endure,' but they had not thought of going further afield than Scotland or Cumberland, ' the most solitary regions of my native land.'

To hold out the promise of a meeting with Byron at Geneva would be a strong inducement ·to Shelley to go there, for he had sent him an early copy of *Queen Mab*, and greatly admired him as a poet and as a revolutionary, mistaking that somewhat pretentious visit to Leigh Hunt in prison for a substantial measure of radicalism and still innocent of Charles Brown's couplet,

> Ah me, what perils do environ
> . The man who meddles with Lord Byron.

Claire may not have needed to let him any further into her confidence in order to gain her ends, for had she not proved to Mary by the visit to Piccadilly

Terrace how intimate she was with the great man ? But keeping such a secret to herself at Geneva in the weeks of suspense before Byron came was more than she could bear, and she must have told Shelley though Mary does not seem to have known until later. She intended Shelley and her lover to be great friends—and Mary something beside : ' . . . You will, I daresay, fall in love with her ; she is very handsome and very amiable, and you will no doubt be blest in your attachment. . . . If it should be so, I will redouble my attentions to please her '— pathetically she offers an altruism that is often the tribute jealousy pays to love.

' I am coming with the whole tribe of Otaheite philosophers,' she had written from Paris, in the vein of gaiety that appealed to him so much more than any tongue-tied yearning. It was not so difficult to be gay now, for she was proud of the secret burden that she bore for him and full of hope that she might stir his heart to love.

And none did love him ; though to hall and bower
He gathered revellers from far and near,
He knew them flatterers of the festal hour ;
The heartless parasites of present cheer. . . .

Surely he would appreciate her loyalty and devotion ! But Byron was to write to Augusta Leigh, his half-sister : ' . . . as to all these mistresses, Lord help me, I have had but one. What could I do ? A foolish girl in spite of all I could say or do, would come after me, or rather, went before me . . . I could not exactly play the Stoic with a woman who had scrambled eight hundred miles to unphilosophise me.'

63

The idol had picked himself up from the dust of the market place and, setting his heart to advantage upon his sleeve, made for exile in the monstrous Napoleonic coach that he had had built. " Besides a *lit de repos*, it contained a library, a plate-chest and every apparatus for dining." Although it stuck several times in the Flanders mud it was still not capacious enough for the luggage or the staff, and at Brussels a *calèche* was bought for the three servants ; the Swiss, Berger, and the English valets who had accompanied him on his Grand Tour in 1809, Rushton, and the faithful Fletcher. " Polly-Dolly," the young Italian Doctor, John William Polidori, travelled in the coach with his master and grew daily too big for his boots.

On May 25th the cumbrous party arrived in Geneva and Byron signed his age as 100 in the Hotel visitors' book. Claire rallied him on it :

' I am sorry you are grown so old. Indeed I suspected you were 200 from the slowness of your journey. I suppose your venerable age could not bear quicker travelling. Well, honour and your sweet sleep. I am so happy——

CLARE.

Direct under cover to Shelley, for I do not wish to appear either in love or curious.'

But Byron was slow to collect his letters at the Poste Restante or to answer them when he did, and Clare could not forbear a complaint :

' How can you be so very unkind—I did not expect you to answer my note last evening because I supposed you to be so tired. But this morning ; I am sure you can't say as you used in London that you are

64

overwhelmed with affairs and have not an instant to yourself. I have been in this weary hotel this fortnight and it seems so unkind, so cruel of you to treat me with such marked indifference. Will you go straight up to the top of the house this evening at half past seven and I will infallibly be on the landing place and shew you the room. Pray do not ask any servants to conduct you for they might take you to Shelley which would be very awkward.

¼ past two. Sunday morning.'

According to Polidori, Byron first met Shelley as he was getting out of a boat, and, after dining together that evening, their meetings were frequent. Polidori described Shelley succinctly in the notes for the Journal which he hoped to sell later to Murray for 500 guineas (and from which he would then no doubt have cut out his private memos. on the looks of the women in the countries through which they passed!).

'Dined, P.S. the author of Queen Mab came; bashful, shy, consumptive; twenty six; separated from his wife; keeps the two daughters of Godwin who practise his theories; one L.B.s.'

Byron and Shelley sailed together round the Lake of Geneva and were nearly capsized in a squall off Meillerie; Shelley, who could not swim, and, only afraid that Byron might risk his life to save him, sat on the locker with arms folded refusing even to take off his coat and boots. They made an expedition to lay laurels on the grave of Rousseau and honoured the garden where Gibbon finished the *Decline and Fall.* Every day they met to sail or to talk, Byron riding down from Diodati, or the Shelleys and Claire walking up from the smaller Villa Chapuis that nestled in the vineyards below. " Albé," the Shelleys called Byron, or " the Albaneser," from a wild howling that he had set up one evening on the Lake and told them was an Albanian national song. " Monk " Lewis came to stay with Byron and Byron and Shelley were witnesses to the will by which the negroes on his West Indian estates were to be humanely provided for. They discussed ghosts and they teased Polidori. ' What is there that you can do that I cannot ? ' ' Why, since you force me to say,' answered Byron, ' I can swim across that river, I can snuff out that candle with a pistol shot at the distance of twenty paces and I have written a poem of which 14,000 copies were sold in one day.'

In the evenings when they all sat in the firelight Shelley and Byron would talk, so that Mary wrote later, ' I can never hear the voice of Albé without expecting that other voice to come in answer,' and on one memorable evening they all decided to write a story of the supernatural. ' Have you thought of anything ? '—Shelley asked Mary every morning, till at last her " mortifying negative " was no longer returned and she could say that she had begun *Frankenstein*.

Not as often as she hoped did Claire go up to Diodati alone, and when she went on the excuse of copying poems, Polidori would not realize that he was *de trop*. She begged her lover to send him out to ' write a dictionary or visit his lady-love,' but Byron did not bother. He was growing restive and wanted his Chapuis neighbours to go away. He tried shocking them : when he was in Constantinople he told them, he had had a girl who was unfaithful to him sewn up in a sack and thrown into the Bosphorus. The Thirza of his poem, he went on, was a young woman he had seduced and had two children by ; when he would not marry her, she committed suicide and was buried at a cross road which was why he could not erect a stone to her memory. ' He said,' recorded Claire (and this is so typical of the man that it almost makes the rest credible), ' he fretted very much about her death, but nothing, not even that, would have made him marry her because she was of mean birth.' They did not take much notice of what he told them, ' it was all untrue,' said Shelley, ' and only a childish love of astonishing people and creating a sensation.' He was very largely right, but another incident that they discounted at the time was not to be so easily dismissed. Claire wrote an account of it :

' . . . Next morning I went up to copy out " Childe Harold " [*sic*] as was my wont—and he asked me whether I did not think he was a terrible person—I said No I won't believe it—and I don't. He then unlocked a cabinet and spread a number of his sister's letters upon a table ; he opened some and shewed them : the beginning was ordinary enough—common news of their friends, her health and then came long spaces written in cyphers which he said only he and she had the key of—and unintelligible to all other people. We gathered them together to put them by, when he suddenly declared there was one letter missing and that I had taken it—he was extremely agitated —I said I have not touched any and begged him to look them again well over—he did so and after a time said he had found it, and made an apology for suspecting me. I mentioned the cyphers to Mary and Shelley but the latter said they most likely were used to convey news of his illegitimate children—I supposed so too and thought no more of Mrs. Leigh . . .'

In her Journal Claire destroyed all record of her association with Byron, and her notes to him at this time afford no evidence of a date when her condition was disclosed to Mary and Shelley, but by the end of July it must have been obvious that the secret could not be kept much longer, and an entry in Mary's Journal may indicate a date on which Byron broke the news to Shelley :

' *August 2nd.* I go to the town with Shelley to buy a telescope for his birthday present. In the evening Lord Byron and he go out in the boat and after their return Shelley and Clare go up to Diodati ; I do not, for Lord Byron did not seem to wish it.'

It would be easier for Byron to discuss it with Shelley alone ; he would not raise a woman's practical difficulties ; the question of money provision, perhaps of divorce and marriage. But even Shelley, idealizing Byron for his genius as he might, must have known something of his character by then and realized that this *liaison* was very different from his own connection with Mary. ' Love caused our first imprudence,' —not glamour, not a casual lust.

But it was not for Shelley to add to Claire's difficulties. There was a lame dog to be helped over a stile and he was ready. She must come home with them and they would care for her so that the Godwins need not know, and when the child was born Byron would make the necessary provision. That it should go to Augusta Leigh had been his first suggestion, but at

68

Claire's protest, he agreed that it should always be with one or other parent until the age of seven.

He would probably have agreed to anything to get rid of her—as he made quite obvious. ' We go, I believe, in two days,' wrote Claire on August 26th. ' Are you satisfied ? It would make me happy to finish " Chillon " for you. It is said that you expressed yourself decisively last evening that it is impossible to see you at Diodati. If you will trust it down here, I will take the *greatest* possible care of it ; and finish it in an hour or two. Remember how short a time I have to teize you and that you will soon be left to your dear-bought freedom.'

To his half-sister, Byron was to write : ' I forgot to tell you that the demoiselle who returned to England from Geneva, went there to produce a new baby B. who is about to make his appearance.'

Part Two

THE MOTHER
OF ALLEGRA

Love were lust . . .
     If Liberty
Lent not Life its soul of Light,
Hope its iris of delight,
Truth its prophet's robe to wear,
Love its power to give and bear.

    SHELLEY, *Hellas*, Chorus, Scene 1.

I

CLAIRE gathered up her self-control and her courage before leaving Geneva to write one more letter to her lover that should make a last good impression on him. She would neither be bitter nor solicitous and unduly tender, for he had shown that he did not like a mistress who sat worshipping, nor one who was too provocative. " Little fiend," he had called her and she had told him that she believed he rather disliked her, not minding, for it meant that he was not indifferent ; and she had been able to laugh as she laughed when the soft voice lost its caress and he told her he was tired, ' Pray go.'

She had been self-confident then, but now the neglect and the snubs at Diodati, his reluctance to be alone with her and his evident relief at her departure, made her doubtful both of herself and of him. But she would not doubt her love :

> Unkindness may do much ;
> And his unkindness may defeat my life,
> But never taint my love.

She wrote carefully, with self-restraint, making no reproaches. There was always the hope that when the child was born, he might turn to her :

' When you receive this, I shall be many miles away ; don't be impatient with me. I don't know

FACSIMILE OF A LETTER FROM CLAIRE
CLAIRMONT TO BYRON QUOTED IN THE TEXT

you would be kinder to me if you could but know how wretched this going makes me. Sometimes I feel as if you were dead and I make no account of Mary & Shelley's friendship so much more do I love you. Think sometimes of me dearest will you. Write to me soon & let me hear of your happiness & health. May you have every thing you like, hear nothing but good news & enjoy the greatest health. Farewell my dearest dear Lord Byron. now don't laugh or smile in your little proud way for it is very wrong for you to read this merrily which I write in tears. I am fearful of death yet I do not exaggerate when I declare I would die to please or serve you with the greatest pleasure nay I should feel as happy in so doing as I now feel miserable. Farewell then dearest I shall love you to the end of my life & nobody else, think of me as one whose affection you can count on & never pray, never forget to mention your health in your letters. May every good & every happiness be yours.

Your own affectionate Clare.

why I write unless it is because it seems like speaking to you. Indeed I should have been happier if I could have seen and kissed you once before I went, but now I feel as if we had parted ill friends. You say you will write to me, dearest. Do, pray, and be kind in your letters. . . . My dreadful fear is lest you quite forget me—I shall pine through all the wretched winter months whilst you, I hope, may never have one uneasy thought. One thing I do entreat you to remember—beware of any excess in wine. . . .

Farewell then dearest, I shall love you to the end of my life and nobody else. Think of me as one whose affection you can count on and never, pray, never forget to mention your health in your letters. May every good and every happiness be yours.

Your own affectionate,

CLARE.'

But she could be devoted and solicitous, or gay and provoking, Byron did not care. He was tired of her, and she, eighteen, romantic, unsophisticated, could not know that the only women of whom he had not tired were Lady Oxford, because she had given him his *congé* for another man, and Augusta, because she laughed at him, her ' Baby Byron.' Augusta had all the Byron casualness that reached callousness without any breath of genius to trouble the shallows of her mind, but in the end even her light inconsequence was not to escape the tide of evil that overwhelmed nearly all who had to do with him.

Claire's last letter, so carefully composed to sweeten her leaving—for to her lover it made only the differ-

75

ence of a few seconds' more *ennui*—was to be the first of many others. Distance lent enchantment, and from the rooms at Bath to which she and Mary had gone, she could not resist writing again. She makes the excuse of giving news about Shelley's negotiations with Murray over *Childe Harold* and gossip about *Glenarvon*—the novel in which Lady Caroline Lamb had sublimated her love-turned-hatred ; assures him that her depression will be better after the New Year, and with badinage talks of his reputation (they frighten the Shelley baby with a new Corsican Ogre, by saying ' the great poet is coming '), his drinking and the *petits pois* he likes for dinner. Still lightly, she refers to Augusta :

' Don't look cross at this letter because, perhaps by the same post, you expected one from Mrs. Leigh, and have not got it ; that is not my fault, dearest.'

But she could not always keep it up ; comfort of writing turns to bitterness when there is never any answer :

' I don't complain of you, dearest Albé, nor would not if you were thrice as unkind. . . . Indeed, my dearest dear, if you will write me a little letter to say how you are, how all you love are, and above all if you will say you sometimes think of me without anger, and that you will love and take care of the child, I shall be as happy as possible. . . .'.

Two or three times more she wrote such letters till in October there was real news to send, for Fanny had committed suicide by taking poison in a hotel at Swansea and Shelley had had to go and identify the body. She had been driven to it, said Mrs. Godwin, by love for Shelley, but it is more likely that she was goaded to desperation by her stepmother's tongue, reminding her that she was no child of Godwin's and a burden 'to his home. Godwin's first anxiety was to ensure that nothing of the affair became public, and he gave out that she had gone on a visit to friends in Wales ; with such success that Charles Clairmont a year afterwards wrote home to Fanny in complete ignorance of her fate.

Claire apologized to Byron for her low spirits :
' Add to this the unhappy state of that poor girl. I passed the first fourteen years of my life with her, and though I cannot say I had so great an affection for her as might be expected, yet she is the first person of my acquaintance who has died and her death so horrible too. . . .'

The Angel of Death was abroad ; his wings darkening the sky as he swooped to destroy, each time striking nearer the heart.

On December 15th a letter came from Shelley's bookseller friend, Hookham, to tell him that Harriet had drowned herself in the Serpentine. She was in an advanced state of pregnancy and had for some time been living away from her father's house in Chapel Street. Shelley hurried to London to claim his children, but had to write to Mary that he had not got them and that Eliza, who seemed to have driven Harriet from home out of jealousy, was determined to prevent his having their custody. ' At least it is consoling to know that if the contest should arise it would have its termination in your nominal union with me—that you having blessed me with a life, a world of real happiness, a mere form appertaining to you will not be barren of good.'

Claire shared in the Shelleys' horror, but lesser clouds had already blackened the sky for her; in November a letter came from Byron to Shelley with no enclosure, not even a message.

'My hopes are therefore over,' she wrote to him, 'I won't teize you with any more letters till after December, when I shall be able to write more cheerfully. . . . Soon I hope we shall see your handwriting again for I shall never know one moment's peace till we have another letter from you dearest.

. Farewell, then, dearest and best. I hope you have heard no bad news from England concerning those whom *you do love*. May you be ever pleased and have no wish ungratified.

Ever your affectionate,

CLARE.'

II

December, 1816.

Claire might assure Byron that she would be more cheerful in the New Year, when her child would be born, but in the meantime it was Mary who had to bear the brunt of her depression—and the romantic attitude did not favour self-restraint. Disappointed, unhappy and more than a little fearful for the future, it was no wonder that she was moody, though she made some effort to work at the books that Shelley set her and roused herself to cheerfulness when he came down to Bath. He had to be in London much more often that he liked, for, besides the question of raising money for Godwin, he was now faced with the far worse threat of the Chancery suit which the West-brooks were bringing to deprive him of Ianthe and Charles. The children had not been with their mother at the time of her death nor at her father's, but had been sent away to a clergyman's family in Warwickshire—a testimony against the " care " of the Westbrooks that should have told against them in the judgment.

Mary looked forward to having them to live with " Willmouse," but there is a presentiment of disaster in her Journal entry :

' *Friday, January 24th.* My little William's birth-day. How many changes have occurred during this little year ; may the ensuing one be more peaceful, and my William's star be a fortunate one to rule the decision of this day. Alas ! I fear it will be put off, and the influence of the star pass away . . .'

Loath as they were to leave Claire, Mary and Shelley decided at the end of December that they ought not to delay any longer going to London for their marriage. It would strengthen Shelley's posi-tion before the Chancellor if his union with Mary were regularized, and he was no doubt anxious to ensure that Mary and her children should have a proper status in the event of his death. For, with all his altruistic improvidence, he had too sound an intelli-gence not to appreciate legal obligations. He had made a will on his return to England after the elope-ment in which he left " an independence " to Claire, so that even Mrs. Godwin, who had reproached him with having ruined her daughter's prospects, had to concede, ' I should never have thought that so harum-scarum a man could have been so thoughtful.'

The ceremony, ' so magical in its effects,' as Shelley wrote to Claire, reconciled the Godwins, who were present at the Church and raised the ban on Skinner Street. But the house was full of unhappy memories and present embarrassments ; there lacked the quiet but somehow healing presence of Fanny, a Cinderella for whom no Prince Charming had come, and it was difficult to talk non-committally about Claire when her mother, to whom she was still " Jane," persisted in her enquiries. There was not even Charles at home to relieve the tension with his inconsequent talk and arguing, for he was in Bordeaux travelling at Shelley's expense for his pleasure or, as Mrs. Godwin said, for his health, so shattered by his sister's share in Mary's " ruin."

Mary and Shelley were as glad to get back to Bath as Claire was to welcome them. She had plenty of questions to ask about the household in Skinner Street and rather enjoyed the mystification of which she was the centre. Shelley stayed in separate rooms at 5 Abbey Churchyard but every day called on his wife and " Mrs. Clairmont " in New Bond Street and over the fire or in leisurely walks the three of them built their castles in the air. There was to be a house either in Wales or in the Thames Valley, where they would settle " for ever." It would be a home for Shelley's children and they would invite their friends to stay ; Byron might come if he ever returned to England and Hogg and Peacock could live with them. The dreams of Pantisocracy fluttered into a new reality.

III

January, 1817–March, 1818.

On January 13th, Claire's baby was born, a little girl, and Mary wrote to Byron ' she is in excellent spirits and as good health as can be. expected.' In her relief at her safety, for she was always a little nervous of herself physically, Claire's hopes soared, and she was as confident as Shelley that Byron would find his new daughter irresistible. ' Miss Alba,' he had written, ' is very beautiful ; although her frame is of somewhat delicate texture, she enjoys excellent health. Her eyes are the most intelligent I ever saw in so young an infant. Her hair black, her eyes deeply blue and her mouth exquisitely shaped.' An exact enough description of a newly-born infant from the Platonist who had astonished his fellow-under-graduate by challenging a baby on Magdalen Bridge, and had shaken his long hair in deep disappointment when the mother protested that he could not speak. ' He may fancy perhaps that he cannot, but it is only a silly whim ; he cannot have forgotten entirely the use of speech in so short a time ; the thing is absolutely impossible.'

If at nineteen Shelley had expected babies to trail their clouds of glory, at twenty-three he knew them from a more familiar angle, sticky at meals, crawling about his library and tearing at his papers, but he did not love them the less and he longed to have Ianthe and Charles to share a home with William and " Miss Alba."

But the Law could not be cognisant of that ; to

Lord Chancellor Eldon it only mattered that the Atheist who was responsible for *Queen Mab* had acted on the opinions expressed in it and was not repentant. He must confide his first-born son and daughter to strangers who were to allow him a visit of a few hours once every month, and see to it that he was not left alone with them during that time.

The judgment was given in March, a few weeks after they had moved into Albion House, Marlow. Its dark aspect where none of the rooms ' receive any sun at any time ' and ' the books in the library are mildewed,' made for depression ; it was not to be a home for the children and it seemed that no good could befall them there.

Even the friends that they had looked forward to welcoming proved disappointing. Peacock dropped in daily, but it was ' *uninvited*, to drink his bottle,' as Mary protested in disgust. The Leigh Hunts, with whom Shelley had made friends after the first notice of " Alastor " in *The Examiner*, came from London, but rather outstayed their welcome. And when Godwin brought William, Claire found her young brother more tiresome than before :

' *Wednesday, January 21st*. William teizes me all day. He is a strange creature. We walk together in the Woods. In the Evening play at chess.'

The most successful visit was that of the Dundee Mr. Baxter who was so completely converted by Shelley that he determined to face his dour son-in-law and insist that Isobel should be allowed to resume her friendship with Mary. But his visit was cut short by the birth of Clara, an event thus recorded in Mary's Journal :

' I am confined Tuesday, 2nd (Sept.) Read Rhoda, Pastor's Fireside Missionary, Wild Irish Girl, The Anaconda, Glenarvon, first volume of Percy's Northern Antiquities. Bargain with Lakington concerning Frankenstein '—so little did the philosophic household let the claims of nature interfere with the duties of literature.

But Mary was not always the imperturbable Madonna that she looked, that Fanny had wondered at ; ' . . . I cannot help envying your calm, contented disposition,' she had written to Bath, ' and the calm philosophical habits of life which pursue you or rather which you pursue everywhere.' Underneath the placid exterior there ran a gamut of emotions, from the melancholy that was the acknowledged legacy of her mother to an occasional access of high spirits that was to render her liable in later years to an embarrassing coyness. There is a foretaste of this in her announcement to Byron that she was married :

' . . . Another incident has also occurred which may surprise you, perhaps. It is a little piece of egotism in me to mention it, but it allows me to sign myself, in assuring you of my esteem and friendship,
MARY W. SHELLEY.'

This is very like her mother's letter to a friend when she was living with Gilbert Imlay : ' Teasing hinderance of one kind or another continually occur to US here—you perceive that I am acquiring the matrimonial phraseology without having clogged my soul by promising obedience, etc. etc.'

With Shelley frequently away to avoid the duns

who were harassing him, the two girls were none too happy together. Mary was in a low state of health (for she had borne three children in three years and was only twenty) and longed to move somewhere where they might be alone, ' give me a garden and *absentia Claria* and I will thank my love for many favours.'

Claire's spirits drooped as no intelligence came from Byron and irritability was the inevitable reaction. *Accidie* gained fast upon her. She grew slovenly in her dress and would only appear at meals and then sometimes not speak a word but retire immediately afterwards to her room or busy herself defiantly with Allegra. She coloured everything with her melancholy. ' Claire arrived yesterday night,' Mary wrote to Shelley in September, ' and whether it might be that she was in a croaking humour (in ill spirits she certainly was) or whether she represented things as they really were, I know not, but certainly affairs do not seem to wear a very good face.'

Mary might have spared Shelley more, but she was young and had not learnt to compromise, and only too naturally was the more impatient with Claire that Shelley always saw her in a better light. With him, she would commute her melancholy into more pleasing sadness and sing again, so that he could forget dull cares and put shining words to the music of Constantia, singing. Her dark eyes would glow with excitement or soften with unshed tears as she gave herself up completely to a song and lived in the world of daydreams it evoked. And when she came down to earth, she would offer to copy his verses, or recite the Italian exercises he set her, or listen while he read aloud.

It was not that she was in love with Shelley, either at this time or any other, for he had none of the qualities to strike the romantic imagination, and Claire " was of imagination all compact." She was not passionate, her infatuation for Byron due to many factors besides sexual attraction, and she had no craving for marriage, an institution from which she revolted : ' I can never resist the temptation of throwing a pebble at it as I pass by.' She may not have been above wanting to keep up with Mary by having a poet-lover of her own, but she never wanted to take Shelley from her. Probably he was the one person in her life of whom she was genuinely fond and, if so, she provided an instance (about the only one !) that proved his rule of love, for he certainly gave to her all that he could in patience and consideration and, in spite of relapses, she responded. Her last thought was to be for a little gift of his.

With her child she was happy when she could forget her over-anxiousness and the shadow of parting that lay over them. She was to tell Byron later that she had worn out her health by constant attendance on Allegra in the first year of her life. She certainly devoted herself to her with all the energy of her nature, but her demonstrativeness was an embarrassment in itself, for it made it impossible to keep up before neighbours and servants the fiction that the child was no relation, but had been sent into the country by friends for her health. Suspicion of her paternity began to fall upon Shelley, and, little as he and Mary might care for worldly tittle-tattle, they had learnt in a bitter lesson that public opinion could make itself felt in more than words. They were terrified of having William and the baby Clara taken from them—an unjustified fear, but one that was real enough to them at the time.

The sooner Byron fulfilled his promise to look after his daughter, the better. Shelley's financial obligations were heavy and not likely to grow less, but, even apart from this, they all seem to have felt, Claire not least, that Byron would be able to ensure the child a brilliant future which they had no right to deny her. Their attempt at worldliness here is a pathetic instance of their real unworldliness : the advantages that Byron offered were such as they all considered worthless, rank, money, fame, but they were determined to secure them for Allegra. They did not ask at what price—perhaps because in their innocence they did not think there would be anything to pay. ' Our upbringing,' as Claire observed in old age, ' unfitted us entirely for intercourse with vicious characters . . . Nothing could be more refined and amiable than the doctrines instilled into us, only they were utterly erroneous.'

In February, Shelley succeeded in getting rid of Albion House and they were free to take Allegra to Italy. They all packed up ; Mary and Shelley with William who was two years old, and Clara who was five months ; Claire with Allegra, just over a year old ; the Swiss nurse, Elise ; and a girl from Marlow, Milly.

Claire's Journal records the events of the few weeks they spent in London :

' *Tuesday, Feb. 10th. Sublime Shelley. Cantor di berdade sorge Queen Mab a ristorar il mondo.* Go with Peacock a shopping. Mary and the Babes come.

86

We all gó to the Opera in the Evening. *Il Don Giovanni* and *Acis et Galatea*. Remove to 119 Great Russell Street, Bloomsbury Square. Mr. Bramsen calls.

Wednesday, Feb. 11th. Read *Il Barbiere di Seviglia*. Spent the Evening at Hunts. Peacock, Hogg and Keats. Music.

Thursday, Feb. 12th. We go with Peacock in the morning to visit the India House Library. Curiosities. See the Panorama of Rome. In the Evening not well. Hogg and Peacock dine.'

A happy time ; Shelley could be ' jocosely horrible ' again and thoroughly enjoy himself, plunging into arguments with men of his own age and interests who, it never occurred to him, might be out of their depths. Hazlitt was shocked and Keats resentful, but the Smith brothers of the *Rejected Addresses* and Leigh Hunt himself saw through the shrillness, the occasional intolerance and obstinacy, to the poet of *Prometheus*.

Claire was encouraged to sing and play the piano at the Hunts' and in their admiration regained her vivacity. ' Spend my time at the Hunts very pleasantly.' And it was pleasant too, to inspect carriages in the city with Shelley or go with Peacock to look at the Apollonicon and other wonders, and on more than one occasion to walk with him ' to Bond Street and in the Park.'

There is nothing in Claire's Journal at this time to show that Peacock was in love with her and it is improbable that the author of *Nightmare Abbey* would want to marry his Stella, but it must have been his attentiveness now and the frequency of his visits to

Marlow when Shelley was away and Mary disgusted with him that were responsible for Mrs. Gisborne's comment to Mary years afterwards, ' How much suffering she might have been spared if she had married Peacock ! '

The last day sums up their visit and adds a name that it is good to have connected with Shelley in kindness, for mischief-makers had unhappily kept Elia from him :

' *Monday, March 1st.* Ride with Shelley into the City. Call on Mr. Baxter. Miss Hunt calls.

From this Monday till the next I was employed nearly in the same way. We saw a good deal of the Hunts. The Children were christened. We went to the Opera. Miss M. Lamb pays us a visit.'

I V

May, 1817–April, 1818.

Meanwhile Byron had been travelling about in Italy, and it was not until May, when he was in Rome, that he received the news of Allegra's birth. With a paternal egotism not surprising in the sentimentalist that he was, he preened himself considerably upon the event. ' They tell me it is very pretty,' he wrote to Augusta, ' and although I never was attached nor pretended attachment to the mother, still in case of the eternal war and alienation which I foresee about my legitimate daughter, Ada, it may be as well to have something to repose a hope upon. I must love something in my old age and probably circumstances will render this poor little creature a great and perhaps my only comfort. . . .'

But he did not trouble to make plans for her coming or relieve the anxiety—and the finances—of the Shelleys waiting on his pleasure. He showed more concern about the purchase deeds of Newstead, ' A clerk can bring the papers,' he wrote to Hobhouse ' (and, by-the-bye, my *child* by Clare at the same time. Pray desire Shelley to pack it carefully) with *tooth powder, red only* ; magnesia, soda powders, tooth-brushes, diachylon plaster, and any new novels good for anything.'

There are none of Claire's Journals preserved for the year of Allegra's birth, nor any of her letters to Byron, but she evidently did not cease writing to him, and on the child's first anniversary could still begin, ' My dearest Friend.'

' I do not say that she is a pretty child,' she wrote of their daughter, ' though she is certainly very far from ugly, but she has good points—pretty eyes of a deep day-time blue, rosy projecting lips and a little square chin divided in the middle like your own. . . . .

. . . My dear friend, how I envy you ! You will have a little darling to crawl to your knees and pull you till you take her up ; then she will sit in the crook of your arm and you will give her a raisin off your own plate and a tiny drop of wine from your own glass, and she will think herself a little Queen of Creation. But there is one delight above all this ; if it please you, you may delight yourself in con-templating a creature growing under your hands ; you may look at her and think : " this is my work ! " . . .'

89

This should have appealed to Byron ! But Claire never knew when to leave him alone, and she goes on—and the letter is very long—to declare that she had observed one thing in him that she likes ; ' let a person depend on you, let them be utterly weak and defenceless, having no protector but yourself, and you infallibly grow fond of that person.'

Where the child was concerned, she was less blinded by illusions, and she is genuinely apprehensive for her health :

' . . . I so fear she will be unhappy, poor little angel ! In your great house, left perhaps to servants, while you are drowning sense and reason in wine, and striving all you can to ruin the natural goodness of your nature, who will there be to watch her ? She is peculiarly delicate—her indigestions are frequent. . . .'

Pathetically—perhaps tragically, as it is to her lover she is speaking—she defends her break from the " tramels of custom ". ' I have loved, it is true, but what then ? '

' . . . Though I have praised myself I am not vain in that—how should I be otherwise, living in the company I do. Indeed I ought to be better. Alone, I study *Plutarch's Lives*, wherein I find nothing but incitements to virtue and abstinence. With Mary and Shelley the scene changes, but from the contemplation of the virtues of the dead to those of the living. I have no Hobhouse by my side to dispirit me with an easy impudent declaration of the villainy of all mankind, which I construe into nothing but an attempt to cover his conscious unworthiness. I must be the veriest wretch if I were wicked, placed in a situation as I am. I have faults—I am timid from

90

vanity ; my temper is inconstant and *volage*—I want dignity ; I do not, like our Mary, sail my steady course like a ship under a gentle and favourable wind. But at thirty I shall be better, and every year I hope to gain in value. . . .'

On their way to Italy, the travellers had little eye this time for France and concentrated their attention less on natural beauty than on the books they had brought with them, succeeding in reading Schlegel and Hunt's *Foliage*, in spite of the presence of three babies and the servants, and the constant risks the carriage ran of being overturned on the steep and often unmade roads. ' We have journeyed towards the Spring, that has been hastening to meet us from the South,' wrote Shelley to Leigh Hunt, unconscious of danger or fatigue, ' we have now warm sunny days, and soft winds, and a sky of deep azure, the most serene I ever saw.'

Once across the Alps, they opened their hearts to the scenery ; the vines become ' peculiarly pictur- esque ', ' unlike the French vines, which creep lowly on the ground, they form rows of interlaced bowers, which, when the leaves are green and the red grapes are hanging among those hoary branches, will afford a delightful shadow to those who sit upon the moss underneath.' And the sight of the white oxen in the fields and the peasants in their bright costumes were all that was wanted to complete the picture they had painted in imagination ; so, that arrived at Milan, Shelley could report to Peacock that they were far from disappointed : ' . . . no sooner had we arrived at Italy, than the loveliness of the earth and the serenity of the sky made the greatest difference in my sensations . . . . with what delight did I hear the woman who conducted us to see the triumphal arch of Augustus at Susa, speak the clear and complete language of Italy, though half unintelligible to me, after that nasal and abbreviated cacophony of the French.'

The cavalcade had halted for Byron to visit them and take Allegra back with him. But he did not come. A whole month went by before he answered the invitation and then he sent a messenger with a letter which said that if he took the child he could have nothing more to do with Claire and she must give up all claim to her.

The unexpected harshness woke Claire to some realization of what she was doing, for she had been too preoccupied with the "advantages" the child would have, and a certain satisfaction at her own sacrifice, to consider what it really entailed. Now for a moment she saw with agonizing clarity what it would be like never to have her again, not to be able to watch the small, fine features broaden and the blue eyes darken to violet when she dropped to sleep ; not to be able to laugh and throw loving arms about her when she struggled with new words or fell over in her play. At eighteen months Allegra had little of the plump featurelessness of her age, for her nose, mouth and chin were delicately cut, and she moved lightly as though her life were meant to be danced to a tripping measure. 'I think she is the most lovely and engaging child I ever beheld,' wrote Shelley to her father, begging him to have some consideration for the mother's feelings.

The messenger was detained while Claire sent

a letter to Byron in which she reminded him 'of the promise made at Geneva that the child should always be with one or other of her parents until she was seven years old, and that her mother should have frequent access to her. She implored him to be merciful :

' . . . Remember what you felt at my age, and think if it is not a lamentable sight to see one human creature beg from another a little mercy and forbearance. You must know that you have all the power in your hands—I entreat you to spare me. . . .'

She was to find that his consideration for dependents stopped short if they were not his complete slaves, but she was not yet disillusioned. She hoped that the harsh letter had been written in one of his fits of bad temper ; perhaps, he had had indigestion, or been drinking too much, or just quarrelled with a new mistress—all *peccadilloes* that she was anxious to forgive. She had made up her mind to the sacrifice and intended to go through with it.

Shelley for once was less optimistic, and rumours about Byron's way of life that he heard in the town made him entreat her to think again before she sent the child : but she rejected his warning, the first of his Sibylline books, and, only accepting Mary's offer for Elise to go with her, she professed satisfaction with Byron's reply, and, on April 27th, let the messenger take Allegra to Venice.

The next day was Claire's twentieth birthday.

With her child she had sent another of her letters, blindly written from the tears that ran down on to the paper and made her smudge the words, sparing herself nothing and completely careless of the impression she might make upon her lover.

' . . . think if it is not a lamentable sight to see one human creature beg from another a little mercy and forbearance. . . .'

' . . . I pray you remember what you have writ that I shall see her soon again. I do not know what you mean by saying that my letters are bad German novels—they may well be bad, and it is my daily fear that they may become worse. . . .

. . . I have sent you my child because I love her too well to keep her. With you who are powerful and noble and the admiration of the world she will be happy, but I am a miserable and neglected dependant. Dearest and best, I entreat you to think how wretched and alone I feel now that she is gone, and write to me that she is well, the darling bird ! . . .'

V

May–August, 1818.

Shelley had great faith in the panacea of travel to promote good spirits, ' Motion has always this effect upon the blood, even when the mind knows that there are causes for dejection,' he wrote, and Claire, determined to be comforted, diligently observed the scenery and wrote descriptions of it in her Journal as they continued southward :

' The scenery to Bologna was flat, but of incredible luxuriancy. The travelling in Italy seems like riding perpetually through pleasure-grounds, where ever the greatest art has been employed to give an air of Nature.

94

Descriptions of Italian Scenery

The weather was delightful ; a full sun in a cloudless blue sky looking down upon the scene of green below. The fields are planted with rows of trees, under which the vine twines and twists till it attains the summit and falls in countless festoons, stretching till it reach another. Under the trees, which themselves are sometimes fruit-trees, waves the high and beautiful corn. The hedges are full of flowers, and swarms of insects buzz in the sun. The motion of the carriage lulls one generally into a state of quiet observation and enjoyment ; and when I travel regularly on I cannot help hoping that the long straight road I see before me will take me to some place where I shall be happier.

The northern side of the Apennines is not highly cultivated. In one thing they differ highly from the Alps. In the latter the road runs along deep and narrow ravines ; the mountains rise on either side, and close somewhat in above, leaving but small portions of the blue sky to be seen ; but among the Apennines one travels along wide flat valleys which form their summits. . . .'

If the entries lack the spontaneity of the impressions of France and Switzerland four years earlier, they do credit to the courage with which she was facing her fate. She had strength as well as resilience of character and, once a decision had been taken and put into effect, she was prepared to accept it. She might cry for the moon, but she did not cry over spilt milk.

But the cheerfulness with which she wrote for news of Allegra would not be the less irritating to Byron because it was courageous :

' How is my Allegra ? Is she gay ? And has she

given you any *knocks* ? I sincerely hope she has, and paid you all your unkindness to me in very innocent coin. Whenever I think of the little creature I feel myself smile. She is so *funny* and yet so pretty. Upon my word, I think you ought to thank me, and instead of calling me *stupid*, be astonished at my *cleverness.* . . . You cannot think how unhappy I have been, but I am now better. I know you will let me see my *chick* again, and I can only hope when you see how *good* I am that you will be kinder to one who can never forget you . . .'

Her tactlessness was not relieved by her ill-timed flattery ('I heard of your extreme charity to the poor at Venice which was lauded by everyone') or her request for a lock of his hair to mix with Allegra's in a locket :

' . . . Now do, *dearest and most amiable of Bashaws*, send me a little ; if you do, I will turn Turk to please you, and forget reading and writing and every other Christian accomplishment. Good God ! If anybody could see how double I am getting with bending lowly to entreat the slightest favour of you. . . .'

This was written from Leghorn where they stayed nearly a month to enjoy the society of the Gisbornes.

Maria Gisborne, who might have been Mary's stepmother and whose influence was always of importance to her, was a woman of great charm and beauty. In her itinerant girlhood she had studied art under Angelica Kauffman and played the violin with Jeremy Bentham who declared that she was the only woman he had ever met who could 'strictly keep time.' On the death of her young architect husband, Reveley, who designed Bentham's Panopticon, she

96

had had no mind to find fame as the second wife of William Godwin and a little later married John Gisborne instead. He seems to have been a man of considerable understanding—if we judge from Shelley's letters *to* him and not from his remarks *about* him—and, though unsuccessful in his merchant's business and without defined ambitions of his own, entertained high hopes of the ,stepson, Henry Reveley, whom he brought out to Italy to educate.

The young man had undoubted ability, but was rather spineless and later involved Shelley in considerable expense over a steamboat engine that he invented and which Shelley wanted to employ in a regular service between Leghorn and Marseilles—for in the 1820's Industry and Economics had not taken all the romance out of mechanical invention. He was also anxious to improve Reveley's English by a course of correspondence, ' You are to write me *uncorrected* letters ; just as the words come.' He would annotate them : ' Do not think me arrogant. There are subjects of the highest importance in which you are far better qualified to instruct me than I am qualified to instruct you on this subject.'

But just as the engine was finally left to rust under the sea wall, so were the letters never sent that might have received the precious corrections on them. Reveley's mother appreciated better the quality of their new friend and introduced him to the reading of Calderon, but even she can hardly have realized when she welcomed the three young travellers to Casa Ricci that in the poem that was to be written from her son's workshop by the delicate-looking, rather excitable young man who had been denounced by the

Lord Chancellor and disowned by Godwin, her name was to be handed down to posterity.

In spite of the Gisbornes, they would not tarry more than a month at Leghorn, for there was much in Italy to be seen and the philosophical life yet to be lived. At the Baths of Lucca they thought they had achieved it ; ' we lead a very quiet and pleasant life,' Mary wrote to Mrs. Gisborne, ' reading our canto of Ariosto and walking in the evening in those delightful woods.' With leisure to turn her mind to a new book and Shelley and the children in good health, Mary was happier than she had been for some time ; the conditions of life in Italy made housekeeping easier and the presence of Claire less irksome than it had been in London lodgings, or struggling to make ends meet in the bleak house at Marlow.

Shelley was contented, too ; the genial climate was repairing the strain of the past year, and if there was little poetic accomplishment (*Rosalind and Helen* only finished at Mary's persuasion by ' taking advantage of a few days of inspiration which the Camoenae have been lately very backward in conceding '), he translated Plato's *Symposium* to give Mary ' some idea of the manners and feelings of the Athenians.' The poetry of a philosopher rendered by the prose of a poet, the translation may rank as one of Shelley's major works.

But Claire could not settle down. Confident as she was that she had made a sacrifice, and made it rightly, she nevertheless yearned for more substantial news of Allegra than was provided by the scant, illiterate letters from Elise. The child was no longer with Byron, but with the British Consul, Belgrave Hoppner, son of the painter, and his Swiss wife was looking after her with her own child of a few months old, the Rizzo to whom Byron had written verses on his birth. Something in a letter from Elise received on August 10th—perhaps the news of her dismissal—decided Claire to set off for Venice.

Shelley had to go with her. It would never do for Byron to think that Claire had come after him ; Shelley must create the impression that they were all at Padua, and that he had simply run over alone to invite Allegra on a short visit.

Actually it took them the best part of five days to make the journey from Lucca, for they had to travel to Florence in ' a one-horse cabriolet almost without springs,' and there they were detained by passport officials, the Austrian authorities as much hated by the Italians as the white-uniformed military. From Florence it was then three days further to Padua, but that was comparatively easy, as they travelled in what Shelley described as ' a comfortable carriage with two mules.' Arrived there, they were able to leave the roads for the water and in the afternoon embarked in a gondola for Venice. But their first sight of the city was not to be in any romantic setting, for the rain drove against the cabin where they huddled together for warmth, and blinded them to everything but the reflection of the lightning in the dark waters, their shallowness calm and undisturbed in eerie contrast to the convulsions overhead.

As undeterred as the laguna, the gondolier regaled them with stories of Lord Byron, the ' *giovinotto inglese stravagante*,' and his life at Palazzo Mocenigo where Margarita Cogni was installed, the Baker's

99

wife who had refused to be turned from the steps and now ruled the household with the tenderness of a tiger. She was to be cast out by doctor's orders a few months later when Byron's health had broken down and he could neither laugh at her nor rescue her when she flung herself into the water, bleeding from a self-inflicted dagger wound and had to be fished out by one of his gondoliers.

That night they spent at an inn, and called the next morning on the Hoppners. They were delighted with Mrs. Hoppner, ('rather Mary-ish' wrote Shelley), and ready to abide by the advice of the Consul who warned them that Byron must on no account hear of Claire's presence in Venice, and that it would be useless to try and see him before the afternoon.

There seemed no end to their kindness. They had rescued the child from her father's very unsuitable *ménage* where Elise had shown herself to be quite helpless, and now they insisted on Claire staying with them, and immediately put off engagements of their own in order to look after her.

Shelley and Claire were enthusiastic at such amiability, but in view of later events it may be doubted whether curiosity was not as strong a motive as kindness; Mrs. Hoppner was as pleased as her husband to have a finger in the Byronic pie.

Bewilderment had robbed Allegra of some of her bright-eyed liveliness, for a child thrives best on habit and routine, and Allegra's nineteen months had seen more changes than were good for her, but Mrs. Hoppner assured her mother that she would soon settle down and her cheeks regain their delicate clear colouring when she had the proper care that Elise, well-

100

intentioned but incompetent, had been unable to secure for her in Byron's distracted household. She would be properly fed now and keep regular hours and wear the sensible clothes that Mrs. Hoppner had already chosen to replace the evidences of La Fornarina's taste.

Allegra had a quantity of expensive toys, but like Papa she soon tired of things, and the baby Hoppner had not long to wait for what he coveted. Claire delighted in her daughter and longed for Shelley's return from the Palace to know if she might take her away and have her all to herself for a few weeks ; compare her with Clara and see if she would recognize her first playmate, " Willmouse."

Hour after hour went by and he did not come back. It was unlike him to delay, for, however vague he might be about his meals or his clothes or anything else that affected himself, he would never keep anyone waiting who depended on his coming. Suppose he had met with an accident, or worse, had had a quarrel, and Byron insisted on a duel, although he knew that Shelley disapproved and would not fight ! She found it hard to attend, as Mrs. Hoppner enjoyed vicarious licence at Byron's expense and chattered inconsequently about her servants, her baby, Allegra ; apologized for not having sent more news, but explained that she had so little time, so much to do . . .

At last Shelley returned. Byron had insisted on taking him in his gondola to the Lido where horses were waiting, and he had had to ride with him across the sands. But the object of the journey had been attained. Byron would let Claire have Allegra for a week. She was not to go to the Shelleys, for if she did he was afraid the Venetians would say that he was tired of her ; but he would put I Cappucini, the villa at Este that he had rented from the Hoppners, at their disposal, and they could all go there.

Claire was overjoyed at the news ; pleased with Shelley, pleased with Byron, effusive in her embraces of Allegra. A whole week ! Surely now that he had been so good, so like his *real self* (the rumours of his bad life were libels, as they had been in London), he would not disappoint her again ; he would extend this week to a fortnight, and every month in the future allow her to have her daughter for a few wonderful days. . . .

V I

August, 1818–March, 1819.

Shelley had to write to summon Mary in all haste to Este and, although it was not very convenient to leave the Baths as the Gisbornes had just come on a visit and Clara was not well, she immediately set off, taking the child with her. The journey did not dismay her—or she had no experience of sick children —and she looked forward to seeing Este. She had heard that it was very beautiful and she would enjoy excursions in the woods and mountains alone with Shelley while Claire was happy playing with Allegra.

Unfortunately Claire was taken ill when she arrived from Venice and had to go in to Padua to consult the doctor, but she did not think much of him and when Mary began to get anxious that her baby's condition was not improving, she and Shelley decided to take her into Venice in spite of the risks of the journey. At Fusina they were detained by the Austrian police, as they had forgotten their passports in their anxiety, but Shelley's impatience was not to be denied and they were allowed to pass. But it was too late ; Shelley rushed to the doctor only to return with him to find the child in a state of coma in Mary's arms.

Once more the Hoppners were kind. With ready sympathy they insisted on the distracted young parents coming to their house and relieved them of the practical arrangements for the burial on the Lido. Mary responded to their kindness, and with eminent self-control forced herself to go about with them sight-seeing. She even brought herself to call on Byron to beg him to extend Allegra's visit, though the mention of one small girl so near the age of the baby she had lost must have cost her dear. Godwin need not have feared that she did him discredit in the ' first severe trial of your constancy and the firmness of your temper.' ' You should recollect,' he wrote to console her, ' that it is only persons of a very ordinary sort and of a pusillanimous disposition that sink long under a calamity of this nature.'

The extension was not granted and Claire had to return Allegra to the Hoppners. Elise came back to be nurse again to William and, after a few days longer at Este, they set out for the South in a carriage driven by their Italian servant, Paolo. The hills around Este had fired Shelley with new enthusiasm for the Italian scene and he longed to absorb all he could of the beauties that each part of the country had to disclose. *The Euganean Hills* did not exhaust his inspiration but provided later the background for that giant of his creation, *Prometheus Unbound.*

After a week in Rome they arrived in Naples in December for a winter stay which was to have important repercussions on their lives afterwards. Certain events occurred there which affected Claire in that they provided the elements for the scandalous reports that Elise later communicated to the Hoppners, accusing Shelley of having had a child by Claire which he sent to the Florence Foundling Hospital. Claire certainly had an illness at Naples, and Shelley evidently undertook to be responsible for some child which afterwards died, and Mary was sunk in a despondency to which Shelley's poems bear unhappy witness, but Mary's denials to the Hoppners and Shelley's open references to " My Poor Neapolitan " in letters to the Gisbornes must dispose of the major accusation in the story. Elise left the Shelleys' service during this stay at Naples, as they found that she was with child by Paolo whom they sent away to a situation in the North, after, with some philosophical inconsistency, making him marry her. The slander seems to have been his revenge ! He got his wife to regale the Hoppners—and therefore Byron—with it, and later went to such lengths in his charges that Shelley was obliged to take legal action against him.

Claire's Journal was resumed on their return to Rome in March 1819. There are none of her letters to Byron for this period, though she no doubt wrote them, as surely as he did not trouble to answer. Her only news of Allegra, therefore, came through Mrs. Hoppner who wrote to Mary in January. After long apologies for her neglect and longer explanations of

104

the arrangements she has had to make for a nursery girl to attend to Allegra at night, she goes on to complain of the child's perpetual coldness. ' *Je crains qu'elle aye déjà la même disposition que sa mère . . . les mains et les pieds sont comme des morceaux de glâce et sont toujours rouges comme du sang.*' This seemed to react on her temperament, for she is much quieter now ' *tranquille et sérieuse,*' and compares unfavourably with Rizzo who is a year younger, ' *mon petit brûle et est toujours gai et sautillant.*' She sees as much of her father as possible, but his debauches are ' *affreuses* ' ; and when Allegra visits him La Fornarina (" *Madame La Boulangère* ") upsets her with sweets and cakes.

' *Quant à moi, je voudrais faire tout ce qui est en mon pouvoir pour cette enfant que je voudrais bien volontiers rendre aussi heureuse que possible le tems qu'elle restera chez nous ;* ' *car je crains qu'après elle devra toujours vivre avec des étrangers indifferents à son sort . . .*'

They did their duty by the child. They did not do more ; ' she was not,' wrote Mr. Hoppner after Byron's death, ' by any means an amiable child, nor were Mrs. Hoppner or I particularly fond of her.'

Her miniature shows that odd resemblance to the Princess of Parallelograms, on which Byron himself remarked (' she is much more like Lady Byron than her mother—so much so as to stupefy the learned Fletcher and astonish me '), with little of the beauty Shelley ascribed to her when he wrote :

. . . A lovelier toy sweet Nature never made,
A serious, subtle, wild yet gentle being,
Graceful without design and unforeseeing,
With eyes—Oh speak not of her eyes ! which seem
Twin mirrors of Italian Heaven . . .

ALLEGRA

*In her miniature she bears an odd resemblance to that
'Princess of Parallelograms,' Lady Byron, with little of the
beauty that Shelley ascribed to her when he wrote :*

'. . . A lovelier toy sweet Nature never made,
A serious, subtle, wild yet gentle being,
Graceful without design and unforeseeing,
With eyes—Oh speak not of her eyes! which seem
Twin mirrors of Italian Heaven . . .'

Perhaps the Hoppners were right and Shelley was
wrong, but, however it was, Allegra at two years old
was paying the price of those advantages for which her
mother had surrendered her to her father.

V I I

March–November, 1819.

When they returned to Rome for the spring
Claire took up her singing and music again with
enthusiasm, (' practise seven hours,' records the Journal
one day) and in sight-seeing and going about among
acquaintances she regained something of her old
gaiety :

' *Sunday, March 28th.* Mr. and Mrs. Bell call.
Walk with S. to the Capitol and the Coliseum. It is
a most bright and beautiful day. Drive to the Borghese Gardens and sit on the steps of the divine
temple to Esculapius the Saviour. See many priests
walking about it. In the evening go to the Conver-
sazione of the Signora Marianna Dionigi where there
is a Cardinal and many Englishmen, who after having
crossed their legs and said nothing the whole
evening, rise all up at once, made their bows and
filed off.

Monday, March 29th. A lesson in music. Walk
with M. across the Capitol to the Forum and Coliseum
—Go to Palazzo Borghese where there is a large collection but only one or two good pictures ; one is the
Sybil of Domenichino, in the moment of inspiration
—it is an exquisite picture—she is very beautiful both

107

in face and form and her head-dress and drapery are arranged with the utmost taste.

In the evening, go with the Signora Marianna to a friend of hers where we hear sung the celebrated *Miserere*. Nothing was ever so beautiful. Words can never express it, for they could only do so by turning to music themselves. Nothing but itself can be its parallel.'

With Mary, as they were driving one day in the Borghese gardens, she met Miss Curran, daughter of the Irish reformer, Godwin's old friend, and with her a real friendship sprang up. She encouraged Mary in her drawing and persuaded each of them to sit to her, including the blue-eyed little William who was always with his mother and father. Of these portraits those of Shelley and Claire are preserved ; Shelley's has been responsible for much of the Ariel legend with its failure to grasp his strength and essential integrity, while that of Claire might well have borrowed some of his lightness, for it has caught nothing of the vivacity which all who knew her declared to be her great charm.

' *Thursday, May 13th*. We go to Tivoli with Miss Curran. We see the Cascades and the Temple of the Sybil. The day then comes on rainy, and we return to Rome. This I shall ever remember as one of the pleasantest of my life and one as only Italy can give.'

Claire could write in some serenity again ; her emotional vitality almost completely absorbed in care for Allegra. At her birth the child had been largely a means to an end, the return of Byron's passion, as her mother's over-anxiousness for her betrays, and in the first months of parting her feelings were distorted by a conscious satisfaction in the sacrifice she was making ; but in the long absences her anxiety for her welfare grew genuine and selfless, so that she became in a sense more balanced than she had ever been. There are no longer any indications of that hankering after emotional excitement which had so horrified Shelley in the London lodgings, and her refusal to accept the offers of marriage that were made to her show an exceptional honesty and strength of will. If only Allegra kept well and she could see her from time to time Claire would make herself happy, wherever she was, with friends and study and music.

In Rome they were all prepared to be content. Mary had thrown off the melancholy of Naples, looking forward to the birth of another child in the autumn, and Shelley was enthusiastic to begin a play on the story of Beatrice Cenci which he had found in a manuscript.

They would go to Leghorn to be near the Gisbornes for the hot Roman summer and would return in the fall of the year.

They delayed leaving until later than they intended and on May 26th " Willmouse " was taken ill. Mr. Bell, a Scottish surgeon with whom they were friendly, was called in, and seemed to succeed in curing him ? (' William better,' records Claire's Journal on May 29th and 30th) but on June 2nd he had a relapse. They nursed him day and night ; Shelley refusing to go to bed and Claire taking her turn with both of them, too distraught to enter up her Journal. There is a blank from June 3rd to June 7th and then one line which sufficed to finish the brief, unhappy story.

 ' *Monday, June 7th*, at noonday——'

Three days later they set out for Leghorn. Shelley bowed down with a grief that anticipated old age ; his " high hope " laid in that Protestant burial ground he had described to Peacock on his first visit ; ' . . . a green slope near the walls under the Pyramidal tomb of Cestius . . . I think, the most solemn and beautiful cemetery I ever beheld.'

Claire, sharing in his agony and that of Mary, incapable now of the philosophic calm her father preached, wondered with sinking heart if it were possible for the Angel of Death to strike any nearer. She was in another world from that in which she had mourned Fanny, ' the first person of my acquaintance who has died.'

Conscientiously she took up the Journal again as they travelled and entered in it the sights they saw, (' the waterfall of Terni, the Lake of Thrasimene now called the Lake of Perugia ') and the books she read, (' Cobbett's *Journal in America*, Birbeck's *Notes on the Illinois*, *Nightmare Abbey*, and *The Heart of Midlothian* by Walter Scott '). They spent a week at Leghorn with the Gisbornes and then settled near Monte Nero in the Villa Valsano.

Here Charles Clairmont came to stay in September. Fresh from travelling in Spain, he had learnt the language and was full of enthusiasm for the literature, so that for once Shelley was to get some return on his money, for Charles read with him every day and helped him to finish the plays of Calderon that he had first discovered with Maria Gisborne.

Lively and handsome, Charles cut a dashing figure in the small colony, and when the time came to leave, Shelley wrote that it was ' not without many lamenta-
110

tions as all true lovers pay on such occasions.' His presence was not unwelcome in the household, for his high spirits were refreshing, and he had a good enough intelligence to be companionable to Shelley. His many schemes for earning a living which had up to now deserved Mary's early description of ' a wild project in the Clairmont style,' had at last settled into a decision to go to Vienna and teach English. This seemed sensible enough ; certainly an improvement on the scheme of two years earlier when he had been travelling in Switzerland and asked Shelley for a competence on which to marry a Swiss girl five years his senior ; with her to ' cultivate a little *métairie* among the mountains, to become a hardy *campagnard*, and to have a sweet association with every sequestered vale and nook within the compass of my ramblings : '— a Wordsworthian idyll which had had to be thrown to the wolves clamouring at the Skinner Street door.

He accompanied Shelley in October to look for suitable rooms for Mary's confinement at Florence where she was to be attended by Mr. Bell. They decided to stay in a *pension*, and it was there at the end of October that they made friends with some other English visitors, among them the Sophia Stacey for whom Shelley wrote the *Lines on a Dead Violet* and " Thou art fair and few are fairer."

Sophia, a very pretty girl, was a connection of the Shelley family and, though simple and *ingénue*, was a good deal more open-minded than most of her Sussex contemporaries. Determined to profit by the Grand Tour on which her guardian had brought her, she kept a Journal, but the sights of Florence are soon

111

neglected for references to the people she is meeting, particularly her Sussex relations. ' Mr. Shelley gives away half his income,' she noted, ' he keeps his carriage, not horses, being more humane to keep fellow men ' ; and of Mary, ' she knows Greek and Latin —is beautifully fair,' and, ' looks very delicate and interesting.' ' He is always reading and at night has a little table with pen and ink, she the same.' Sophia was soon being taught Italian by Shelley and invited upstairs in the evenings to sing ; a Carbonari song and an air well known at the time, called " Why declare how much I love thee," being the favourites. ' I played and sang with Mr. Chaloner and was in good voice. Mr. Shelley praised me much—also the other gentlemen.'

She was to benefit by that practical ability of which poets are capable so much more often than is accounted to them, for when she had ' dreadful toothache ' it was Mr. Shelley who came downstairs and put the cotton in her tooth. But the flutter this gave her, and being helped by him twice into her carriage had not time to develop into more serious heart-trouble before she was taken off to complete her Tour. ' Mr. Shelley saw to the arrangement of everything for our journey and was excessively kind ' ;. Mary exchanged promises of correspondence, and, her verses carefully packed, Sophia Stacey went away. She lived to marry happily and to treasure her poems—and her memory of the wild heir to the Shelley estate, so unlike what she had expected to find.

How little personal emotion there may be in a lyric which seems to be a *cri de cœur* is well shown in these poems of Shelley's ; they were simply presented in fulfilment of a promise and in the case of the " Dead Violet ", written on a half sheet of a letter from Mary ! Meanwhile Percy Florence had been born on November 15th, giving his mother as little trouble in his entry into the world as he was to cause her anxiety afterwards. ' Mary,' wrote Shelley to Leigh Hunt, ' Mary begins for the first time to look a little comforted. . . .'

V I I I

January—September, 1820.

Winter in Florence can be deceptively severe, the bright sun reflected in the Arno gives little warmth, and when the sharp Tramontana sweeps over the mountains, powdered with snow, it spares no corner of the city. The lofty rooms which the Shelleys occupied were not conducive to comfort with their stone floors and the tiny fireplace that no Italian could be persuaded it would be healthy to use for providing warmth ; and after four months of it, they decided to move to Pisa where the climate was milder and the waters had been recommended for the pain in his side to which Shelley was becoming increasingly subject. With their capacity for infinite discomfort in travelling they decided to go by water in the early morning :

' *Wednesday, January 26th.* Set off at eight. Mr. and Mrs. Meadows and Zoide walk with us to the side of the Arno where we begin our navigation. The weather was at first very severe. A keen wind blowing all the time. The Banks of the Arno are very beautiful, somewhat like those of the Rhine, but of a much softer character. We see hills the whole length of our course, now hanging over the River, and now receding in long green valleys to meet others. We arrived at Empoli about two, having done thirty miles in five hours. There we landed and took a carriage for Pisa, which city we reached about eight at night. We lodge at *Tre Donzelle.*

Thursday, January 27th. Walk with S. about the town seeking lodgings. Call on Mrs. Mason and the pretty Laurette. The weather most exquisitely warm and sunny. Read an Irish pamphlet. Horrid dream about Skinner Street and apoplectic fits.'

In the Mason family Claire was to find a sympathetic companionship similar to that of Mary with the Gisbornes. They were, as might be expected, no ordinary people. Mrs. Mason to whom Mary Wollstonecraft had been governess in Ireland, was really the wife of Lord Mountcashell, from whom she was separated, and Mr. Mason's real name was Tighe. They had two children, Laura and Nerina, though there must have been nine others somewhere as Claire referred to Mrs. Mason having ' brought up eleven children successfully,' when she was to plead the value of her advice on Allegra.

She was a woman of strong and independent intellect who wrote several books (one of them published by the Godwins' Juvenile Library ran into a thirteenth edition) and in later life was the leading spirit of a literary club in Pisa to which Italians as distinguished as Giusti and Leopardi belonged. She must have been interested to see the two girls about whom she had heard so much from Mrs. Godwin at the time of the elopement. The accounts she had received of them had been flattering : ' No man of forty,' Mrs. Godwin had written of Mary, ' is more steady than she is at any business you set her to do ; however difficult she succeeds in all she undertakes except music ; ' and she lamented Claire, ' with her cheerful temper and obliging disposition ; always pleased to be sent here and there and make herself useful.'

But of Shelley Mrs. Mason must have found it hard to make head or tail. He was an opinionated young man, she had been told, who even contradicted Godwin. On one occasion when a Saint was quoted at him he had ' laughed and said he would listen to Socrates or Plato, but not to a Saint as he could not see any merit in past ages except in the Pagan republic of Athens,' and he had called Mrs. Godwin a ' vulgar, commonplace woman without an idea of philosophy,' and refused to allow her to see her daughter. This had brought the name of Mrs. Mason herself upon him as Mrs. Godwin told her :

' . . . Perhaps you will be vexed with me, but I mentioned you to him as our friend and, being distinguished for your genius, your liberal opinions and every virtue and yet how different you were from him, for, let a woman be as poor or ignorant as possible, I was certain you would consider her maternal feelings as worthy of as much care, consideration and respect as those of the most refined and educated lady . . .'

This must have made an impression which it says much for her personality that she dispelled, for Shelley liked her at once and began to read with her the classics of the ' Pagan republic of Athens,' as earlier

115

he had read Spanish with Mrs. Gisborne. ' Very unprejudiced and philosophical,' he called both of them : high praise, for, as Claire recorded, ' it was one of Madame M.'s rules to consider a prejudiced person as one labouring under a serious illness.' She was gaunt in person and brusque in manner, with an Irish directness that was not softened by much Celtic charm. But besides being ' unprejudiced ' she was extremely kind and her influence was wholesomely astringent. She insisted on Claire taking part in social interests, with the result that the Journal entries become livelier and more expansive ; anecdotes of Mrs. Mason's interspersed with information from the works that she is reading :

' *Saturday, February 5th.* A letter from Charles. Practise. Walk with Laurette and call in Casa Silva. Vacca calls and says I am scrofulous and I say he is ridiculous.

M. and S. drink tea at Casa Silva. Answer Charles' letter. Read Paine's letters to the Abbé Raynal. Read Travels before the Flood which I like much. The Copts, who have a thinking Sultan, discharge God as superfluous. The Sublahers (*sic*) keep him on account of his being a grand, mysterious poetical subject. In the Alcoran are there words speaking of Poets. Bereft of their senses they run about in the Valleys and talk what they do not perform. An ambassador of St. Louis, King of France, met a woman in the streets of Damascus carrying water in one hand and fire in the other. The Ambassador asking the reason of so singular an appearance, she answered, " With the fire I will burn Paradise, with the water extinguish the fire of Hell that men may

116

worship God for his own sake and not as mercenary labourers.'''

On February 13th she recounts Mrs. Mason's visit in London to the shop of Hardy the republican shoe-maker who had narrowly escaped a sentence of High Treason. He made her a pair of shoes which she had to return saying, ' My feet are democratical and your shoes are aristocratical ; and they don't agree at all.' He refused payment for the next pair and they parted with mutual admiration.

This is followed by a story of Fanny Holcroft, a daughter of Godwin's friend the radical dramatist who was also involved in the treason trial. She was governess for a time with Mrs. Mason :

' *Sunday, February 13th* . . . But Fanny was of that kind which goes by the name of " luckless." She could not take anything into her hands but she let it fall. She thought herself handsome, tho' a very plain girl, and her dress and affectations excited the ridicule of the whole house. She attended nothing to her pupils but was for ever writing poetry. Did a great man enter the House she wrote Poetry, a little one, she wrote poetry—was there a party to dinner, she wrote poetry, was there no party to dinner still she wrote poetry—and such poetry ! She was called down by one of the servants on the arrival of a party of strangers. She rushed into the room breathless and with a pen in her hand. " Ah ! my God " said she, " have the kindness to excuse me, I have left my heroine in my hero's arms and I must fly to relieve them." So saying she disappeared to the great astonishment of all the company. She was found missing one morning, sought for and pursued. She had run away with a gentleman and all the account she could give of him was that he wore a *great coat.* Yet with all this, she was the best creature in the world, of a sweet and equable temper and very generous disposition.

As we walked to Casa Silva we met the Rev. Colonel Finch—a sight I did hope never to see more. A letter from Miss Stacey who is at Naples.'

There is another anecdote, this time of Lady Oxford, which evidently owed its circulation to Mrs. Mason :

'*Sunday, February 27th.* Walk with S. in the Cascini. Dine in Casa Silva. Lady Oxford used always to travel with an English doctor in her suite. She said one day to a large párty, " Well I do not know what I should have done last night. I was so thirsty, had not Bickerstaff, my doctor, who slept in my room got me a glass of water, I should have perished." When she was at Vienna, she used, on the pretence of delicate health, to make this Bickerstaff carry her to and from her carriage in his arms, and she always danced with him which astonished the Germans who thought it " *très drôle que Miladi dansoit toujours avec son accoucheur.*" '

But Mrs. Mason had other accomplishments than those of *raconteuse* :

'*Saturday, February 19th* . . . Mrs. M. has the power of shutting up her nose so that she need not smell bad odours. Vacca thinks it is the muscle which prevents the food from going from the mouth to the nose which she closes tight. Madame Vacca by long practise had acquired also this faculty—so at least she says.'

Reading included some dabbling in Science and other subjects less serious than philosophy and the classics.

'*Monday, April 10th.* Salt is composed of the metal Sodium and of a green air called Clorine. It is possible to procure efficient manure by digging in the stalks and leaves of plants, which is better than aid of beasts. Soda is composed of the metal Sodium and oxygen gas.

A lesson in dancing. Call in Casa Silva. Write letters from Italy. Read the Germania of Tacitus and begin his life of Agricola.'

'*Sunday, June 25th.* Practise. Read *Edinburgh Review.* Walk out with S. in the evening. Write to Tetta. Read a *History of England* written in French by a Jew after the manner of the Bible. " *Or les faits du Roi Henri, les lamproies qu'il mangea et les enfans qu'il engendra, ne sont-ils pas écrits dans le livre de Baker l'historien ?* " Of the miracles performed at Becket's tomb : " *Que celui qui croit ces choses, continue de les croire ! et que celui qui en doute reste dans son Incrédulité, et soit damné. . . .*'

It is a pity she could not record with her naïve acumen more impressions of another poet in Pisa.

'*Friday, May 5th.* Finish *Agnès de Lilien.* Breakfast in Casa Silva. A lesson from Legerino. Account of the odd English at present in Pisa. Walter Savage Landor who will not see a single English person —says he is glad the country produces people of worth but he will have nothing to do with them. Shelley who walks about reading a great quarto encyclopedia with another volume under his arm. Mr. Tatty who sets potatoes in Pots, and a Mr. Dolby . . .'

119

Claire still went for walks with Shelley, though she was a little uncomfortable sometimes when his careless appearance made them conspicuous, and she never knew when she might not have to contend with the quixotry that in Oxford days had embarrassed Hogg. Mary described one of their adventures to Mrs. Gisborne :

‘ The other day Clare & Shelley were walking out, they beheld a little dirty blacksmith’s boy running away from a tall long-legged man running with an umbrella under his arm after him crying *fermatole fermatole*—the boy got into a house & cried *son nella mia botega ! non tocami ! son nella mia botega*— Shelley approached & asked *cosa chè* ; for the tall umbrella gentleman had seized the boy by the collar—He (the tall man) cried " *Cercate il governatore—subito cercate il governatore.*" ' " *Ma perché ? che cosa è :* " " *Signor non fa niente che cosa sia —cercate il Governatore—subito cercatelo !* " & this with greatest vehemence—A crowd collected—Clare twitched S(helley) & remonstrated—Don Quixote did not like to leave the boy in thrawl but, defeated by the tall strider’s vociferations & overcome by Clare’s importunities he departed—& the(n) Clare out of breath with terror as you may well suppose said " for mercy’s sake have nothing to do with those people it’s the Reverend Colonel Calicot Finch ! "—so they escaped the attack.’

This Colonel Finch (‘ Calicot ’ was a nickname that Mary gave him from Moore’s Fudge family) was one of the " boon companions " like Hobhouse, to whom Claire objected for his bad influence over Byron. She was afraid that her story, which was kept secret from all but the most intimate friends, might get abroad and she was super-sensitive at encountering anyone of Byron's *entourage*.

It was natural that she showed some morbidity, for the last year had brought no sight of Allegra and very little news of her. In May, at Rome, she had heard from the Hoppners of the offer made by a Mrs. Vavasour to adopt the child and had written to Byron that she was willing to consider it—no stranger could be harsher in depriving a mother of visits and at least she would be with somebody who wanted her. But Byron's paternal vanity did not rise to putting the child's good first, and he refused the offer, as later he did no more than ' ponder ' the Hoppners' proposal of a family in Switzerland. Nothing more was heard until October when, from Florence, Shelley was prevailed upon to write to the vice-consul asking formally for news, as the Hoppners had left Venice.

Claire had certainly not been tactful when she wrote about Mrs. Vavasour ; her badinage as ill-timed as her remonstrance and the extraordinary request for a promised portrait :

' I am very unhappy over Allegra . . . really I think I shall never see her again. And if Shelley were to die there is nothing left for us but dying too. All the good you can do for me is not to hate me, but for Allegra everything depends on you. Do not make me mention what you *ought* to do for her, for I know that every word that falls from my mouth is serpents or toads to you, like the wicked sister in the fairy tale. It is not mine, but your fault that they are not pearls and diamonds. . . . I opened the letter to say that we think of being at Pisa this summer—if so perhaps

I shall come to Venice. *Bada a voi* in that case. The French nurses used to still their crying charges with " Marlborough's a'coming." If you are not good the Fornaria will get hold of my name to frighten you into order.'

But when she heard that Allegra had gone with Byron when he accompanied his new mistress, Teresa Guiccioli, and her father, husband, and brother, to Ravenna, she wrote not at all unreasonably asking for the child to be sent over to Pisa :

' I am afraid it is almost impossible for me or S. to fetch her. To Shelley it will be a most serious inconvenience in money should he be obliged to do so. I think it is not asking too much of you to beg you will send her to us at Pisa, where we are comfortably settled. This visit will be of the greatest advantage to her, for I shall take the greatest pains to teach her to read, and also we are going to the Baths at Lucca, a very cool place which may prove of service to her health, as she is delicate.'

She received no answer and wrote again on April 23rd :

' . . . If you force me to come to Ravenna against the reason of everyone and my own desire, I shall nevertheless be careful not to molest you, and any of your wishes concerning my darling, whether written or in words, will be carefully minded by me.

Farewell—all health to you,

Affectionately yours,

CLAIRE.

Pray kiss my dear child many times for me.'

This letter crossed with one from Byron forwarded by the Hoppners, ' concerning green fruit and God,' as Claire described it in the Journal. Written in some irritation with what he supposed were the Shelleys' theories on vegetarianism and atheism, he had not spared them the unkind jibe on their upbringing of children, ' Have they reared one ? ' But Claire replied with careful dignity, for there was much to lose, and at all costs the threat of putting Allegra in a convent must be avoided. She offered to have her at Leghorn where the sea air would be good for her and promised to pay every respect to his wishes regarding her diet :

' Your fears concerning the child's religious principles are quite unnecessary,' she wrote, ' as I should never allow her to be taught to disbelieve in what I myself believe, therefore you may be assured that in whatever way you desire, she shall be taught to worship God. Though my creed is different from Shelley's, I must always feel grateful for his kindness (to which I am perhaps indebted for my life), and every day convinces me more of his moral virtue . . .'

And Shelley, forced to take a hand, summoned his humour to supplement his tact :

' . . . I smiled at your protest about what you consider my creed. On the contrary, I think a regard to chastity is quite necessary, as things are, to a young female—that is, to her happiness—and at any time a good habit. As to Christianity—there I am vulnerable ; though I should be as little inclined to teach a child disbelief, as belief, as a formal creed. . . .'

So far had Shelley outgrown the young man who

contradicted Godwin and lectured Mrs. Godwin on philosophy.

However tactless Claire's letters may have been, and as irritating in their Griselda-like affection as in their banter and protest, they hardly deserved Byron's reception of them. ' . . . Claire writes me the most insolent letters about Allegra,' he told Hoppner, ' see what a man gets by taking care of natural children !   Were it not for the poor little child's sake, I am almost tempted to send her back to her atheistical mother, but that would be too bad ; you cannot conceive the excess of her insolence. . . .'

I X

August, 1820–March, 1821.

Fresh places brought fresh hopes, but the bright opening of Pisa became overcast as the prospects of Allegra's visit faded.   Entries begin to appear in Claire's Journal in a new tone of bitterness ; morbid dreams of Allegra and caustic references to Byron. Under " Hints for Don Juan," she collects quotations and occasionally adds her own comments.   In the following the criticism of Leigh Hunt is interesting for, to the Shelleys at the moment, he was without reproach :

' " *Quand la vanité se montre elle est bienveillante ; quand elle se cache, la crainte d'être découverte la rend amère, et elle effecte l'indifférence, la satiété, enfin tout ce qui peut persuader aux autres qu'elle n'a pas besoin d'eux.*"   Pride is concealed vanity and

124

that is what makes it so odious. Two examples we have in Albé and Hunt.'

Her series of suggestions for Caricatures for Albé were suppressed by Shelley's biographer, Professor Dowden, who called them " bitter in feeling and revolting in conception." Elegant they are not, nor kind, but they have point and are securely based on that foundation of truth which is the essence of a good caricature :

' *Wednesday, November 8th.* Caricature for Albé. He, sitting writing poetry, the words *Oh ! faithless Woman* round the room, hearts are strewed, inscribed, *We died for love of you.* Another—he catching a lady by her waist, his face turned towards her, his other hand extended holding a club stick in the act of giving a blow to a man who is escaping. From his mouth

> The maid I love, the man I hate—
> I'll kiss her lips and break his Pate.

Another to be called Lord Byron's receipt for writing pathetic History. He sitting drinking spirits, playing with his white mustachios. His mistress, the Fornaria, opposite him drinking coffee. Fumes coming from her mouth, over which is written " garlick ; " these, curling, direct themselves towards his English footman who is just then entering the room and he is knocked backward. Lord B. is writing, he says. " Imprimis, to be a great pathetic poet. First prepare a small colony, then dispatch the Mother, by worrying and cruelty, to her grave ; afterwards to neglect and ill-treat the children—to have as many and as dirty mistresses as can be found ; from their embraces to catch horrible diseases, thus a tolerable quantity of discontent and remorse being prepared, give it vent on paper, and to remember particularly to rail against learned women. This is my infallible receipt by which I have made so much money."

. . . Three more to be called Lord Byron's Morning, Noon and Night. The first he looking at the sky, a sun brightly shining—saying : " Come I feel quite bold and cheerful—there is no God."

The second towards evening, a grey tint spread over the face of Nature, the sun behind a cloud—a shower of rain falling—a dinner table in the distance covered with a profusion of dishes, he says—" What a change I feel in me after dinner ; where we see design we suppose a designer ; I'll be, I am a Deist."

The third—evening—candles just lighted, all dark without the windows (a cup of green tea on the table) : and trees agitated much by wind beating against the panes, also thunder and lightning. He says " God bless me, suppose there should be a God—it is as well to stand in his good graces. I'll say my prayers to-night, and write to Murray to put in a touch concerning the blowing of the last Trump." Pistols are on the table, also daggers—bullets—Turkish scymitars . . .'

She has a sally for Shelley, not malicious but apt enough :

' Caricature for poor dear S. He looking very sweet and smiling. A little Jesus Christ playing about the room. He says :

> Then grasping a small knife and looking mild
> I will quietly murder that little child.

Another'. Himself and God Almighty. He says :
" If you please God Almighty, I had rather be damned
with Plato and Lord Bacon than go to Heaven with
Paley and Malthus." God Almighty : " It shall be
as you please, pray don't stand upon ceremony."
Shelley's three aversions : God Almighty, Lord
Chancellor and didactic Poetry . . .'

The threats of a convent for Allegra had added new
fear to Claire's anxiety and this reacted on her spirits,
so that the old friction broke out with Mary.

> Heigh, ho, the Clare and the Ma
> Find something to fight about every day,

Claire had written in her Journal in July, and things
had not improved since.

Mrs. Mason in her wisdom—they called her Claire's
Minerva—saw that the only way to relieve the tension
was for Claire to go away, and she accordingly took
the matter in hand and arranged for her to go to
Florence as a paying guest in the family of the German
Professor Bojti. That she did not go as a governess
to the children there, is shown by the entries ' Pay the
Bs,' which occur regularly in the Journal. Later she
was able to secure a few pupils for English, but the
frequent references to German exercises and reading
indicate that she received more lessons than she gave.
She went in October, but indulged herself in such an
orgy of complaint and misery that at the end of a
month Shelley advised her to risk Mrs. Mason's
annoyance and come back to them.

She found new excitements in Pisa ; Pacchiani,
the professor-priest-adventurer who boasted that his

127

clerical hat was a Tartuffeometro or measure of hypocrisy, had already introduced them to several of the more outstanding inhabitants of Pisa, among them the handsome Prince Mavrocordato who had become Mary's inspiring tutor in Greek ; he was now to provide for them a figure who was the embodiment of all their youthful dreams of a persecuted heroine. He took them to call on Emilia Teresa Viviani, the lovely eighteen-year-old daughter of a governor of the city, confined to a convent by a jealous young mother who was determined to have her out of the way of her own lovers until a suitable husband had been found for her—and suitability was to be measured by age and money-bags.

The consequence of the encounter for Shelley is well known in the passionate eloquence of *Epipsychidion.* A whirlwind friendship, it caught up all three of them in a storm of emotion where pity and admiration blinded their more reasonable faculties, with the inevitable result that disillusion followed, and a year later Shelley referred to the ' Juno who had turned out to be a cloud,' and Mary wrote acidly to Mrs. Gisborne of his ' Italian platonics.' Claire was less disappointed, for her judgment had early been tempered with the astringent of a slight jealousy that Shelley's attention should not be reserved for her own affairs, and her conversation with the captive had been on less high minded planes :

' *Monday, July 23rd* . . . Emilia says that she prays always to a Saint, and every time she changes her lover, she changes her Saint, adopting the one of her lover.'

While it lasted the friendship provided her with

an enthusiastic correspondence and kept her employed on daily visits to take flowers and books or to read English and Italian—and did nothing to lessen her convictions of the evils of a convent education.

Claire may have realized that it was her pursuing *accidie* that had made her paint Florence in such gloomy colours, and in repentant mood—or at Mrs. Mason's strong persuasion—she decided to take the opportunity of travelling with Pacchiani, to return there in December. Her effort to control her spirits was successful, and in a congenial and admiring circle of acquaintances she recovered much of her natural vivacity, for she had ' an *esprit de société* rare among our countrywoman,' as Shelley's cousin Tom Medwin noted when he called on her. ' Though not strictly handsome,' he wrote, ' she was animated and attractive and was much courted by the Russian coterie, a numerous and fashionable one in that city.'

Besides the rounds of visits, Claire entered with enthusiasm into learning German :

' *Friday, January 12th.* Allegra's Birthday, 4. In the morning Call upon the Princess Montemileto. In the Evening in Casa Butterlin and Schwasoff.

Saturday, January 13th. Walk with Luisa and Annina to the Cascina and the Gallery. Wrote to M. and to S. and to Madame M. Study German.'

References to Allegra in her Journal are rare. When she wrote the entry above she did not know that on that very day, the child's fourth birthday, her father had sent her with a Guiccioli servant to the Capucine convent at Bagnacavallo. She only heard of it two months later :

' *Thursday, March 15th.* Rainy day. Letters

CLAIRE CLAIRMONT

" Though not strictly handsome," wrote Shelley's cousin, Tom Medwin, " Claire was animated and attractive." The portrait of her by Miss Curran hardly does justice to this vivacity which all who knew her declared to be her greatest charm.

from Emilia, Shelley and Mary with enclosures from Ravenna. The child in the convent of Bagnacavallo. Spend a miserable day. Begin the Hero and Leander of Schiller. News from the Austrians who are advanced through the defile of the Madonna della Grotta to the city of Aquila which was evacuated by the Neapolitan troops and were received by its inhabitants with open arms.'

Force of habit was strong. At Skinner Street only those of a ' pusillanimous disposition ' sank long under calamity, and Shelley had insisted on daily study whatever else happened. Claire followed the Neapolitan revolt and read her Schiller, but the peace of mind was shattered that she was so hardly coming by.

X

March–November, 1821.

In Byron's household, the human child had occupied a place a little higher than the animals ; ' the child Allegra is well,' her father wrote to Augusta, ' but the Monkey has a cough and the Crow has lately suffered from the head-ache.' He remained pleased with her, but his attitude to the child of four was no more wholesome than it had been to the baby ; she was still the means to an end : to satisfy his paternal vanity and provide a comfort for his old age. From this it naturally followed that she would always come second to the mistress of the moment. In Teresa Guiccioli she was fairly lucky ; the young woman liked to pet her, or liked Byron to see her pet her, but she

151

was jealous that she had no child of her own by her lover and in no mind to revolutionize his household by introducing a proper nurse into it. Very naturally Allegra was, as Byron said, ' four years old complete and quite above the control of servants ' and this, combined with the dangers of his flirtation with the Carbonari to which the Guiccioli attachment led him, provided the half excuses, half reasons that he gave for putting Allegra into the convent.

There is no need to think that Claire was justified in accusing him of wilfully endangering the child's health and character. He undoubtedly intended her to be turned out a little Teresa, than which nothing could be more desirable in woman, though his immediate object in sending her away was to save himself trouble—of which a great part was provided by Claire's letters. Such was his preoccupation that he could not even take her himself, but sent her with a Guiccioli servant. Never once did he make the journey to visit her. So far might the Byron casualness overtake callousness and leave it far behind.

To Claire's frantic letter reminding him of his promise that Allegra should always be with one or other of her parents until the age of seven he vouchsafed no answer, but forwarded it to the Hoppners with the remark across the top :

' The moral part of the letter upon the Italians, etc., comes with an excellent grace from the writer now living with a *man* and his *wife*—and having planted a child in the F. Foundling, etc. . . .'

This was the calumny for which Paolo and Elise were responsible, and which Byron was to repeat to Shelley in spite of his vows of secrecy to the Hoppners.

Shelley wrote at once to Mary to refute it, which she did in a letter of searing sincerity ; how could they, who had seen Shelley, believe that he would abandon a child or abuse his wife ? She implores the Hoppners, who had been kind, to be just. Of Claire she wrote : ' It is all a lie—Clare is timid ; she always showed respect even for me—poor dear girl ! She has some faults—you know them as well as I—but her heart is good, and if ever we quarrelled, which was seldom, it was I, and not she, that was harsh, and our instantaneous reconciliations were sincere and affectionate.'

The letter was never answered ; either Byron never forwarded it to them (for he would not like to admit to breaking his word), or they thought the matter too unimportant to trouble about. Whichever way it was, the letter was found among Byron's papers after his death with the seal broken : and when, many years later, Mary met Mrs. Hoppner and her daughter in the street, she cut them dead.

Between the lines of Claire's Journal it is easy to trace the cause of the general malaise which she tried to defeat by an intensive study of German and for which the doctors prescribed sea-bathing. She was willing to obey them so far as to go and stay for a few weeks with the Gisbornes at Leghorn.

Here an opportunity offered for escape from some of her troubles, for Henry Reveley wanted to marry her. Matrimony would have given her a defined position and she could have had little loyalty left for the principles of which she had boasted naïvely to Byron, showing off her Italian learning at the same time : ' *Anzi, vivendo in noi sempre talento, di stare insieme crescesse il disio*—is a blessing which I think the goodness of God ought to have bestowed upon married people, since he has imposed such an evil on the world.' But she had too much courage to take the easy way out. Her experience of real love, as she had thought it, had ended in disillusion; but that was no reason for pursuing counterfeits. The concentration of her emotions on Allegra gave them a complete integrity.

It was at Leghorn that she had hoped to have Allegra with her, but there was not even news of her, and Shelley, more worried than he let her know, was accepting Byron's invitation to Ravenna in order to have an opportunity of visiting the convent. He stayed a night on the way, and Claire entered the next day in her Journal :

' *Saturday*, *August 4th*, S.'s birthday. 29 years. Rise at five. Row in the harbour with S. Then call upon the Countess Tolomei. Then we sail out into the sea. A very fine warm day. The white sails of ships upon the horizon looked like doves stooping over the water. Dine, at the Giardinetto. S. goes at two . . .'

At Geneva Shelley had been dazzled by Byron's genius but now it oppressed him, ('the sun has extinguished the glow-worm,') and he was uninterested in the tales of debauch that compensated the simplicity of life under the Guiccioli dispensation. Ill at ease and haunted by pity for Claire (' the foolish and weak are in this respect Kings, they can do no wrong,') he was anxious to return home, but he had to be careful not to quarrel with his host, and he would not go without seeing Allegra. Alone he went over from Ravenna to the convent.

He found Allegra quite happy, though paler ' from the effect of improper food,' and more obedient, ' but not at the expense of much severity.' ' . . . Before I went away,' he wrote to Mary, ' she made me run all over the convent like a mad thing. The nuns, who were half in bed, were ordered to hide themselves, and, on returning, Allegra began ringing the bell which calls the nuns to assemble. The tocsin of the convent sounded, and it required all the efforts of the prioress to prevent the spouses of God to render themselves, dressed or undressed, to the accustomed signal.'

Shelley made the best of a bad job ; but even if the nuns, who had accepted her at double fees three years younger than the other boarders, were kind, and with latin cogency refrained from visiting upon her the venial sins of a rich, nobleman father, the convent was no place for a child of four. It was unhealthily situated near fever-breeding marshes and in winter would be bitterly cold. Her mother was not being " insolent " or hysterical when she wrote :

' He [Byron] robbed her of her liberty and shut her up in a building dark, gloomy and forbidding— she was never allowed to see a glimpse of the outer world, never a field, a wood, a rivulet—she was cut off from Nature which is the great Nurse, Comforter and delight of Children—an hour every day she might enter the garden of the Convent which was surrounded by high gloomy walls and looked upon the burying place of the Nuns also surrounded by walls 30 feet high.'

Claire went back to Florence from Leghorn later in the month, hoping against hope that when Byron came to the palace opposite the Shelleys at Pisa, he would bring Allegra with him, but on October 3rd she received a letter from Shelley telling her that the child would not be coming. Knowing what her disappointment would be, he went over in the week following to fetch her for a visit to the Williams' at Pugnano. She must have been too pleased to see him to worry what he looked like !

These friends, Edward and Jane Williams, had come to Italy at the suggestion of Tom Medwin and proved much more congenial to the Shelleys than he had been himself. Plans were already being made for the two households to spend the summer together by the sea, for Edward had stimulated Shelley's love for boats by providing a one-sailed craft that carried them on the Arno and Serchio, and was promising more adventurous sailing when his friend Trelawny, the Cornishman, should arrive.

Edward had been in the Army in India, where he had met Jane who was unhappily married to a man called Johnson and they had since lived together. She was an exceedingly pretty woman, with a talent for music and a gentleness of manner that was very soothing, even if it owed less to a steadfast than to a lymphatic temperament.

They had one child at this time, Edward Medwin, and were a devoted couple. Edward was intelligent though not intellectual, in spite of encouragement from Shelley who wrote of his play *The Promise*, ' if not a dramatic effort, of the highest order, [it] is one of the most manly, spirited and natural pieces of writing I ever came across.'

There was plenty of coming and going between the

two households and Claire was welcomed again at Casa Silva where Mrs. Mason thoroughly approved of a plan she was now turning over in her mind to become *dame de compagnie* to some German lady of rank. Shelley was less convinced of her qualifications and not altogether sympathetic towards her ' predilection for Germany, German literature and manners,' but he hoped that they ' would answer her expectations.' He always had to be wise for her and look ahead ; he was too fond of her to let her jeopardize her future if he could prevent it, and beyond everything he did not want her to feel that she ought to work in order to be independent of his support.

The matter did not have to be decided in a hurry and in Florence she was meeting influential people who could give her the necessary introductions. She decided to return there, as she could not risk daily encounters with Byron in Pisa, and did not like to accept the Williams' offer to remain with them.

On November 1st she went back. Coming out of Empoli the public coach in which she made the journey had to draw to the side to make way for a travelling cavalcade headed by a magnificent coach with four horses, to which the smaller carriages behind had difficulty in keeping up. The Italians crowded to admire the foreign *milord* and his suite ; it was Byron. Claire may have caught sight of that handsome head, wondered how she had ever come to love it so, and remembered how she had hoped there would always be a place for her at his side. But she was beyond that now ; irony and sentiment left behind where only tragedy lay ahead.

137

XI

November, 1821–April, 1822.

With Claire a calm usually presaged a storm, for activity was natural to her, and when she was passive or resigned it was likely that trouble was brewing. At Lynmouth as a girl—only six years before, but how long ago it seemed !—she had used her rural solitude to plan her meeting with Byron and now in Florence she was brooding in secret on a new scheme. It matured slowly and no evidence of it is allowed to appear in her Journal, which baldly records her lessons and her visits to friends. ' Translate Goethe ' is an entry which occurs from the beginning of April and refers to some translation that Byron wanted done and which, unknown to him, Shelley had procured for Claire. ' Bad spirits,' she records on several occasions, but, on the whole, secret activity was keeping her from *accidie* and she put a good face on things. She was genuinely anxious to earn her own living and only decided to relinquish the *dame de compagnie* project in favour of going to Vienna to join Charles who had assured her that there were excellent openings there for English teachers.

She could not go without seeing Allegra and on February 17th she wrote to Byron. It should have been a well-timed letter, as the recent death of Lady Noel had brought a considerable increase to his income and enabled him to adopt the initials N.B. which mightily pleased his Napoleonic vanity :

' . . . I am sensible how little this letter is calculated to persuade, but it is one of my unhappinesses that I cannot write to you with the deepness which I feel ; because I know how much you are prejudiced against me and the constraint which this inspires weakens and confuses all I would express.

. . . The weather is fine, the passage of the Apennines quite free and safe. The when and where of our meeting shall be entirely according to your pleasure, and with every restriction and delicacy that you may think necessary for Allegra's sake. . . .

. . . My dear Friend, I conjure you, do not make the world dark to me as if my Allegra were dead. In the happiness her sight will cause me I shall gain restoration and strength to enable me to bear the mortification and displeasures to which a poor and unhappy person is exposed in the world. I wish you every happiness.

Claire.'

When she received no answer, she hurried over to Pisa to consult with Shelley and Mary. She hardly liked to tell them all that was in her mind, but she confided freely in the Masons and in Elizabeth Parker, a girl who was staying with them recommended as companion by Mrs. Godwin. All that the Shelleys did to soothe her was undone by the rash sympathies of her friends, and the reports that Mr. Tighe gave of his secret visit to Bagnacavallo owed more to sympathy than tact. She returned again to Florence disquieted and with her mind so charged with suspicion that it only wanted an unexpected visit from Elise to put a match to the flame. The woman now took back all the story she had told the Hoppners and at

Claire's dictation wrote two letters, one to Mrs.
Hoppner and one to Mary, denying that she had ever
said anything. She did protest too much ; Claire in
her anxiety to clear herself of any charge that might
afford Byron an excuse to keep her daughter away
from her, was too impulsive to choose her ground with
care.

For one slander disowned, Elise teemed with plenty
more, and Claire tortured herself by listening to them.
Byron, she was assured, had said at Venice that
Allegra would be a pretty woman when she grew up
and he would take her for his mistress, and on remonstrance had declared that she was not his child anyway
but Shelley's.

Claire made up her mind to brook no more delay,
and wrote off to Shelley. He must rescue Allegra by
force.

Shelley was amazed. He replied firmly and with
some sternness to recall her to reason ; then, fearing
that he was himself forgetting that the weak and
foolish are Kings, tried to comfort her. ' It seems to
me that you have no other resource but time and
chance and change. Heaven knows, what sacrifices
I could make, how gladly I should make them, if
they could promote our desires about her . . . Come
and stay among us—If you like, come and look for
houses with me in our boat—it might distract your
mind.'

Although superficially their relationship was not
altered, Claire never really forgave Shelley for his
refusal to adopt her wild scheme ; disappointment,
as it so often irrationally will, withered the affection,
the kindness and the sacrifices that had gone to build

up the understanding between them over years. And to Mary's dispassionate account of the convent's situation and her plain warning that Byron was strong and they were weak, may be attributed Claire's strange accusation in old age that she had revelled in the execution of a child at Pisa and shaken hands with the hangman. This must refer to Allegra and Mary's later softening towards Byron's memory.

The sympathy and encouragement that she craved were supplied by the Masons and Elisabeth Parker, and they remained gratefully in her mind when their irresponsibility was forgotten or ignored.

'I was for decided measures,' wrote Claire in later life, ' and so were Lady M. and Mr. Tighe —so also was Elisabeth Parker who was my best, firmest and most affectionate friend—and has ever been so. Elisabeth constantly averred that nothing but the death of L.B. would free the child and that were she its mother she would stab or shoot him— she would lose herself but she would save her child. And had she been me, my firm belief is she would have done it—but I was not cast in that mould—a deed of blood was abhorrent to me—or indeed even one of unkindness to even my worst enemy would have been difficult for me to perform . . .'

Wrought up as Claire was, her anxiety taught her a new cunning ; to outward appearances her life followed its routine and she affected to acquiesce in Shelley's refusal to help her. She even accepted his invitation to come to Pisa as soon as Byron went to Leghorn.

On April 25th she left Florence for Pisa, where the Shelleys and the Williams' had flats at the Tre Palazzi

141

one above the other in the Italian fashion, round a courtyard where flowers grew luxuriant and bright, and the ground floor was left free for storage. With them again she could think herself back in those young days when they had all been light at heart together. She went for walks and practised her singing and worked with Mary at a table piled high with books, as though the dingy Skinner Street's schoolroom had never been changed for a large white-washed living room where the sun poured in through open windows and the distant sea seemed to be sparkling at the bottom of the garden.

Shelley still walked about with a book in his hand, not looking where he was going, and read or wrote for hours together in his room, with his dinner left untasted on a shelf, and in the evenings drank down the large cups of tea that he took without sugar because it was produced by slave labour, talking as enthusiastically as of old. He was full of plans for the new paper, *The Liberal*, which Leigh Hunt was to edit when he came with his wife and family to live in a floor of Byron's *palazzo*, and with Edward he never tired of discussing the boat that was being built for them and which they would sail in the Bay of Spezzia in the summer.

Mary was not so enthusiastic for the move, as she was expecting another child and would have preferred to remain quietly in Pisa, but neither she nor Jane liked to oppose the scheme on which their husbands were so set. They listened as sympathetically as they could to the plans that were made, and when the talk was exhausted Jane would sing, or play the guitar that Shelley had given her. The " magnetic lady " hands would hover so lightly over the strings that she seemed to compel the sounds from them by a charm, as her voice was a breath of evening wind ; for she had the intense femininity that suggests the elemental and for hours together Shelley would watch her, fascinated.

But Claire had no jealousy for Jane, " Miranda " where she had been " Constantia," for she had no feelings beyond her hope of seeing Allegra. She was not even roused to interest by the new visitor, Trelawny, who was the embodiment of all the heroes who had stirred the girlish imaginations at Skinner Street and who immediately showed for her an obvious admiration. Although she unfortunately did not record her first impressions of him, a much later letter describing one of his numerous portraits in the hands of one of his numerous women friends provides a detailed description of his appearance.

' . . . She has got a portrait of Trelawny—as like as like—yours is as handsome as he is, but the wildness which is real in him, seems in the picture to have been affected in accordance with the costume of the sitter : West's was too smooth and sleek, though resembling : hers is Trelawny and in his most Trelawny mood : his sunken eye, gloomy with reverses, but indelibly beaming ; that intense hardihood and genius which seem to command the whole world and even Fate itself : and then the delicacy of his nostrils and beauty of his lips which contrast so strangely with the severity of his brows, and his capacious forehead and dark thick locks are all to the life.'

About the same age as Shelley, Edward John Trelawny came of unbroken Cornish ancestry and

E. J. TRELAWNY

... " *West's was too smooth and sleek, though resembling,*"
*wrote Claire of this portrait, describing another now apparently
lost, which showed* " *his sunken eye, gloomy with reverses, but
indelibly beaming ; that intense hardihood and genius which
seem to command the whole world and even Fate itself ; and
then the delicacy of his nostrils and beauty of his lips which
contrast so strangely with the severity of his brows, and his
capacious forehead and dark thick locks are all to the life.*"

had lived through adventures as romantic as his looks. He had run away to sea and become lieutenant to the famous pirate De Witt, but if he was a Hero, he was also something more ; he had a fine natural taste and an instinct for the first-rate as much in literature as in life : he was generous and would spare himself no pains to be of service to those to whom he was once attached. And he admired Shelley more than Byron :

' Mary, Trelawny has found out Byron already. How stupid we were—how long it took us.'

' That,' she observed, ' is because he lives with the living, and we with the dead.'

It was Mary who was the most interested in him. She was attracted and at the same time repelled, for he was in many ways her opposite ; the opposite of that Mary she was always trying to live up to ; the Mary she looked like ; Madonna-gentle, serene and single-hearted. She disapproved of his philandering and the negligence that he sometimes affected with a certain Petruchio brutality, and she wished that he would not encourage Shelley in his wanderings away from the house, wearing shabby clothes, and being completely oblivious of the time. He undid all the good example of Edward Williams who was unconventional in more convenient ways. ' Still we like him,' Mary wrote, ' we believe him to be good.'

Claire had more natural affinity with Trelawny, although she was in no mood to develop it and was genuinely indifferent to his admiration. Her type of beauty appealed to him, for he was too experienced to be attracted by the obvious prettiness of Jane, whom he saw through as easily as Byron, and he appreciated having, for the first time in his rough career, the companionship of a woman of education and liberal views. Her story won both his pity and his respect ; he admired the courage that it showed and he felt for what she had suffered, for if he talked lightly of his love affairs, he had never betrayed a woman and left her destitute, and of children he always spoke simply and affectionately. His matrimonial affairs were a little complicated even at this stage ; as a youth on an expedition against slave raiders with De Witt he had rescued a beautiful young Arab girl, Zélla, whom he found to his dismay he was expected to take for his wife. The story of the development of his affection for her and their happiness together which was only destroyed by her tragic death is told with poignant sincerity in his *Adventures of a Younger Son*. But his railings in that book against the institution of matrimony as practised in the West, and his practical experience of it with a Miss Addison on his return to England, did not prevent him from marrying twice more in the course of his career and, although the experiences ended disastrously, his several families kept up with each other to the end without undue animosity.

Lively surroundings always cheered Claire and to the others at Tre Palazzi it seemed that she was contented enough. She no longer picked quarrels and she was ready to fall in with anything that was suggested, so that when the Williams' proposed that she should accompany them to look for two houses for the families at San Terenzo on the Bay of Spezzia, she willingly accepted.

She had only just left when news of Allegra came

to the Shelleys. They put everything else aside and determined that at all costs they must get away from Pisa and take Claire to Spezzia, whatever house accommodation offered ; for the news was to say that Allegra had died at the convent. Typhus had been raging in the district and for weeks she had been ill, but no one had thought to summon her mother.

In the little bed that she had shown Shelley in the bleak white-washed dormitory she must have struggled with the choking heat of her fever, imploring water and a cool breath of air from the coiffed figures who crowded round her, sometimes talking excitedly and then suddenly falling silent and wiping their eyes, until one afternoon they had to make way for the priest in his long black coat who hurried across the room to make the sign of the cross and put a little water on her forehead.

There was no handsome Papa, as there had been last time she was ill, to come in and dose her with a bitter tasting medicine, looking fierce one moment and speaking in a low caressing voice the next ; no Fletcher trying stiffly to play with her, and no soft and fair-haired lady to call her pretty names and leave a lingering trace of scent when she took her in her arms. Not that she wanted any of them, nor the mother she had seen too long ago to remember ; she only wanted the awful stuffiness to stop and her throat not to burn. She wanted to get up and play outside : to run all over the convent again with that strange man who had laughed so loudly when she rang the convent bell and the nuns had begun to hurry out.

Allegra was five years and three months old when

she died at the Capucine convent in Bagnacavallo on April 19th, 1822.

Byron wrote to Shelley that ' the blow was stunning and unexpected, for I thought the danger was over,' and Teresa Guiccioli declared in her Memoirs that he was overcome with grief when she broke the news to him. ' He desired to be left alone and I was obliged to leave him. I found him on the following morning tranquillized and with an expression of religious resignation on his features. " She is more fortunate than we are," he said, " besides, her position in the world would scarcely have allowed her to be happy. It is God's will—let us mention it no more." '

XII

April–September, 1822.

Mary and Shelley had not wanted to break the news to Claire until they were farther from Byron's neighbourhood, and therefore when the Williams' returned and announced that there was only one house available, Casa Magni, they decided they must share it with them. Shelley stayed behind to arrange about their furniture and, accompanied by Trelawny, Claire went with Mary and Percy Florence to Lerici.

But postponement did not make the telling any easier, and when Shelley arrived with the Williams' it was agreed by common consent that he must be the one to break the news. They were all sitting together discussing it in Jane's room at the back of the house when Claire suddenly came in upon

148

them and, from one look at the faces they turned to her, guessed what it was that she had to be told.

In her first grief and despair she wrote to Byron ; searing words to burn into the heart like an acid, sentences of withering reproach and bitter gibe, promises broken and warnings neglected flung into his face. It is one of the few letters that she wrote him which does not survive ; not because he immediately tore it up instead of casually tossing it into a drawer or passing it round with remarks scribbled across the top, but because he sent it to Shelley.

' I had no idea that her letter was written in that temper,' Shelley answered, ' and I think I need not assure you that, whatever mine or Mary's ideas might have been respecting the system of education you intended to adopt, we sympathize too much in your loss, and appreciate too well your feelings, to have allowed such a letter to be sent to you had we suspected its contents.'

If it should never have been written, it should never have been shown to anyone else, and Shelley made sure that it should not be.

But Byron could take punishment, for a bully is not always a coward, and in his essentially masculine nature he respected a just blow. It was typical of him to ask for sympathy from Shelley, the stronger man, but he bore no resentment, and for once he did not procrastinate in granting Claire what she asked for ; he sent her a miniature of Allegra and a lock of hair and gave permission for her to regulate the funeral. She did not avail herself of this nor go over, as had been her first intention, to see the embalmed

149

body. It was sent therefore directly to England where Byron had arranged for burial in Harrow Churchyard. He wanted a plaque to her memory put up in the church, but the vicar of the day could not allow a Natural Daughter to be remembered within holy walls.

The first storm of her grief over, Claire rose to her full stature. With a determination and self control that those who were nearest to her had hardly looked for, she insisted on relieving the discomfort of Casa Magni by returning to Florence and continuing to make her plans for Vienna.

The catastrophe had made her grow up ; a process which is entirely independent of years and to some people never comes at all, not because the opportunity does not offer, but because they are not capable of accepting it. In her child's death, Claire found the passion of her life. As her genuine care for Allegra grew, her infatuation for Byron had weakened and begun to show itself for what it was, something compounded more of vanity and glamour than affection. Often there is no date to be put to the death of love which sickens unnoticed until the day its corpse is found and the wonder grows that it was ever fair, but Claire was made free in a day—a costly freedom and one that in the years to follow she would often gladly have foregone, secure her maturity as it might. She had never really loved Byron, though for a time his strong physical attraction had intensified the glamour and excitement of their relationship ; for, like many women of her vivacious type who do not appear cold, she was not really passionate and her enjoyment of a sexually exciting situation was entirely mental. She was speaking more truth than she knew at the time when she wrote in an early letter to Byron, ' I have no passions ; I had ten times rather be your male companion than your mistress.' She was emotional from the head and not the heart.

The thing that was real in her life was Allegra's death, and because it was real it enabled her to discard sham sentiments and to show herself in her full strength of character. There was to be much for her to bear afterwards and often she complained and often, she revolted, but fundamentally she achieved a balance that she was never to lose ; she might sometimes dissipate her energies in regrets and sometimes in self-pity, but she was no longer the prey of moods and empty longings and always she controlled herself before outsiders. She was in equipoise ; her love for her child balanced by the memory of her being. She had borne Allegra ; she could forget the ugliness and the pain that went before and after.

Determined not to stay to let the irritation that often succeeds grief jangle her nerves and revive the old friction with Mary, Claire returned to Florence and only came again to Spezzia for a farewell visit on June 7th.

The evening after her arrival Mary fell dangerously ill and a week later suffered a miscarriage. In so isolated a place it was not easy to procure a doctor, and only Shelley's promptitude in placing her in ice to stop the hæmorrhage, saved her life. For days she lay weak and ill, miserable if Shelley left her, and yet, when he was with her, unable to control her depression and the sense of foreboding with which the place filled her. She had hated it from the moment they had come into it, beauty of open sea and dark wooded hills overcast for her by the isolation and wildness. The roaring of the waves that threatened to break upon the verandah that ran along the house and overhung the water drove her frantic, and she loathed the uncouth shouting of the natives who gathered for wild dances on the shore. The place boded no good.

Claire felt no uneasiness about it. "Quick natures run out to calamity in every shadow of it thrown before," but at this time her consciousness was too concentrated on facing her own tragedy to be sensitive to atmosphere. With the others she put down Mary's depression to her physical condition and did her best to cheer her with a determined brightness that was probably little better than her old moodiness, for it oppressed even Shelley who had put up with much in the old days. But there were no outward quarrels, and Claire at least helped to keep the peace with Jane, who was being rather Martha-ish, sighing for her own pots and pans and blaming the Shelleys' servants for everything that went amiss in the common kitchen.

For the most part Shelley was unconcerned with all this ; he loved the bay and was happy as he had never been before in the possession of his little schooner, the "perfect plaything for the summer." In every possible weather she was taken out, and when it was too rough to venture in the open sea, Shelley would drift about the shore in the fragile dinghy that Edward had shown him how to make out of reeds and canvas. For the first time in his life he cried to the flying instant, *Verweile doch, du bist so schön.*

News came on July 1st that the Hunts who had

arrived at Genoa about a fortnight before, were due to leave for Leghorn where Shelley could sail over to meet them and help them to settle in at Palazzo Lanfranchi. He had bought their furniture already, but that, he had begun to suspect, was to be by no means the end to what he might be called upon to do. With Edward and their sailor boy, Charles Vivian, he set sail on Monday, July 1st, at noon.

Mary was more low spirited than ever, determined that some ill was about to befall her little boy, Percy Florence. She could not maintain even an appearance of courage and wrote in deep melancholy to Shelley, although he had said that he would be back under the week.

Letters came from him, but they contained no good news; Marianne Hunt was very ill and the plans for the paper were all upset, as the Gambas had been ordered to leave Italy and Byron was going with them. 'Everybody is in despair and everything is in confusion.' He could not return home until he had nailed Byron down to some definite financial arrangement and then he hoped he need have nothing more to do with him. For, as Claire was to declare years after, his adoration for Byron's genius had turned to a conviction that it was ' a fatal gift, that developed in him inordinate pride and a dryness of heart and fierceness of feeling most dangerous in theory as in practice.'

Mary received Shelley's letter on the Friday; on Monday Jane heard from Edward promising her that, if Shelley were detained any longer by his friends, he would come over by felucca on his own; ' you may expect me on Thursday at furthest.'

But Thursday came, and then Friday, and still there was no sign of the *Don Juan* in the bay. Jane was so worried that she determined to be rowed across to Lerici and go by land to Leghorn for news. It was very rough and no boatman would put out, so that she was still there at midday when the letters came.

One was from Leigh Hunt to Shelley and Mary tore it open.

' . . . Pray write and tell us how you got home, for they say that you had bad weather after you sailed on Monday . . .'

They must have sailed, then ! But if they had sailed they must have arrived by now, and if they had put back there would have been letters to say so.

' Then it is all over,' said Jane.

Mary would not hear it ; she forgot her weakness and took the initiative ; made a sailor row them across the bay and secured post horses to drive, without a stop, to Leghorn. Claire must stay to look after Percy Florence and the Williams' babies and explain what had happened if unexpectedly the two men returned.

On the Saturday evening Mary and Jane came back, Trelawny with them. He and Captain Roberts had seen the *Don Juan* set sail on the Monday, but had been turned back from accompanying her by customs officials. He would not have it that all was hopeless, a contrary wind might easily have driven the boat out of her course, to Elba or Corsica. He would send messengers along the coast ; they could do nothnig but try to be calm and wait patiently at Casa Magni. He brought them back to the house.

It was *festa* in San Terenzo when they crossed the bay ; the little village was all lighted up and the

154

natives assembled on the shore to dance their wild dances ; men, women and children in separate groups singing a raucous chorus as they flung themselves into frenzied reels. Mary's nerves were worn to snapping, but for five days more she had to endure suspense ; the clamour on the shore and the howling of the waters against the house mocking her agony.

Trelawny left on the Thursday to get news, telling Mary to open any letters that might come for him from Leghorn or from his naval friend, Roberts, who was scouring the coast. ' On Friday I was very ill,' wrote Mary afterwards, describing the events of the week to Maria Gisborne, ' but as evening came on, I said to Jane, " If anything had been found on the coast, Trelawny would have returned to let us know. He has not returned, so I hope." '

But news had already come to Claire, for she had intercepted a letter from Roberts to Trelawny which said two bodies had been cast up on shore. It was more than she could bear to break the news to the other women and she wrote to Leigh Hunt begging him to help her, begging him to say that the news wasn't true.

Friday evening.

' . . . Outside the letter he [Roberts] has added " I am now on my way to Via Reggio, to ascertain the facts or no facts contained in my letter." This then implies that he has doubts, as I also doubt the report, because we had a letter from the captain of the port of Via Reggio, July 15th, later than when Mr. Roberts writes, to say nothing had been found. For this reason I have not shown his letter either to

155

Mary or Mrs. Williams. How can I, even if it were
true ?
I pray you to answer this by return of my messenger.
I assure you I cannot break it to them, nor is my
spirit, weakened as it is from constant suffering, capable of giving them consolation, or protecting them
from the first burst of their despair, I entreat you to
give me some counsel, or to arrange some method by
which they may know it. I know not what further
to add, except that their case is desperate in every
respect, and death would be the greatest kindness to
us all.

Ever your sincere friend,
CLAIRE.'

But she was to be spared being the messenger of evil
tidings, for it was Trelawny, the Hero with the roving
eye, the Pirate, who boasted of extravagant feats, it
was Trelawny who came to the two women ; tried
to choose words that would spare them, but gave away
the tragedy in his face, and went without speaking
from the room to send a maid with their children to the
stricken women. When words had to be spoken, he
found them with fine tact. ' He did not attempt to
console me,' wrote Mary in gratitude afterwards, ' but
he launched forth into, as it were, an overflowing and
eloquent praise of my divine Shelley, till I was almost
happy that I was thus unhappy, to be fed by the praise
of him, and to dwell on the eulogy that his loss thus
drew from his friend.'

The house that had always oppressed Mary was
unbearable to all of them now ; the waves moaning
beneath the windows and the howling of the sirocco

cruel reminders of the toll that sea and wind had taken, while the barbaric chants of the natives seemed a dirge fraught with the horror and mystery of Shelley's death. They did not know if the boat had simply capsized (for Edward was not the experienced sailor he thought he was) or had been run down in the storm by accident, or deliberately, by sailors who thought that Lord Byron's money was on board. Trelawny undertook to make enquiries, but first he helped them move back to Pisa, and then went to Via Reggio where he had to conform to the State regulations by burning the bodies that had been cast on shore. Williams' ashes were to be sent to England and Shelley's laid beside Keats and " Willmouse " in the Protestant Cemetery at Rome ; ' . . . the most solemn and beautiful cemetery I ever beheld.'

Byron and Leigh Hunt went with Trelawny. Leigh Hunt lay exhausted in the carriage that waited, with the two horses nearly dropping under the heat of the midday sun, but Byron stood out with Trelawny on the shore where brushwood was piled high on the bier, more moved than he would admit.

" Is that a human body ? " he exclaimed, " why, it's more like the carcass of a sheep, or any other animal, than a man ; this is a satire on our pride and folly."

The police and coastguards kept curious strangers away, while Trelawny performed the last rites unhindered, pouring wine and salt and frankincense upon the flames.

It was too much for Byron : ' Let us try the strength of these waters that drowned our friends,' he cried, and with Trelawny swam out to sea as the flames still

SHELLEY'S FUNERAL RITES

The police and coastguards kept curious strangers away, while Trelawny performed the last rites unhindered, pouring wine and salt and frankincense upon the flames.

Louis Edward Fournier
1854

curled and leaped upon the bier on the sands behind them.

Then Trelawny, who had loved Shelley with surpassing love, returned to look after those who had depended upon him. They clung together, the three women, in their misery ; Pisa almost more unbearable than Spezzia with its memories of the plans that had been so unconcernedly made there for the summer's sailing.

But they could not nurse their grief ; money had to be found to send Jane to England with her children and Claire to Vienna, and Sir Timothy Shelley had to be approached for an allowance for Mary. Byron offered to be banker and employed his London solicitor to help Peacock who was Shelley's executor with the negotiations. Godwin wrote to invite his daughter to her old home, and the Hunts asked her to live with them.

' After Shelley's death we all degenerated apace,' wrote Trelawny. This was not wholly true ; Byron began to haggle over the payments for the Goethe translations when he found out who had done them and regretted his rash money promises to Mary : and Jane on her return to England found a speedy consolation ; but Trelawny himself did not let die the flame that Shelley had lit ; Mary was to prove herself in her widowhood and Claire kept to her resolution.

Vienna seemed far off and hostile ; the Royal and Imperial city whose cold winds had tempered the cold steel that put down the Neapolitan revolt and restored the treacherous Bourbon to the throne, but "sanctions" had yet to be invented, and Claire was not deterred by her principles from seeking her fortune in the

Absolutist capital. She got her passport issued from the British consul at Leghorn on September 14th and a visa from the representative of his Royal and Imperial Majesty at Florence on the 17th, and, as there was no convenient party travelling which she could join, set out by herself for Vienna.

' I shall not be overstocked when I arrive,' she wrote with wry wit to Mary, ' unless, indeed, God shall spread a table for me in the wilderness. I mean to chew rhubarb all the way, as the only diversion I can think of at all suited to my present state of feeling, and if I should write you scolding letters, you will excuse them, knowing that with the Psalmist, " Out of the bitterness of my mouth have I spoken." '

The Journal, which had seen no entries since April 13th, a week before the death of Allegra, now recorded the last of Italy.

' *Friday, September 20th.* Get up at five. Pack; breakfast. It pours with rain. The carriage comes at ten with a Russian gentleman and a fat Bolognese woman, who looks to be a Jewess. Toto and Giuseppe and Francesco for Vetturini. We set out for Bologna. During the first part of the road, I was too occupied with my own thoughts to attend to the scenery. I remembered how hopelessly I had lingered on the Italian soil for five years, waiting ever for a favourable change, instead of which I was now leaving it, having buried there everything that I loved. We stopped to dine at Tagliaferro, where we rested two hours and then again set forward. Notwithstanding the rain which came by fits very heavy, I walked up the steep hills, hoping by fatigue of body to dull the painful activity of mind with which I found myself troubled.

160

The Road to Bologna

The scenery was pretty of itself, but rendered to me beautiful by the dark and gloomy character it had borrowed from the fast approaching wintry season. Small hills rise on every side, and the road winds mounting through the innumerable and yet lovely valleys which sometimes widen into a plain, and whose greatest charm consists in the varied scenery they present. Platforms of green fertility and groves of the chestnut-trees, mingled with the more tender green of poplars, ash and beech, are sprinkled here and there over the almost immeasurable prospect and relieve the eye from the contemplation of its otherwise barren rocky soil. I saw one or two monasteries situated as is usual in the most choice spots. One near the roadside from which it was separated only by a line of cypress trees of the most venerable appearance. To the left it looked across the road over an undulating plain richly cultivated and of the most varied appearance, and on the right over the heads of smaller hills heaped in masses around unto a boundary line of majestic Apennines darkened into the deepest hue by the shadows of the black clouds which hung over their summits. We continued thus our journey until about seven in the evening, the white fog, which as we mounted has been always increasing, now became so dense as to hide the road from our eyes. The Vetturini got down and led the horses step by step when we reached a cottage where we were obliged, nay even glad, to take up our night's rest. It was very poor and so dirty, the dark vaulted kitchens looked like a cavern of Hell.

I did not attempt to go to bed, but lent ' . . . [here this Journal ends].

Part Three

THE WOMAN

It is not much praise to the supreme Lord of Life what I am going to say, which is, Thank God, I can never be young again. At least that suffering is spared me.

Claire Clairmont in a letter to Mary Shelley.

VIENNA 1822–1824.

CLAIRE tried hard to appreciate the scenery on her way to Vienna, but it was not so easy to admire Nature at Mrs. Mason's behest as it had been with Shelley in that lyrical first expedition across France and Switzerland. She had been full of enthusiasm then, the raptures that Byron called " entusamusy," and in the years that came after Nature had remained the Comforter ; the betrayed mistress and self-sacrificing mother could still indulge the romantic idiom, but now it was inadequate. We get no more out of Nature—or anything else—than we put into it ; as Coleridge knew when he gave away the whole romantic case in his *Dejection Ode* :

> O Lady, we receive but what we give,
> And in our life alone does Nature live.

With the sheer misery of a heart trying to be brave, Claire wrote to Mrs. Mason :

' . . . I tried the whole journey to follow your advice and admire the scenery—dearest Lady it was all in vain—I saw not mountains or vallies, woods or rushing streams, Mrs. K. admired them, so I suppose they were there—I only saw my lost darling . . . I am not in need of money, all the expenses of my journey paid, I have over £10 still in my purse and my brother says that he will soon find me a situation as governess, as English governesses are very much in request in Vienna.'

She did her best to respond to the warm Clairmont welcome that Charles gave her ; he was eager to show her the sights and to introduce his friends, and confident that he could find good openings for her in the families to whom he taught English. Too much her brother and too intent on his own affairs to pay much attention to the alteration in her looks since he had last seen her in Pisa he still could not but feel a certain disappointment that she showed so little enthusiasm for his schemes. But he made what allowance he could, found her accommodation with friends in the Kärntnerstrasse, and tried to take her mind off her troubles by visits to the *Paradies Garten*, a popular pleasure ground outside the walls, or his favourite *Kaffee Haus*, " Zum Jüngling."

He was thoroughly at home in Vienna. He had always made friends readily and never had they been more accessible. He could sit and argue over the tables of a *Kaffee Haus* or *Wein Stube*, stroll along the broad walks under the chestnut trees of the Prater, or amuse himself in the evening at one of the numerous dancing-halls where for a few pence any partner could be his for the choosing, and in the set he might find himself beside the beauties of the town or ladies of established rank and virtue, for, in their pleasures, all classes mingled freely. " Light," said some disapproving English visitors born before the mid-Victorian epoch to which they spiritually belonged ; but others compared Austrian morality much

166

Life in Vienna

to the disadvantage of Covent Garden and the Prince Regent's Piccadilly.

It appealed to Charles ; the gaiety and *bonhomie* of the life where the prevailing Habsburg might dominate from the Hofburg within the city or from the seat of his new magnificence at Schönbrunn beyond the walls, but at the same time allowed the populace to wander freely in the royal gardens, so that in the Prater the ornate barouche of a merchant or the hired fiacre of humbler citizens might jostle with the Emperor driving his Empress in a phaeton with a single servant standing behind. Approachable were the Habsburgs if not amenable ; a tradition they maintained down to the later days of the Emperor Francis Joseph, when kings had begun to be less hedged by divinity than bureaucracy, but the meanest subject of the polyglot empire had still the right of personal petition. At the same time the *carrière ouverte aux talents* was obstinately opposed and there was no admission to court circles without sixteen quarterings.

Charles lived in a big block of flats built up against the Biber Bastion, one of the ramparts whose name is still preserved in the Bibergasse that runs parallel to the Stubenring. A typical building of its kind, it had windows at the back that looked out on to the flower-walks and trees planted along the tops of the ramparts and in the *glacis* below, but from the street entrance it seemed uncomfortably high and dark. The common staircase had to be lit all day by oil lamps and there was an outer door guarded by a *Hausmeister* who locked it sharp at 10.0 every night and was not to be persuaded to open again until he had been

167

propitiated with coin. The population was thus for the most part early to bed and the authorities ensured against the disaffection that breeds in midnight conferences. For, beneath all the *insouciance* of the city's life there ran one complete proscription, Politics. No books or papers could be published with any adverse comment on the government and there must be no criticism even in discussion. The net of Metternich's police system was flung wide.

A few weeks after Claire's arrival, Charles was caught in it. His cheerful argumentativeness which had been encouraged to range far and free at Skinner Street had not always avoided the suspicion of politics, and an anonymous letter had only to accuse him of being the son of Godwin and Mary Wollstonecraft and the friend of Shelley and Byron for him to find himself involved with the authorities. Peremptorily he and his sister, " Clarissa," were ordered to leave Vienna within five days.

Charles protested vigorously, rallied his influential patrons, and, with their guarantees of his respectability, presented himself for examination at police headquarters, (*Hochlöbliche Kaiserl. Königl. oberste Polizei und Censur Hofstelle*). Besides the accusations of the letter there were two other counts against him ; one accused him of failing to secure a confirmation of the permit to give English lessons for which he had applied on arrival, and the other asserted ' not only that he was a superfluous foreigner but also an immoral person ' on account of a woman, Caroline Lucas, who claimed to be supported by him. The first charge he answered by ' candidly admitting his neglect through carelessness and so much business and many acquaint-

168

ances ' and the second had to be dropped when it was proved that the woman had only resorted to a favourite ruse of her class in order to avoid suspicion as a *Dirne*.

By the police investigator, one Spreitzenhofer, Charles was described as follows : 'This language master of small stature, 28 years of age, seems to be of genuine French extraction as his name indicates. He is arrogant and argumentative about everything, contradicting all that does not fit in with his ideas ' (' *anmassend und raissonirend über alles, absprechend über alles, was nicht seinen Ideen anpasst* ').

But Charles was already *persona grata* in several great families, the Esterhazys, the Choteks, the Dietrichsteins among them, and their recommendation, combined with the failure of the police charges, persuaded the Foreigners' Commission to rescind the expulsion order. In the revised report Charles was found ' to behave modestly in the expression of his opinions and to give vent to nothing but favourable ideas and to proclaim aloud the earnest desire to be allowed to set up permanently here in Vienna where he is so comfortable. This is also the express wish of many householders and respectable persons who have lately signed a petition to the Government since he is admittedly at present the ablest English Language Professor.' He was still to be subject to discreet supervision and a few years later ' day reports ' were again made upon his movements and a new cross-examination held, for Englishmen were particularly suspect under the Absolutist régime on account of the extraordinary tolerance (*pace* Lord Eldon) allowed to Freethinkers in their native island.

The dossier of these enquiries is preserved in the

DOSSIER OF CHARLES CLAIRMONT

The dossier, which is preserved in the Vienna State archives, is a written document on thick paper of about ninety pages with edges badly burnt and in parts undecipherable as it only narrowly escaped destruction in the fire of 1927 when many of the state papers were lost.

Charles Clairmont was suspect to the Austrian police for a time on account of the following anonymous letter :

' Mr. Claremont who it is supposed will once more endeavour to come here for an outward avowed purpose namely to give lessons but for a concealed one as the writer firmly believes is the son of the authoress of the ' rights of Women '—his father was prosecuted in England some years since for sedition—his sister married Shelly—the author of Queen Mab Shelly was a deist—was deprived of his rights of a father by the Lord Chancellor of England—was the intimate of the late Lord Byron—Claremont is not his real name—it would be adviseable for the police to refer to the affair [*word crossed out*] with him at Presburgh.'.

Namen.	
Geburtsort.	
Character oder Beschäftigung.	
Alter.	
Kömmt von	
Paß.	
Wohnort.	
Aufenthaltsfrist.	
Anmerkung.	

Vienna State archives. It is a written document on thick paper of about ninety pages with edges badly burnt and in parts undecipherable as it only narrowly escaped destruction in the fire of 1927 when many of the state papers were lost. The examinations were close, but fair—Vienna, the stronghold against the Turk, had not then fallen to the barbarians of Europe, and Charles was allowed to continue in his profession.

As for Claire, this, to Spreitzenhofer, was Shelley's " Constantia," the mother of Byron's Allegra :

' Klara Clairmont of London, daughter of a Bookseller, aged 24, spinster.

This Englishwoman was in Pisa with her married sister and has come here for the first time in order to see Vienna and her brother who is professor of English here. She proposes to stop about four weeks and during all her stay has resided with Frau von Henikstein in the Kärntnerstrasse, whom she got to know this summer in Pisa. Moreover she has been recommended as shown in the annexed sheet, from the city of London to Herr von Schwab . . .'

But even without this incident and the disappointment of Charles' hopes of securing her an appointment with Frau Fürstin von Esterhazy, wife of the Royal and Imperial Ambassador in London, Claire would not have found Vienna congenial. After Italy she was sensitive to the climate and could not stand the autumnal winds that blew in from the Kahlenberg, dust-laden and cold, for the *Föhn* to which the Austrians attribute so much of their native *Schlamperei* caught up a heavy burden of dust from the unmade roads in the villages that lay beyond the elegant

171

suburbs outside the walls, and sometimes the atmosphere was as thick as a London fog.

The city itself she found oppressive ; grey under its northerly sky and made the darker by high buildings crowded in the *Stadt*, which was enclosed by ramparts much less extensive in circumference than those of Florence. ' The walls can be walked round by a party of ladies chattering all the time, within the hour ' wrote Mrs. Trollope in 1836. Twelve years later, after the Revolution, they were pulled down, and the Ring that took their place gave an air of essential spaciousness where there had been constriction before.

Indefatigable sight-seer as she had always been Claire must have explored the town, still mediæval and yet burgeoning into belated renaissance, where the deaf Beethoven could be seen any day sitting at his favourite *Kaffee Haus*, and in the afterglow of the Congress the young King of Rome declined into consumption at the Hofburg. She must have wondered at the Stefansdom with its one tower that springs straight from the earth to heaven and forever lacks its twin, the apex of the city as it is the landmark for miles around ; and, skirting the *Fleischmarkt* that lay as close to Charles' flats as Smithfield to Skinner Street, she must have visited the shops in the Graben and gazed sceptically at the Plague memorial that stands there, the quintessence of Austrian baroque. But, jealous as she was for Italy, the architecture had little charm for her ; she recorded no impressions of it, and some years later when she stayed in Dresden drew comparisons very unfavourable to Vienna. Her Gothic sensibility was probably a little dismayed by that element of latinity in the Viennese which combine with their *Schlamperei* to make them seem at once the most civilized people in Europe.

She fell seriously ill soon after her arrival and Trelawny wrote urgently begging her to return to Italy from ' that gelid out-of-the-way place.'

' You do me wrong—to make engagements which affect your health and happiness without consulting your best friend . . . I could only read the first half sheet ; your exile and illness filled my mind with sorrow, I had thought it possible you might find peace or gather some kind of happiness amongst your German friends—which I was anxious not to mar—had I known your real situation—think you I should have so ill fulfilled the charge I so gladly undertook on the era of your losing your noble-minded friend Shelley ? '

He deplored her new plan for going to Moscow, and insisted that she should accept the money he would send for her return to Florence ; ' remember, Clare, *real* friendship is not nice-stomached or punctilious—we are too far apart for tedious negotiation—give me these proofs of your attachment.'

There might have been some comfort in the knowledge of Trelawny's admiration, for in the weeks following the loss of the *Don Juan* he had fallen more and more deeply in love with her. Life does not stand still for death, and he had begged her to become his mistress if she would not marry him, but she had had no heart for such things, and too much head to imagine that there would be any happiness for them together, good friend as he had proved himself, and tempting though it was to stay in Italy.

VIENNA IN 1822

. . . the Stefansdom with its one tower that springs straight from the earth to heaven and forever lacks its twin : the apex of the city as it is the landmark for miles around.

THE GRABEN, VIENNA

Claire must have visited the shops in the Graben and gazed sceptically at the Plague memorial that stands there, the quintessence of Austrian baroque.

To Charles it must have seemed that if this Trelawny, who wrote such devoted letters, wanted to marry her she might do worse than accept him ; for, to his resilient temperament, she dwelt unduly on painful memories and was unnecessarily homesick for Italy and the friends she had known there. But Claire would not compromise with marriage. Travel was to be the panacea, and from Vienna, where so many races mingled in the streets, from the Hungarian officers in magnificent uniform to the peasants in a variety of national costumes rumbling over the paving stones in carts drawn by white oxen, it did not seem so far to Moscow.

To go as a governess to Russia was used by Mrs. Gaskell in *Wives and Daughters* as the equivalent of taking the veil, or a lady-like form of suicide, and Trelawny, who was about to add to his adventures by going with Byron to fight for Greek Independence, was horrified. But in spite of his protests and Charles' entreaties to give him a little longer to find her a place among his aristocratic connections she insisted on keeping to her decision, her ' compulsive emigration to the North ' as Trelawny called it, and early in the summer of 1824, she set off for Russia.

II

MOSCOW 1824-1828.

Very different from the crowded and hill-encircled city of Vienna was the open plain where Moscow's crowded cupolas glittered in the sun, golden cross

MOSCOW IN 1822

. . . the walls of the Kremlin flank one side of the Red Square where a gorgeous mosque-like church celebrates the final defeat of the Turks by Ivan the Terrible.

mounted over golden crescent on mosque and church alike to prove the victory of Christianity over the Tartar—a victory whose symbol might well have stood less for a gallant repulse of the Infidel than for the insidious incursion of a priesthood that was stifling the population with superstition and bigotry. Conspicuous in long black robes and their distinctive *kamelaveke*, the priests with patriarchal beards and the shaven monks might be counted every day in their hundreds passing through the centre of the city, the Red Square, where the walls of the Kremlin flank one side and a gorgeous mosque-like church, Holy Basil, celebrates the final defeat of the Turks by Ivan the Terrible.

Moscow was the Holy City where rich old ladies came to die, boasting to sympathetic father confessors of their sins in the *parvenu* St. Petersburg, but in no part of the country was there a lack of churches or congregations to fill them, for masters liked their servants to be pious, and servants were not inclined to disobedience under a law that gave employers the right to send them to the police station for the knout without further enquiries.

Wealth in the aristocracy was counted in terms of serfs (14,000 was a moderate number) for there was often very little land by the time it had been divided among numerous inheritors, none of whom contributed to its enrichment either by industry or providence. When there were no serfs left to sell to defray gambling debts a landed gentleman had to live on rich relatives, or politely shoot himself. Among the merchants wealth was counted in other ways and spent on ostentatious display in the cities, as if to spite the shabbiness of the aristocracy whose ranks were closed to them. There was little middle-class, for the professions were mostly filled by foreigners, particularly Russophil Germans, and the military and civil services were drawn from the younger sons of the aristocracy and lived much the same lives, dependent less on merit than on chance and favouritism for promotion.

The family to which Claire went was that of a well-to-do lawyer with aristocratic connections, Zachar Nikolaevitch, and his wife, Marie Ivanovna (for the married woman in Russia kept her patronymic) with their two children, John and Dunia. They had a house in Moscow and an estate outside at Islavsave on the Moscow river. In their position it was to be expected that they would have resident foreign teachers, and besides Claire there was a Mr. Gambs whose duties seem to have extended to organization of private theatricals and the delivery of lectures to the family—not a far cry from the office of Fool which still persisted in some big households.

Education was in fashion. Academies were being founded by the state, and numerous governesses and teachers employed to impart languages and a smattering of facts that would provide a veneer of culture without risk of producing too reasoning or political an animal. And indeed, if the education was intended to keep the young from inconvenient thinking, it was well qualified to do so from the cramming of which it exclusively consisted.

But, allowing for the vagaries of the Russian temperament, the teachers imported for this mission of cultivation were treated with a hospitality and

178

respect that might have served as a model to western society. Claire's position with the Nikolaevitchs' was very different from what Mary Wollstonecraft's had been with the Kingborough family when Mrs. Mason had been her pupil and the governess only descended from her attic to be seen and not heard with the children. · ·

Claire's Journal which she resumed after a year or so in Moscow reveals something of the life she led :

[1] ' *Sunday, June 14th—26th.* Mr. Gambs the children and I cross the little bridge and penetrate into the woods beyond—a narrow path sunk in the soil and with grassy banks on each side, from which the pines spring up, one behind and beside the other in countless graduations, runs straight thro' it upwards. A long strip of blue sky seemed to repose upon the top of the pine trees. The children run about, find *vergiss minnichts* and strawberries.

After tea we return home on foot. The whole face of the country is now beautiful. The wide space around is covered by the high green corn, beyond, one sees on every side, the dark pine woods, stretching forwards, in a broke irregular line into the verdant plain.; the sun sets without a cloud, a quiet ocean of golden light—the flocks eating their evening meal proceeding with us on our return home to the village and each one turned in the village at the well known stable door.

I spent a very agreeable evening—except that some

---

[1] The Russian calendar was twelve days behind that of the Western. Claire gives old and new styles.

of the people who were with me, fell into quarrels and ill humours, that all the strict rules of etiquette were not followed in a country walk.'

Her nerves, she complained in letters to Mary and Jane, were worn out by perpetual " scenes."

' *May 2nd.* (O.S.) *May 14th* (N.S.). . . . They attack you, you defend yourself, a thousand names are called· on each side, the quarrel ends. The Russians think no more about it and are ready to quarrel with you again for fretting over such trifles, because with them it is as habitual as the bread they eat, but to a person accustomed to a quiet way of life such perpetual agitation, violence and ill humour destroys one's peace completely. You will naturally say—why do you quarrel with them, why do not you blunt the edge of all their malice by not answering them. But this silence which in other countries would be a sign that you were a well-educated person and would infallibly procure you respect, would here put you on the same footing as one of their slaves who stand quietly before them and either dare not answer or answer only by mild reasonings and you would instantly be treated just like a common slave. The mark of your dignity here, is that you dare dispute and upbraid them. You should hear what villainous reproaches I make them sometimes. I will relate the following scene as a specimen of Russian manners.

I lived lately with a Russian lady ; she is accounted here a woman of vast understanding and most prudent conduct : the latter she always avowed she owed to her ugly face, for as she would often say before a large company of gentlemen when she was trying to make *aimable*, " I'm a perfect Messalina by nature." This declaration she used to make at every moment to my great horror in public and I used to entreat her if it was the case, that at least out of decency she would endeavour to conceal it. On Mondays she used always to have a large party to dinner : she brought up likewise two or three of her nieces in the house and each of these young ladies had two or three other young girls attached to them as *desmoiselles de compagnie.* After dinner on Sundays we always had to play at The Ring, that is to say, a circle is formed round a cord which each holds in his hand : then there is someone in the middle who tries to give you a tap on the hand. If he succeeds you take his place and tap in his turn. It seems to me this game is innocent enough. One evening we were thus engaged—she came in from a visit and in a great ill humour because she had not been able to borrow the money she wanted. So she fell upon us. She called all those poor young girls by the most infamous names : who but a *fille de joie* would ever be so indecent as to give a gentleman a tap on his hand ? and declared she would turn them all out in the street to starve. You may imagine the scene. About sixteen young ladies began to howl for forgiveness : the gentlemen stood aghast and I fell into such a fit of laughter at the strange sight that she grew furious and advanced up to strike me—however, one of the gentlemen interposed and saved me. The young ladies' howling still continued, the gentlemen tried to console them and one of the girls by a strange sympathy seeing me laugh so excessively could not

181

help laughing with me and hearing the howl of her companions could not help mixing a slight howl with her laugh. So the thing continued till we went for the old nurse to come and make peace. She came waddling in and with many Lack-a-daises condoled with us—in vain she remonstrated with the mistress of the house and bid her remember a thousand times how often she had played at the game herself both before and since her marriage : but the other swore it was not in that indecent manner and began to howl also in her turn that the reputation of her house was done for. As a last remedy we sent for the priest —he came and luckily the lady happened to be preparing to take the sacrament—when he recalled this to her recollection, then a new scene began for she gave herself up to despair to think she had allowed herself to offend against the Lord—she cried and wept, threw herself on the mercy of all those she had offended and begged pardon a thousand times, the old priest making the sign of the cross the whole while—then at last she came sobbing to beg my pardon and the whole of the company was scandalized because instead of entreating her to calm herself and of assuring her that she had said nothing at all particular I said, " I assure you, Marie Ivanovna, that I have nothing to pardon ; what harm did you do to me ? You neither pinched nor beat me, therefore I have nothing to pardon." This stupid game lasted till twelve at night. And so it is almost every day. The Russians console themselves for all their *scappature* by saying, "after all I have a good heart," but that is but poor consolation for the unhappy persons around them whose nerves they destroy by their perpetual agitations.'

Even when tragedy overtook the household in the death of Dunia, the little girl, it is obscured by the incompetence and the hysteria that lies on either side of it. Claire's bald narrative accentuates its real quality and her reserve is a measure of the depth of feeling for the memories it aroused :

' *Wednesday, September 23rd—October 5th.* Dark cloudy weather. Dunia has spent a very bad night and in the morning a blister is applied to her throat. Receive after breakfast a long letter from Miss Weston at Penya. Read the *Edinburgh Review.* At one o'clock Mr. Zuvarubov goes away. Walk in the garden before dinner ten times up and down the great alley with Nicolas and Mr. Gambs.

After dinner we are alarmed at Dunia's state, one of restless listlessness. No consciousness, yet perpetually tossing from side to side. I went to her at eight o'clock and did not leave her till five the next morning when she expired. She lay in utter insensibility, would taste nothing, her chest more oppressed at every moment, her cheeks of a burning pink, and all round her mouth of an ashy pale. At twelve o'clock at night call up Mr. Gambs and he sets out to fetch the German doctor at Klinsic—Her difficulty of breathing increased every moment and we were obliged to hold her upright to prevent her from suffocation, and it was thus he found us when he returned at five in the morning. He brought orders to apply leeches behind the ear and infusion of mustard on the legs. We did so, but she gently expired while it was being applied. To describe the scenes that followed would be impossible. The wretched mother threw herself on the ground and writhed there in an agony of grief, and the lovely child, smiling and brilliant as a star, lay not in death but in a sweet stillness before us.

Thursday, September 24th—October 6th. At six, in the midst of these terrible scenes, Mr. Gambs departs for Moscow to announce this unhappy loss to Zachar Nicolaevitch. Dunia is dressed in white and laid out upon a table and tapers in tall candelabras are burning around. The angelic smile of death is soon lost, the brilliancy of her complexion as if animated by the sweetest pleasure soon gives place to the yellowness of death, and a hollow leaden vacancy looks out from the once beaming countenance. Church service is performed, all the peasants come and take leave of her, and the whole morning was spent in weeping and wailing. Mr. Henkin, the German doctor comes at eleven, he says she was lost by neglect, that the first drowsiness which succeeded to the restlessness which prevailed before, was the first symptom of inflammation on the brain. Zinovy Ramamitch had left her ; we did not know that we ought to apply leeches, and if her drowsiness still prevailed, ice upon the head, and the inflammation carried her off in twelve hours . . .'

In some ways Claire, the Romantic, might have felt at home in the atmosphere of general sensibility, and at times she does revert to emotional meditation and nature worship (with the reaction of a bad temper and a head-ache next day !) but a sound instinct in her was repelled by the fatuity in what she saw. It was a very different thing for Shelley to be "romantic" with the definite achievement of his poetry, his social indignation and his practical goodness ; or the elderly

Wordsworth hard-walking on his fells; or for Trelawny with his melodramatic adventures that had at least been lived and not dreamt on—there was backbone to these, but in the life around her at Moscow Claire saw nothing but futility and unreality.

It was no wonder that her thoughts often turned to Trelawny (' if Ynwalert had been different I might have been as happy as now I am wretched ') for he was not only a link with the old life but a man whom for all his faults she could respect. He had left Byron and Mavrocordato soon after they had reached Greece and joined the more active faction under Odysseus, so that he was not at Missolonghi when Byron died, the rueful Childe and incompetent Don Juan become one of his own Heroes at last.

In his death Byron rose above melodrama; for, if he was not to fall, "the foremost fighting," but be done to death by the bungling of his doctors, his death liberated Greece. Hobhouse and the dilatory Greek Committee in England were shocked into action and public opinion insisted on Greek independence as an atonement for Byron's sacrifice. The whole of Europe was stirred and in Russia Claire must have read of the tragedy long before she could hear of it from friends. To her his actual physical death meant as little as the words that Fletcher ' imprudently let fall ' to say that his Lordship had wished to do something for her in his last moments.—So Mary, who had seen Fletcher at Nottingham, wrote to Trelawny : ' Did he mention this to you ? ' For Trelawny had arrived a week after Byron's death, heard the first account of it from the valet and with him lifted the pall to examine that deformity that had wrecked Byron's physical beauty.

He went through his papers and rescued the sentimental treasures strewn about the floor (' a cambric
handkerchief stained with his blood, and marked with
a lady's name in hair ; a ringlet ; a ribbon ; and a
small glove ') and when he had written an account
of it all for Mary to make up into an article for Hunt's
Examiner went back to Odysseus with what volunteers
he could afford to re-enlist. This was not the Trelawny who had presided over Shelley's funeral rites
on the sea-shore, but then it was Byron he was dealing
with, not Shelley.

News of his progress with Odysseus came to Claire
through the papers where she was to read with much
concern a year later that he had fought a dangerous
duel with a fellow Englishman. This in fact was
the attempt made upon him by Whitcombe when he
was disabled in the cave on Parnassus, and which only
his iron constitution had enabled him to survive,
without dressings or attention as he was.

' *Sunday, September 13th–25th.* From Saturday
September 5th to this day I have neglected to write
my journal, for I have had a terrible relapse of
melancholy inactivity such as I used to experience at
times when my mind was wholly devoted to sorrow
But this happy day, all the clouds which have lately
hung over my horizon disappeared. After breakfast
in a mood hopeless of good and careless utterly of
my future fate, the newspapers were put, by Catherine
Ivanovna, into my hand. I glanced over them hastily
as is my custom to see if there is anything about
Greece. I saw my dear friend's name, I did not dare
to read, yet notwithstanding with a horrible feeling
of dread and yet hope—I read—that he was well and

186

still in his cavern. Who shall describe the happiness I felt? Thus sudden relief from horrible inquietude to all the sweet certainty of his being well.

I went then instantly into the garden and sat myself on the balcony to enjoy all the fullness of my happiness. The whole sky was dark and portentous, the grove was agitated by a rushing wind which poured thro' its bared form and shook the dying leaves to the ground in showers. Not a single bird was heard, the whole grove was solitary, its leaves abandoned it and were strewed on the plain. But I in this wasted scene was full of joy and life. I spent the whole day in silent happiness—Many people dined—Madame Zimmerman, Madame Vercouroff and her daughters and many officers. I sat with Johnny afterwards. After tea they all went. I sing *Figaro* with M.G. At nine in the evening a letter from Charles telling me of the birth of his little Pauline on the 28th of July, enclosing one from Madame Moreau begging me to come to Vienna.'

Her anxiety was not without a certain self-consciousness, knowing that the family must wonder what sweet, secret sorrow was hidden in the bosom of their dark-eyed and lively young governess, and in the evenings, when they gathered in the living-room to drink tea from the heavy silver samovar, she let them conjecture what they would from the way she fell upon the newspapers and devoured the news from Greece. With her old sense of mischief, she sometimes fetched deep sighs and employed a sentimental head-ache as an excuse for escaping to her room ; but more often she had to sit and take her part in the tedious gossip of the women, or the

187

uplifting conversation that they attempted when the men were with them. Spurious as these philosophical discussions often were, Claire sometimes enjoyed them and grew vivacious and, to the Russian idea, a little bold, as she plunged deeper and deeper into abstruse problems. For nothing had been barred in the talk that she was used to ; that Shelley had described to Maria Gisborne :

> And then we'll talk—what shall we talk about ?
> Oh ! there are themes enough for many a bout
> Of thought-entangled descant.

But she had to be careful ; it must not be known that 'the charming Miss Clairmont, the model of good sense, accomplishment and good taste,' as she described herself, 'was brought, issued from the very den of Freethinkers.'

Occasionally she found a congenial friend. There was a Mr. Harmonn, of whom she wrote to Jane (who probably did not appreciate the comparison), 'What you felt for Shelley, I feel for him. He is like all Germans, very sentimental, a very sweet temper, and uncommonly generous. . . . His attachment to me is extreme, but I have taken the greatest care to explain to him that I cannot return it in the same degree.' There was also an Englishman who befriended her ; a Professor at the University, he had been an associate of Lockhart, but he had very rigid principles, ' and is come to that age when it is useless to endeavour to change them. I however, took care not to get upon the subject of principles and so he was of infinite use to me both by counselling and protecting me with the weight of his high approbation.'

188

Sensibility and a Music Master

A certain amount of the prevailing *Schwärmerei* was allowed to affect her estimate of a handsome pianist, a Monsieur Genichsta from whom she afterwards took music lessons :

'He is a divine musician and the first that, as a man, pleased me. He seems a world of music, he breathes, he speaks on the piano, and his soul as he expresses it there seems composed of harmony and fire, Nature and art. . . . We hang speechless upon his notes, Silence was enchanted to lose her being in such sweet sounds. His countenance is very original—his features, hair and complexion very feminine ; an open forehead and a soft smile, a low gentle voice and sensibility trembling in every fibre render him truly interesting.

At night I was as fatigued with listening to him as if I had lived a thousand years. When I came to my own room, all seemed a desert solitude for there was no power in myself to keep alive the exalted thoughts and feelings his music had awakened and I fell as it were from a commanding height into a mean confined flat.'

Accidie was not to be kept permanently at bay by sentimental reflections on music-masters ; daily entertaining ('officers dine ; the General comes from Moscow '), or philosophical arguments and picnics on the Sparrow Hills. Pleasant enough as it might seem recorded in her Journal, the life she was leading soon bored her and was therefore interpreted for the sum of horror. The people, she complained in her letters to England, were stupid, ignorant and vain and the children little barbarians :

'If they fall into their father's or mother's way,

189

and are troublesome, they are whipped ; ' she wrote of a family whom she taught after the Nikoleavitchs', ' but the instant they are with me, which is pretty nearly all day, they give way to all their violence and love of mischief because they are not afraid of my mild disposition . . . I never saw the evil spirit so plainly developed. What is worse, I cannot seriously be angry with them, for I do not know how they can be otherwise with the education they receive.'

Nor can she altogether blame the parents, for the *régime* makes them lead an unnatural life, waited on hand and foot, with social responsibility that ended at a monthly visit to the steward of the estate and a sense of public duty that went no further than lip service to the Czar. It was no wonder that they had no word for "Honour" in their language, as she commented in a story she wrote later called *The Pole*.

Through the strawberry picking and the mushroom expeditions, the sledge drives by moonlight and the rides on the native linieke *to drink milk at the estate saw-mills, those who had ears might have heard the clang of hammer and sickle where Versailles caught the rolling of the tumbrils at her* fêtes champêtres.

Claire wanted to move on, a decision that was hastened by her frequent changes of situation after the death of Dunia and a most unfortunate occurrence when a Miss Frewin who had met Mrs. Godwin in London came back to Moscow primed with Claire's history and broke it to the over-principled professor.

' I see that he is in a complete puzzle on my account,'

Claire wrote to Jane Williams, ' he cannot explain how I can be so extremely delightful and yet so detestable.' He made some effort to be broad-minded, but he felt that he could not conscientiously recommend her to be in charge of an only daughter in a family where she wanted to go and where his word was law, ' because he settles every little dispute with some unintelligible quotation or reference to a Latin or Greek author.'

She had no mind to succumb to the fate of elderly governesses as she had recorded it in the first entry of her Russian Journal :

' *Tuesday, May 12th—24th, 1825.* I have long resolved to recommence my Journal and provided myself accordingly to-day with a book. My life flows so swiftly away and so unobservedly that I have need of a Journal to mark a little its progress.

Early in the morning I read Madame Roland— then I called upon Princess Ourousoff. She was as usual surrounded by a set of old, ugly governesses all ravenous and open-mouthed after places . . .'

As the doctors suggested German baths for her health, as much affected by her employers' chronic *crises de nerfs*, as by the climate, she relinquished her idea of going to India, ' or anywhere warm,' and in 1828 left for Toeplitz as companion to a Madame Kaisaroff and her daughter Natalie. No doubt Claire's disgust with the girl's grumbling on the journey was influenced by the intense discomfort of travel in a coach where she could not lie down herself and had to nurse the feet of the recumbent girl, for, in later life, she became quite fond of her and when she was left an heiress cherished hopes of finding her a suitable husband from among Percy Florence's Cambridge friends.

I I I

LONDON 1828.

When she came back to London from Russia, Claire found the Godwins moved from the derelict Skinner Street to 195 Strand, where the bookshop survived in the Juvenile Library publishing house—a venture still to be redeemed by hard work, according to Mamma, and a goldmine for the investments of his richer friends, according to Godwin's irresponsible optimism. Her stepfather had changed little, his speech perhaps even slower and more deliberate as he sought for the exact words to round his flowing periods and his dislike of contradiction a little increased, but this was less a sign of the hardening of his mental arteries than evidence of the persistence of his vanity. He was true enough to his theories to be proud of Mary and not to patronize her ; indeed, he was pleased to capitalize her literary success by using her to negotiate for him with publishers.

Mrs. Godwin was still bustling, but a little more prepared to admit that there might be things in Heaven and earth that she had not dreamt in her philosophy, among them her daughter's liaison with Byron which she only reluctantly gave up thinking had been a shield for some enormity of Shelley's. She had been told that he called her a ' vulgar woman with no idea of Philosophy ' and she could not forget it.

Her hopes and interest were concentrated on

At Home in England

William now, and she was annoyed that her husband did not appreciate him more ; he was stable and conscientious—his contributions to Anarchy finished with his schoolboy absconsions—and he held an interesting appointment with Rennie, the architect. ' Comparing him with other young men,' wrote Claire later, ' his frugality, his industry, his attachment to his wife, and his talents, raised him, in my opinion, considerably above the common par. But in our family, if you cannot write an epic poem or novel that by its originality knocks all other novels on the head, you are a despicable creature, not worth acknowledging.'

Mary, for reasons of economy and health, lived in Kentish Town which was still salubrious and not much changed from ' the village on the way to Highgate,' described by a writer in 1780, ' where people take lodgings in the summer, especially those afflicted with consumption and other disorders.' She had grown handsomer, fulfilling in her womanhood all the promise of her beauty as a girl, and her character had matured into something of that serenity to which her looks had always held up the mirror.

Percy Florence, whom Claire had last seen as a very small boy muddling his Italian and English in baby talk, was now nine years old, finely built and tall with the bright blue Shelley eyes. He was never at a loss for interests and had an equable temperament that showed little evidence of his disturbing heritage of genius. Since the death of Charles Bysshe in 1826 he had been heir to the Shelley baronetcy and was occasionally taken out from his day school by his grandfather, Sir Timothy Shelley, who was now 76 ;

but the allowance which Mary received had not been increased to the extent she had hoped, and she had to work hard to earn money by her pen. The Godwins made constant claims upon her to which new and old friends alike were not backward in adding their own, and even Everina Wollstonecraft, who had done nothing to help her nieces when the means had been in her power, now had no compunction in demanding help with the abuse and reproach that is a relative's prerogative.

Claire paid tribute to the success that Mary had made of her life ; the laurels might not flower for her again but she did not refuse to go into the woods. She had an established literary reputation and had made a wide circle of friends : Caroline Norton ; the Novellos, and the eccentric dilettante Lord Dillon ; Tom Moore, Samuel Rogers and Fred Reynolds among others of the set that gathered in John Murray's famous drawing-room. They were pygmies after the giants that she had known, but life had to be lived and old friends had not always kept faith with the dead.

Jane Williams had been early consoled by Hogg ; a typically predatory woman, she was accustomed to exacting a toll of admiration from all about her (Mary called her "Beauty" in letters, and Claire sent offerings from abroad of the little yellow handkerchiefs she liked to carry) and very soon she was enlivening the devoted, if illicit, domesticity of her new *ménage* by hints that exaggerated Shelley's feelings for her at Casa Magni and accused Mary of having made his last days there unhappy. Candid friends naturally repeated the story and Mary faced Jane with it.

Tears and repentance followed—for Jane cried and repented easily—and Mary promised forgiveness and consented to stand as godmother to the daughter by Hogg so aptly named Prudentia, but there was no healing the hurt she had suffered. In some ways it went deeper than any other wound she had borne, perhaps because it festered, poisoning memories that had been pure and sweet.

Claire visited Jane and duly admired the children, the house and the appointments, but she found it hard to admire " Blue Bag." Although he had lost no time in extending to Jane that protection to which Mary recommended her when she went back to England, he had scarcely been an ardent lover. ' How I long, dearest Jane,' he wrote in an early letter, ' to add a few more chapters to our secret history and surprising adventures and to taste once more as much happiness as is consistent with discretion.' He had kept nothing of the rebel who defied Oxford for his friend but had hardened into the complete second-rate lawyer, vain and cynical, beginning to be as ashamed of his association with Shelley as he was coy and clandestine in his relations with Jane.

Claire was filled with no desire for second best ; but Jane had what she wanted :

> To sit at head of one's own table,
> To overlook a warm familiar landscape,
> Have large cupboards for small responsibilities. . . .

Trelawny was also in England, submitting to some lionizing with a genial growl and adding Caroline Norton and Fanny Kemble to the tale of his more platonic conquests, but remaining untamed enough to sit in Hyde Park showing his ankles and challenging critics with a ferocious, ' What do you want socks for ? ' He went on to America where among other enterprises he bought and freed a slave and swam Niagara—a feat that deserves to be celebrated as much for the trenchant prose in which he described it as for the achievement itself. But his adventures did not satisfy him and his ingrowing energies were beginning to make him a very difficult companion. Claire had not been far wrong when she had written from Russia in answer to Mary's plea that she should consider marrige with him :

' He likes a turbid and troubled life, I a quiet one ; he is full of fine feelings and has no principles, I am full of fine principles but never had a feeling ; he receives all his impressions through his heart, I through my head. *Que voulez-vous ? Le moyen de se recontrer* when one is bound for the North Pole and the other for the South ? '

She knew him well : in a letter to Jane she does justice to his discontent at the intimacy with Moore which was involving Mary in contributions to his *Life of Byron*, at the same time as she makes merry at the expense of his temper.

' . . . He is quite right in thinking she ought not to be acquainted with Moore : it is a privilege he has no right to, having expressed so cruel and unjust an opinion of Shelley. The letter containing this opinion was read to her : but she says as the reader was a man of suspected veracity on account of an incurable love of embroidering every subject that fell in his way, and since she did not herself see Moore's signature attached to it, she has no right to believe him capable

196

of sentiments so unworthy of his general reputation. This is a very amiable and just feeling towards Moore, and if it had been followed up by shunning his intimacy out of an equally amiable and just feeling towards Shelley would have been the right thing. But he being divine was doomed to see the most unworthy things preferred before himself.

. . . Write therefore to him, dear Jane, and to use his own favourite expression, " pour oil and balm into his wounds." To hear him calling out so often for this as he does, it would be natural to judge it did him good—I however must confess I never saw any other effect follow the application besides a hissing sound returned by his volcanic heart as the drops fell, then a smouldering pause of consideration and when cooled it hardened into the irrevocable lava. With Trelawny once parched is always parched and rather than allow his irritated affections to bloom again he would sooner turn into stone and give himself like Vesuvius to the neighbouring town to be made into pavement. But this, I hope, will not cause you to hesitate. If you do not succeed in softening him, it will still be a consolation to remember that you did all on your part to prevent petrifaction from taking place.'

She could always illumine a situation with a flash of wit and Mary, the professional author, readily admitted the superiority of her letters : ' Your letters are so amusing and clever that I thank you much for writing them—and am sorry that I send such stupid ones in return—but I never was a good letter writer and you always were.' If at times Claire's correspondents grumbled at her for not writing to them as often as they wanted to hear, it was no

wonder. ' Tell Trelawny,' she wrote once to Mary
' he ought not to think I am angry when I don't write
if he were a governess he would never put pen to
paper.'

She had need of all her resources ; her wit, her
courage, her mental integrity, for it was to be a long
time before the payment of Shelley's £12,000 legacy
brought release from an interminable round of travelling, teaching and money trouble.

When Claire left England again in 1828 she was
thirty ; that age which had seemed so far off when she
wrote to Byron at nineteen . . . ' My temper is
inconstant and *volage* ; I want dignity ; I do not,
like our Mary, sail my steady course like a ship under
a gentle and favourable wind. But at thirty, I shall
be better, and every year I hope to gain in value . . .'

The years were to be longer than she knew, but
for whom is it to say how much she gained in value ?

I V

1828–79.

For the rest of 1828 Claire was in Dresden ; then
in Carlsbad the next year for her employer's *Kur* ; in
Nice in 1831 ; back in Pisa in 1832 ; in London in the
1840's—so the passage of the years can be glossed
over in a few lines that make light of their burden
and compensate, perhaps, for the other process of
biography,

> When men will call the golden hour of Bliss,
> " About this time "—or " shortly after this."

But Claire had to live through the months that made up the years and sometimes they were very long. For days together she would see no one of any interest and pupils became unbearable. ' I never thought children could be so hideous or vicious, they never cease brawling, squabbling and fighting, from morning till night, but I cannot describe them. The very idea throws me into a fit of the horrors.' She admits that she sometimes let herself go : ' I dress every day worse and worse,' she wrote to Jane in acknowledging a dress rather grudgingly, ' It is by far too elegant for me, consequently I have put it by in the piece and shall only make it up in case of wanting to be fine for some very particular occasion. This is not likely to happen and you really would have done well to have kept it for yourself.

' I dress every day worse and worse. I think I see your horror. " What worse," Dina asks, " than when she was here ? " Yes, a great deal worse. My gowns of that period were ball dresses to those I now wear. I make it a rule never to buy anything for a gown that costs more than a paul a *bracchio*—12 *bracchi* serve me and my gown costs 12 pauls. To be sure it is dark and coarse, but then it only costs 12 pauls. I am in the land of silks but they are not for me.'

In desperation she once considered taking Trelawny at his word and going to keep house for him to bring up Zélla, his daughter by the sister of Odysseus. ' Does the bread of strangers please you better ? ' he had urged, but that was in 1823 ; now in 1831 Trelawny could not bear the thought of being tied, even as loosely as Claire proposed.

' I really know of nothing which could give me such

199

entire satisfaction as realizing the plan you have laid ',
he answered, ' and I acknowledge with gratitude for
your considerate kindness in proposing it, that all the
benefits which would accrue would fall to my share
—your society would be to me a never failing source
of comfort ; and to my child it would be an inestimable
advantage ; but as I have often said we are the slaves
of circumstances. I have struggled all my life to break
the chains with which fate has manacled me—but it
is in vain—this letter will give you no less pain in
reading than it has me in writing.'

Their friendship survived the episode ; they bore
each other no ill will, but kept up for the rest of their
long lives a desultory correspondence that flared into
greater activity in the 1870's, when Trelawny was
writing his *Records* and wanted her to supply details
of Shelley and Byron.

· In 1832, (' that nasty year which could not go over
without imitating in some respects 1822 and bringing
death and misfortune to us',) when she was at Pisa,
Claire was less concerned with the memories the place
might evoke than full of anxiety for Mary and Percy
Florence who she was sure would fall victims to the
cholera epidemic in London. She begged Mary to
get from William Godwin the money that Mrs. Mason
was making over to her from the profits of her book,
Advice by a Grandmother, and when she heard that
by mistake it had already been forwarded to Italy
she offered to send instead her half year's salary, 24
napoleons,[1] for Percy to be taken to the sea.

In the event it was William who died. The shock
unnerved Claire. ' His death has changed all my

[1] A napoleon = 20 lire = 16 shillings.

200

plans,' she wrote to Mary, 'I had settled to go to Vienna, but as the cholera is still there, I no longer considered myself free to offer another of my Mother's children to be its victim.'

She wanted to get away from Italy and asked Mary to rescue her with an introduction to Lady Mulgrave whose husband had been appointed Governor of Jamaica. With a wit a little hardened since Russia she wrote of herself : ' Many people would be glad of a well informed person, who can read to them in various languages, teach them German, write their letters, and of a lively, sprightly disposition, one who neither minds heat nor cold, nor hunger nor thirst, nor fatigue nor hardship of any kind.' But the situation fell through, as did a projected post with Lady Dorothea Campbell, a friend of Trelawny's, and she had to stay in Pisa, ' dull now since the death of Vacca as people will not come to a place without a respectable physician.' She lived with the Masons and went daily to various pupils. ' I must be out at 9 in the morning and not home before 10 at night. I inhabit at Mrs. Mason's a room without a fire, so that when I get home there is no sitting in it without perishing with cold. I cannot sit with the Masons, because they have a set of young men every night to see them and I do not wish to make their acquaintance.'

Although in later life Claire came to depend much on one of these young men, Bartolomeo Cini, who married Nerina, and wrote him most affectionate letters in gratitude for the help he gave her, at the moment Casa Ricci had lost something of its charm —perhaps its memories were still too keen—and the Masons are even guilty of " prejudice."

' They had rather damn all their fellow creatures in a lump than allow the vile manners of the Italians. I never met with people so prejudiced in certain ways as the Masons. They abhor despotic governments on account of the blighting influence they have on the subjects of them, but when you make their conclusions turn upon the Italians, they deny it—no ! no !—they have all the honour and uprightness which distinguish republicans.'

Release was farther and farther off, for Sir Timothy appeared to be immortal. ' I can never think of him,' Clare wrote to Mary, ' without seeing his grey hair growing into fine clustering brown locks ; his bent form assuming manly straightness and strength, and the most glowing pink creeping over his once aged, but now youthful, cheek. He is quite an Adonis in my eyes.'

She raised a small annuity on her expectations under Shelley's will and tried to make some money by writing. A story, *The Pole*, which she sent to Mary to finish and suggested might be signed " Mont Obscur," appeared in *The English Annual* for 1836, attributed to the Author of Frankenstein. Although less diffuse than most of Mary's own fiction, and with some lively observations, it is still completely in the Gothic-Godwin tradition—influence as dangerous in literature as in life. There is a handsome hero, a lively, musical and melancholy heroine and, somewhat autobiographically, a rebel younger sister who acts as " guardian angel " to the lovers ; the scene is laid in Italy and beyond a few expressions, she does not make much use of local colour from Russia. Mary was also able to place for her an article on Naples in the *Metro-*

politan when Marryat was Editor. It had not been accepted by Lord Lytton to whom she first offered it for his *New Monthly* because, as she wrote to Trelawny enlisting his help when he was in London, ' I have an idea that Lady Blessington is the person who is furnishing them with articles on Italy, and compared with Claire's they must be poor. Do let Marryat see them ; and make him be pleased with them—print them in the number for November and desire more.'

Such desultory success did little to eke out Claire's meagre earnings in Italy, and in the later 1830's she was back in England with a family at Wingfield Park.

Well might Trelawny write to her :

' My dear Clare where are you ; and what doing with the Bennets or the Sandfords ?—are you to be always in this vile servitude—and condemned for life —to this worse than galley life ? and what for ? what have you done to merit such damnation ?—are your fetters never to be knocked off ?—your pettycoats I mean. . . .'

In 1840 she was in London and what her life was can be judged from a letter to Mary :

' I am so worried I fear I shall go out of my mind —this is now my life—I go by nine to Mrs. Kitchener's house where I give lessons till one—then I rush to the top of Wilton Place and get a Richmond omnibus and go to Richmond to give a lesson to the Cohens— their daughter is going to be married to a Genoese and must have an Italian lesson every day . . . that vile omnibus takes two hours to get to Richmond and the same to come back and so with giving my lesson I am never back before seven.'

Hurrying for the horse-tram with dark and rather shabby skirts picked up to avoid the mud, Claire cannot have looked very different from a hundred other governess-gentlewomen ; perhaps a little less careful of the gentility of her appearance but more alert for the integrity of her mind ; still unconquered in courage, with the old wit not failing in her letters and her conversation.

Only when the long-awaited release came did Claire's spirit break, the wit give place to querulousness and the courage to defiance :

' It is certainly a strange inexplicable feeling to receive a letter say Sir Tim. is dead ' ; she wrote to Mary, ' it is but a common bit of news and analogous to what happens every day, yet my first emotion was utter disbelief ; the most hard, unyielding disbelief. The idea of that man has been so long my companion, that it seems tearing half my mind out to convince me I have no occasion to think of him any longer.' ·

She was characteristically impatient with the family lawyer :

' . . . He makes you dance attendance upon him day after day, as if he were Prime Minister and when you come, your heart beating, your pulses in a commotion expecting your fate from his lips, he begs you will read The Times and goes scratching on for an hour with his pen, and then says he is very sorry but you must wait another 3 weeks. He ought to consider the world was created in a week, and therefore a law affair which is a fragment of the world has no right to take 3 weeks in doing. If haberdashers and cooks and all the other trades of life were to go on in this way, what an utter overthrow of life would ensue and

Charles' Success in Vienna

I don't see why lawyers should be privileged and monopolize dawdling to their own use.'

With the money she inherited Claire made unfortunate investments : an opera box in which she bought a share failed to pay, and she was persuaded by Charles to make Austrian investments which caused her considerable anxiety after the revolution of 1848. She resented Mary's warnings ('Charles, like me, is *immensely prudent* as regards money '), as she resented Mary's new position and security. Certainly it is odd to find Mary writing that ' for Percy to live as a gentleman on £2,000 a year is only barely possible,' but then it is odd for Claire, whose half-year's salary was 24 napoleons, to declare that a legacy of £12,000 will not add a penny to her income.

On the defensive she turned from Mary and the son who was now the Shelley baronet to her own family ; to Charles with his wife and children in Vienna. He had done very well there. From the newcomer who had neglected to confirm his teaching permit he had become a Professor at the Theresianum, an honorary appointment, as he was a foreigner and a protestant, but one which was invaluable in advancing his position.

A contemporary guide-book (*Picture of Vienna containing Historical Sketch and Map*, Witwe and Braumüller, 1839) has a reference to him :

' English gentlemen or ladies intending to pass some months in Vienna and wishing during their stay to acquire a knowledge of German cannot do better than apply to Professor Clairmont, Wallnerstrasse No. 267.'

Both he and his wife published text-books which are to this day the equivalents of *Reading Without*

Tears, for teaching English to German children. By 1848 when Claire joined him he was one of the tutors to the Archdukes Ferdinand Maximilian and Karl Ludwig, younger brothers of the heir to the throne, Franz Joseph. His name is not to be traced in the records of the Court education, but English could only have been a subject of minor importance in a curriculum that ranged from the three chief languages of the Empire (German, Czech and Magyar) to philosophy, music and military strategy. Charles Clairmont seems to have provided something of a respite, for the time-table began at six in the morning and went on for the rest of the day with no break except the breakfast *mocha* and the tedious afternoon dinner from four-thirty to six.

' Charles is at Olmütz,' wrote Claire to Mary in 1849, a year after the young Franz Joseph had been crowned there, ' and will stay till the Court goes to Schönbrunn. He gains tolerably and is so much better in health because he has but little work to do. He sees the young brothers of the young Emperor every day, and they are so fond of him and always have Willy's letters read to them and are as much interested in him as if he were their brother. Willy is furious at this because the old Emperor their uncle disarmed the students and Willy cannot forget or forgive their having taken his sword from him . . .'

Claire lost none of her faculties with old age, although she invited some surly sympathy from Trelawny for her eyesight when she was copying Shelley's letters for him, and she kept up all her interests, particularly her music. ' Does your passion for it still last ? ' she wrote to Percy Florence, ' Mine does—I find it comes nearer my soul than poetry or philosophy or patriotism or even love.'

She became somewhat erratic in her attachments, both to places and to people, her first enthusiasm for them quickly turning to impatience with their feet of clay. When she was settled in Paris for a time she discovered a one-time Egeria of Shelley's, Mrs. Boinville, and wrote of her coterie to Mary : ' I cannot tell you how much I am enchanted with all the Rue de Clichy lot—what rare people ; how handsome they are, how intellectual, how good!' but a year later she finds them tiresome and dull, and complains that she sees no one and goes nowhere. This in Paris, of which she had written to Mary :

' . . . It is not only impossible to lead a quiet life in Paris, but also impossible to have one day in which you have not twice as much to do as you can possibly get through. In England a woman is doomed to *ennui*, if she does not take to methodism she has nothing to do—not even a visit to pay—but here, leading the most retired life, you find acquaintances swarming in on you like locusts, and society forces itself in an overwhelming torrent into your solitude . . . How I long to get to England for a little quiet. There everyone lives like an oyster, each shut up in his shell.'

Her capacity for impetuous friendships was to entail some unfortunate consequences when it was allowed to run riot in the colony of Italian exiles. Two leading members of it, Guitera, who was married, and Gatteschi, a bachelor, were both prepared to exploit their misfortunes and their good looks to obtain more substantial supplies than were brought in by giving language lessons. Meeting them through Claire,

Mary fell a victim to the eleemosynary passion and, besides giving money to Gatteschi, wrote him letters so unwise that they had to be retrieved later by a friend of Percy Florence, A. A. Knox. That there are no letters of Claire's referring to this *dénouement* suggests that they were deliberately destroyed with other papers referring to the affair, for it is unlikely that Claire would not have expressed her opinion on it freely. She had written to Mary frequently and with intimate details over the whole period of the acquaintance, from her first not displeasing discovery of Signora Guitera's jealousy of her intellectual companionship, to her naïve surprise that Gatteschi, who does not seem to give many lessons, yet is always to be seen at the theatre. She expresses a dispassionate opinion that his hopes of a successful career as an Italian master in England are likely to be disappointed (' he is too handsome '), and she reports after Mary's visit, ' He is quite in despair at your departure '— a despair he tempered with romantic confidences of a blighted youth, for which the jealousy of his father's and his brother's mistress was responsible. But the advent of a Lady Sussex displaced both Mary and Claire, for she was willing to make a more generous distribution of her favours—and her money—to each of the fatal exiles in turn.

(*Dec. 28th, 1844*) . . . ' Madame Guitera,' wrote Claire to Mary, ' came to Lady Sussex's and made a scene and rushed out of the house finding Gatteschi and Guitera at dinner there unknown to her, and they all three rushed after her in the dark and ran up that lonely boulevard I showed you—and when they reached home Madame Guitera beat her head, poor woman, on the floor and wanted to throw herself out of the window, Martini and servants all assisting to hinder her and only getting her calm by asseverations from Lady S. and the two G's that their mutual sentiments were entirely platonic and the dinner was quite platonic and their dining there unknown to Madame Guitera quite a thing by chance.'

An atmosphere of intrigue and excitement was by no means wholly unacceptable to Claire. When this fruitful source dried up she busied herself with protégées, for she was fond of young people, provided they were not pupils. She wanted Knox to marry Natalie and when he did not pursue his advantage forwarded the suit of a young man disapproved by the Kaisaroff family. With Shelleyan quixotry she offered to sacrifice her Shelley papers to give ' a tolerable education ' to a girl called Georgina in whom she became interested, and refused an invitation from Mary and Percy Florence to join them in Italy, because she was looking after Dina Williams, 'who must forget Henry.' Her efforts were apparently not successful, as Dina afterwards married Henry, a son of Leigh Hunt's, and, for her fairy godmotherliness, she received scant thanks from Jane ; all her possessive instincts were aroused and she found occasion years afterwards to vent her repressed animosity in a churlish letter.

' . . . Even in my own house,' she wrote to Claire, ' and particularly during your last visit there, you made use of language to me so harsh, so violent, so undeserved and so entirely incomprehensible to me, that had I been a man, I should have resented it on the spot, as it is, I have done that which it befits a woman to do on such occasions—and have withdrawn from you ! I know my own entire worth and am proudly gratified to find it appreciated by the good and wise ; and if it fails to obtain recognition when it is doubly due towards me and would be doubly welcome to my heart, the fault lies in the withholders, not in me . . .'

But Claire had already summed up her Jane with pungency : ' . . . alas, poor Percy, my poor dear Percy—at last he will know what it is to be liked by Henry and Dina—that it will cost him Jane's love and esteem. Always now will he be viewed by her as a suspicious person, and wished away—and lucky will he, be, if on some slight occasion lending itself, she does not get up a little calumny to deteriorate his merit. Thus I know it happened to me . . . Could I do what is just, I would have a board stuck up before Mrs. Hogg's door, warning anyone who cared for their happiness, to have nothing to do with her.'

Claire as the Maiden Aunt, a prototype of that peculiarly British Institution which flourishes in the *pensions* of Italy and the Riviera, conducted a busy clearing-house for the affairs of the Clairmont nephews and nieces and it was on account of them that she finally broke with the Shelleys. For some time her defensiveness had made visits difficult ; ' Our clothes are shabby, that I warn you of,' she had scribbled across the top of a letter when invited to bring Cleary and Willy to Field Place.

'. . . Only I cannot imagine what you want to see these two children for, and I am afraid of their not pleasing, and incurring the criticisms of your *superfine wit*. And poor dears, they have to earn their livelihood— and are such well disposed young people that it would be a pity to turn them from the right path and make them miserable for life, which often happens when poor people frequent the society of the rich . . .'

And she had been a little sarcastic about the estate : ' I hope you will get through and if your young people are [*word omitted*], I think you will—they are very well disposed to economy—especially Lady Shelley— for she told me she did not care for the luxuries of Life and wanted only Bread and Cheese.'

With a love affair between Cleary Clairmont and a friend of the Shelleys, hard words passed that could not be taken back and the links of thirty years were broken, so that when a friend of Robert Browning's tried to sell some papers for her to Percy Florence he replied : ' You are right in supposing that the relations between Miss Clairmont and myself are not those of intimacy. . . .

In answer to your application therefore I have simply to say that I decline to purchase these documents—and I may add that I feel the less disposed to make a move in the matter inasmuch as Miss Clairmont, being a stranger in the Shelley family, received £12,000 from money raised upon the Shelley estates. I have no right or wish of course to grudge the payment of this legacy but I think the sum above named ought to have satisfied the lady.'

They had gone through much together, Claire and Mary ; shared their poetry and shared their prose, but always in uneasy fellowship. . . .

' One of the reasons I always say disagreeable things to you and Percy,' Claire had written to Mary in the letter giving the news of Charles's success in Vienna, '[is] because I cannot bear that anyone should

211

think I am paying my court to you and taking advantage of your love of agreeable sensations.

I hope you are all well—leave off your stays—eat no potatoes—take ginger and you will be well.

Ever yours,

CL.

Although they admired her ('She is a small, distinguished, very English lady with white curls') the way of the young Clairmonts with their Aunt cannot always have been easy.

'She likes you all very much already,' reported William to his wife, when he was confined by malaria to Florence and Aunt Claire sat by his bedside, ' and says she will come to see us next summer because she is so desirous of knowing you—but on this I throw cold water because I know Aunt would be very much disappointed with the Banat and would find it nasty and get ill and be discontented, for she makes a great many pretensions and has a great many whims— although she herself has no idea of it and believes herself to be the most unpretentious person in the world.'

The nephews visited her from time to time to discuss the estates that she had bought and which they farmed, and when she settled in Florence it was arranged that Paula should become her companion. She brought the disturbing problems of youth with her. ' I am troubled by circumstances,' wrote Claire to a friend on Christmas Day, 1869. ' My niece during and after her Mother's sickness and death was very much assisted by an elderly Austrian retired Major—he wishes to marry her ; he cannot leave

Austria or he would lose his pension—if they marry
I must either go to Austria or live on here without
one relation near me. So I know not how to decide.
Could May Moulsen who has lived the last year and
a half with me, still continue to do so, I should stay
on here ; she is a charming girl and likes me, and
would have every care of me. But she must go home
next Spring and then I should feel too lonely and
unprotected. I have told Pauline to do exactly what
she thinks will be best for her happiness. I will
give no advice or take any responsibility on myself
in her affairs. My nephew is, thank God, pretty
well at present . . .'

For a time Aunt and Niece were separated—not
because Paula married, for she had enough of the older
woman's temperament to decide that Matrimony
would be too great a risk for her ; but on account of
a quarrel, and Claire, who had been converted to the
Roman Catholic faith, retired for a time to a convent.
' My own firm conviction after years and years of
reflection,' she wrote to an unresponsive Trelawny,
' is that our Home is beyond the Stars, not beneath
them. Life is only the prologue to an Eternal Drama
as a Cathedral is the vestibule of Heaven.' She considered writing a book to ' illustrate from the lives of
Shelley and Byron the dangers and evils resulting
from erroneous opinions on the relations of the sexes,'
but beyond a few fragments the work was never
carried out. " *La fille aux mille projets*," as Shelley
had called her in the Pisan days, could not settle down
to the consecutive effort of writing—or perhaps, for
once, she lacked the courage.

Paula returned to her later and for the rest of her

213

life they lived on together in Florence, first in the Via Valfonda and finally at 43 Via Romana. 'I find a great consolation,' wrote Claire three years before her death to Bartolomeo Cini, 'in how many distinguished and excellent and virtuous friends I have had. *Nudrirmi di memoria piu che di speme* is my daily occupation. And in this way I banish from old age that stupid Melancholy which generally accompanies that stage of life.'

Her house at 83 Via Valfonda was on the same street where she had first stayed more than half a century before at the *pension* Palazzo Marini, though the Central Station had been built in the square behind it and steam-trams ran along the roads where she had walked with Shelley and the charming Sophia Stacey, and Mary had 'begun for the first time to look a little comforted' as she carried Percy Florence in her arms.

Their paths had been trodden since by others ; the Brownings had come to Casa Guidi and the "half-angel and half-bird" been laid to rest in the English cemetery, and Walter Savage Landor lived out his truculent life in the lodgings on the Via Nunziatina where Swinburne came to offer *Atalanta*. But all that Robert Browning knew of the girl who had seen Shelley plain was from Percy Florence's letter, and Landor never spoke with her, though he put Trelawny in one of his *Imaginary Conversations*, and blushed for the 'prejudice and injustice' that had kept him from meeting Shelley at Pisa ; and only when it was too late did Henry James discover at one of his tea parties that he had been in Florence with Claire Clairmont.

The Tale of Life Told

Claire died on March 19th, 1879, at the age of ninety-one, and Paula entered in the Journal that she kept :

' This morning my Aunt died at about 10, calmly, without agony, without consciousness—as she had predicted herself, she went out like a candle . . . She was buried as she desired, with Shelley's little shawl at the Cemetery of the Antella.'

V

> First our pleasures die—and then
> Our hopes, and then our fears—and when
> These are dead, the debt is due,
> Dust claims dust—and we die too.

In Shelley's verse is the tale of Claire's life told. Her Pleasures had been short-lived. Of them she might have sung, white-haired at her window where the notes rose straight into the Italian blue, as once she had sent them winging across the Holborn rooftops, thick dark hair blown back from a young brow,

> Plaisir d'amour ne dure qu'un moment
> Chagrin d'amour dure toute la vie . . .

' A happy passion,' she had written to Jane Williams on hearing of her union with Hogg, ' a happy passion like death has *finis* written in such large characters in its face there is no hoping for any possibility of a change. You will allow me to talk upon this subject, for I am unhappily the victim of a *happy passion*. I had one ; like all things perfect in its kind, it was

215

fleeting, and mine only lasted ten minutes, but these ten minutes have discomposed the rest of my life.'

Her Hopes had died in Allegra.

Her Fears she had outlived : poverty, boredom, despair. For over fifty years she wrung a living from life and contrived to outwit the old enemy, *accidie*. Perhaps it is the most poignant comment on one who could call ' Passion, the high tide of the mind ' that in old age she should be thankful for the release it brought from feeling. ' Poor boy, but I pity him,' she wrote to Mary when Percy Florence was an undergraduate, ' and all young people of his age whose heart is just opening, who pine to expand themselves, and find unsurmountable barriers placed everywhere. It is not much praise to the supreme Lord of Life what I am going to say, which is, Thank God I can never be young again. At least that suffering is spared me.'

She had outlived old friends ; all except Trelawny, who lived till he was ninety-one. ' In my youth I railed at age as hard and crabbed and so I find it.' But he was allowed to go down fighting. ' He was a splendid type of vigorous and intellectual old age,' wrote Richard Edgcumbe, visiting him in 1875, ' though he stooped a little he was a man of colossal proportions, and his movements denoted great force and energy, which was the more surprising after all that he had suffered in his youth.'

To the last day of his life the Sompting villagers could watch ' the tall gentleman, always alone,' stride from his cottage to the shore for the bathe that he never missed summer or winter, and little know that their admiration had been shared by the painter of the favourite *North-West Passage* that hung in

216

many of their homes. ' Mr. John Millais, our best painter,' he had written to his daughter Laetitia in 1872, not insensitive to the honour done him, ' asked me to sit for a great picture he was composing of strenth [*sic*] and meekness, he wanted a resolute man and gentle girl, he had sought in vain over Town and could not find one—I was the only one that would do—it's a £2000-er and he has done it. The likeness is perfect.'

Mary died in 1851 ; she had come to terms with the world in which she had to live, not quite the ' conventional slave ' of Trelawny's disgruntled saw, but certainly not easy to recognize for the daughter of Mary Wollstonecraft who had worshipped at the shrines of the French Revolution with Shelley. In 1848 France was spreading ' wicked and desolating principles amongst all the nations,' encouraging the Irish and the Chartists who were alike ' full of menace,' and Percy Florence was standing for Parliament as befitted a Sussex country squire. Though her fears had for long brooded over him more than her hopes, it was in her son, with his equable temperament, warm affection and quizzical humour that she found a happiness which did not betray her. She left him with the contented knowledge that he was married to an ideal wife in Jane St. John, a woman who cared for Mary as no friend had ever cared.

Jane Williams lingered on until the age of eighty-six, when a biographer of Shelley met her, still gracious, with the memory of her beauty fragrant about her, a little deaf and the powder forgotten on one side of her face.

Hogg had died seventeen years before ; grown more

217

and more crotchety, until he finally broke with Mary
and Shelley's son when he compensated the failures
of his own life in the impertinent biography he wrote
of his friend. And Peacock, who would have been
the only possible second-best for Claire, his astringent
intelligence capable of keeping their affection fresh,
Peacock took a disgruntled leave of life :

' He will not long survive his old friend,' Jane had
written to Claire in December 1863. ' He has this
conviction himself and is declining in the same way
that poor Dah [1] did. He has taken a dislike to Halli-
ford, to his books, in short to everything he once liked,
and like Dah his appetite is failing him . . . What
a sad and solemn thing life is at our years, my dear
Claire ? How very fortunate are those who die under
their first great grief ! '

And Byron, who had died in Greece in 1824, had
died to Claire long ago ; nothing of him that she
wanted to remember survived the day when she heard
the news of Allegra's death and wrote the last letter
that he sent back to Shelley.

She summed up her feelings towards him dis-
passionately to Mary in 1835 when she was convinced she was going to die of the cholera in Florence :·

' . . . As you are a great analyzer of human
characters, and fond, like your father, of speculating
upon them, it strikes me you might be curious to
know whether, in leaving life, my sentiments experience any change with regard to Lord Byron.—Not
at all ; so far from it, that were the fairest Paradise
offered to me upon the condition of his sharing it, I
would refuse it. At the same time it would give

---

[1] A name for Hogg used by him and Jane.

me pleasure to know that he was happy, for I am not revengeful and desire pain to no one, not even to him. But for me there could be no happiness, there could be nothing but misery in the presence of the person who so wantonly, wilfully, destroyed my Allegra.'

She regretted that Shelley had not broken with him : ' From the continuation of that intimacy has arisen all we have suffered since, and ah ! how much it is ! What years of poverty and humiliation, of exile from all that is dear to us. . . . His genius extinct, the greatest that was ever known, and the noble system he would have established therewith fallen for many ages to the dust. All this for his ill-advised gentleness.'

But she was not always so detached, and on the publication of Mary's novel, *Lodore*, had protested with indignation :

' Mrs. Hare admired *Lodore* amazingly ; so do I, or should I, if it were not for that modification of the beastly character of Lord Byron of which you have composed Lodore. I stick to *Frankenstein*, merely because that vile spirit does not haunt its pages as it does all your other novels, now as Castruccio, now as Raymond, now as Lodore.

Good God ! to think a person of your genius, whose moral tact ought to be proportionately exalted, should think it a task befitting its power to gild and embellish and pass off as beautiful what was the merest compound of vanity, folly, and every miserable weakness that ever met together in one human being ! '

In the fresh burst of her correspondence with Trelawny—in the seventies as they both were—

when he accused her of having a " bee in her bonnet,"
she replied with spirit. It was all very well for that
magnanimity which had made him pardon Whitcombe to prompt him to say a word in extenuation
of Byron, but he did not know the facts. ' If you
did, you also would judge L. B. with the severity he
deserves.'

It was hardly to be expected that she should be
objective, and there was enough element of truth in
her arguments to exacerbate them. The convent *was*
unhealthy, the nuns *were* casual, and she had every
reason to believe that the children came of poor
parentage, although later researches have shown this
not to be the case.

' You may think what pangs of anguish I suffered
in the winter of '21,' Claire wrote, ' when I saw a
bright fire, and people and children warming themselves by it, and knew my darling never saw or felt a
cheerful blaze and was more starved with cold than
an English pauper Child in our Unions. And how I
trembled for the consequences and lived every day and
every hour in fear of bad news, and went about wildly
from one to another, imploring them to help me to
get her out, and received everywhere a refusal to
do anything, and the advice to be patient and wait
more favourable events. In this life, one dies of
anguish many times before one really dies. And not
the promise of cycles and cycles of unbroken felicity
could bribe or win me to live over again that period
and re-suffer what I then suffered.'

She was wrong in believing that Byron tried to get
rid of Allegra ; he did not want the comfort of his
old age to die, but he took no steps to see that she

didn't, and for his remorse afterwards, Claire's criticism of the ' prosy commonsense ' of his letter to Shelley is not unjustified; passing easily from his grief in a sentence, as he does, to an account of his visit to an American man-of-war and his flirtation there with an American lady.

On Byron's relations with Augusta she wrote to Trelawny that she had read the articles in the *Saturday Review* on the history of Medora Leigh, and from the internal evidence of the girl's character judged that she might well be Byron's daughter !

' Poor Mrs. Leigh ! What with her Brother, and what with her two daughters, she must have undergone torture. There is no positive proof that the connexion between L.B. and Mrs. Leigh existed ; but his verses to Augusta, by a Brother to a Sister—then his fit of hysterics at Bologna when he witnessed the performance of Myrrha—then Manfred and Cain— all form presumptive evidence against him. It is also so odd that he never went to England to see Ada though he was so fond of her ; was it because he knew that Lady Byron had full power to forbid his seeing her ? '

Sensual without passion and sentimental without tenderness, Byron wanted a " Sophie " and, his grasp never being far beyond his reach, he got a Teresa Guiccioli. In her, rather than in Augusta, or in Lady Jersey, who might have qualified when she braved London Society to give him a farewell party, he found the slave girl to plant a rose on Nero's grave. Teresa was faithful unto death ; standing always in deep mourning underneath his portrait to receive the guests in her noble drawing-room. She faded in fidelity,

221

not wholly unaware that it was only his death had saved her from his desertion.

Byron was not the man to foster a great love ; had he been less crude a Don Juan he might have made much of Claire. Her vitality, her courage, her wit would have flowered under the hand of a sensitive lover ; he might have ridden away but he would have left a memory to cherish. " Love's proved in its creation, not eternity."

But for Claire, who thanked God that she would never be young again, Death had always proved more real than Love, so that when it came to her it held no terrors. She had her memories and there was nothing of which she could be robbed : no pleasures, no hopes, no fears.

> These are dead, the debt is due,
> Dust claims dust—and we die too.

AUTHOR'S ACKNOWLEDGMENTS
NOTES TO THE TEXT
APPENDICES
INDEX

AUTHOR'S ACKNOWLEDGMENTS

FOR this biography of Claire Clairmont I have had access to the following papers and have been allowed to quote from them :

The Journals of Claire Clairmont in the Ashley Collection now at the British Museum. These Journals (described in Appendix A) are unpublished except for a few extracts used by Dowden. I have worked from transcripts of them made by the late Roger Ingpen, whose widow, Mrs. Ingpen, received permission from T. J. Wise to hand them over to me. I am grateful to the Keeper of MSS. at the British Museum for allowing me to examine the originals.

Claire Clairmont's letters to Lord Byron in the possession of Sir John Murray. These letters cover the period of her first meeting with Byron and the later struggle for Allegra. Some of them were published by Prothero in his edition of *Byron's Collected Works* (1899) and others appeared in the *Cornhill Magazine* (August, September, 1934). For permission to use these and certain others that have not been hitherto published I am indebted to the kindness of Sir John Murray, who also found for me the portrait of Byron which he has allowed to be reproduced as a frontispiece.

Claire Clairmont's papers. Some of the papers bought from Claire's niece, Paula Clairmont, by the late H. Buxton Forman, have remained in the possession of his son, Mr. M. Buxton Forman, who has most kindly allowed me to make quotations from them.

Police *dossier* of Charles Clairmont. This is a document preserved in the State Archives of Vienna which I was able to trace there on a visit in 1937. As the archives were badly damaged by fire in 1927 and the work of sorting and replacement had only reached a much earlier date it was entirely through the gracious assistance of a lady curator to whom I was introduced that the papers were found and a copy and photostats made for me. Besides the information it affords with regard to the Clairmonts' life in Vienna, the *dossier* provides interesting evidence of Metternich's police administration.

I am very grateful to the owners of original Shelley papers which I used in *Mary Shelley* (Oxford University Press, 1938), for allowing me to transcribe further material from Boscombe MSS.A., and to Bodley's librarian and the Curators of the Bodleian library for permission to examine their reserved Shelley MSS.

I should like to acknowledge with sincere thanks the great kindness I have received from descendants of men and women described in this book and from those who have also made studies of their lives.

The Marchesa Origo, author of *Allegra* (Hogarth Press, 1935), has most generously allowed me to reproduce the miniature of Allegra which she acquired after her book was published. This belonged to Byron, and was sent to Claire after the child's death.

I am also indebted to Frau Alma Crüwell, granddaughter of Charles Clairmont, for sending me information with regard to Claire's later life and the old prints of Vienna which I have been able to

Author's Acknowledgments

reproduce ; to Mrs. Rigby, a great-niece of Trelawny, for allowing me to use an unpublished letter of his about Millais' *North-West Passage*, and for allowing me to reproduce a hitherto unpublished portrait by West ; to Signora Farina-Cini and her husband (a descendant of Lady Mountcashell through her daughter Nerina Tighe, who married Bartolomeo Cini), for permission to make use of their letters from Claire to Lady Mountcashell. Signora Farina-Cini also very kindly took photographs of Claire's grave which have been most useful to me, and I am very grateful to the Marchesa R. Viviani della Robbia (author of a delightful life of Shelley's " Emilia," *Vita di una Donna*, not yet translated into English) for sending me further particulars of the cemetery at the Antella.

Through Mrs. Belisario of Sydney, N.S.W., I have come across new Mary Shelley letters in the possession of Mr. Alex Hay, a descendant of the Alexander Berry who married a sister of Edward Wollstonecraft and was his partner in business in Sydney. I am very grateful to him for his permission to quote from these.

I am indebted to Mrs. Rossetti Angeli for allowing me to make use of the transcript of Sophia Stacey's diary which she made when she was writing *Shelley and His Friends in Italy* ; to Mr. C. M. Trelawny Irving for giving me information about his great-grandfather ; to Mr. A. C. Grylls for work at the British Museum ; to Mrs. May Wedderburn Cannan and Mr. Ronald Fuller for advice and help in reading proofs.

I am also grateful for the opportunity I have had to discuss points of interest in correspondence

227

with Professor Newman I. White of Duke University, North Carolina, who has informed me of material of great interest in Shelley biography which he will incorporate in his forthcoming life of the poet. I owe to Professor Frederick L. Jones of Mercer University, Georgia, several introductions to others interested in the period and in particular to Professor Miss Nitchie of Goucher College, Baltimore, who has allowed me to make use of information she obtained in her researches at Bodley, and most kindly initiated enquiries about Claire for me in Florence.

★ ★ ★

I acknowledge, with gratitude to the memory of their authors, my indebtedness to the following books :

The Life of Percy Bysshe Shelley, by Edward Dowden, LL.D. (1886).

The Life and Letters of Mary Wollstonecraft Shelley, by Mrs. Julian Marshall (1889).

The Letters of Percy Bysshe Shelley, edited by Roger Ingpen and Walter E. Peck, Julian edition (1926).

The Works of Lord Byron, edited by Rowland E. Prothero, M.A., M.V.O. (1904).

Lord Byron's Correspondence, edited by John Murray (1926).

Recollections (1858), *Records* (1878). Trelawny, E. J.,

Where quotations have been made from other authorities in the text, they have been acknowledged in the Notes and referred to in the Index. Many printed sources have contributed to my information about the period, but as any list can easily be compiled from the appropriate volumes of a library catalogue, I have refrained from the superfluous display of a Bibliography.

NOTES TO THE TEXT

For purpose of reference in the Notes and Appendices I have called the MSS. sources by the following terms :

Claire Clairmont Journals . . . . *Ashley*
Claire Clairmont letters belonging to Sir John
 Murray . . . . *J.M.*
Claire Clairmont papers belonging to Mr. Buxton
 Forman . . . . . . *C.P.*
Vienna Police Report . . . . *Dossier*
Shelley papers belonging to heirs of Lady Shelley
        Boscombe *MSS.A*

PART ONE

PAGE

3. Claire's singing Master, Corri, likened her voice to " a string of pearls." Dowden says in a note, Vol. I, Chapter X, ' Yet I am assured, by competent authority, that her sense of time was very defective.' Cf. Shelley's poems " On Constantia Singing " and Byron's " There be none of Beauty's ,daughters . . . "

4. Description of conditions at Skinner Street from *William Godwin*, C. Kegan Paul, 1876.

8. Letter quoted from *William Godwin*, C. Kegan Paul.

9. Description of Skinner Street shop from *Old and New London*, Thornbury.

12. For the name of the house at Dundee and the description of it I am indebted to Mrs. Hamilton Fyfe, who lived there as a girl.

12. See Claire's description of Mary, Appendix B.

13. Verse quoted from Byron's poem *Genevra*. Cp. the description by Mary and Shelley of the ' only pretty

229

women we met ' in the *Six Weeks' Tour*. ' She had lately recovered from a fever, and this added to the interest of her countenance, by adorning it with an appearance of extreme delicacy.'

13. Mary's tartan dress is described by Hogg in his *Life of Shelley*, Vol. II, p. 10. Her hair is done in this way in the miniature reproduced in *Mary Shelley*.

14. Jane's description of the walks is quoted from her unpublished papers to Trelawny. See Appendix D.

16. I take the view that Jane knew of the journey beforehand and was not rushed into it as she stated later. See Letter 7, Appendix C.

17. It was St. Sepulchre's clock that Bill Sikes and Nancy heard in Dickens' *Oliver Twist*.

18. The desk was a Secretaire or writing case. It may not have been the desk which caused the delay, but it would have been so like them to have risked the whole escape for the sake of papers ! Shelley's Journal states : ' I watched until the lightning and the stars became pale. At length it was fair. I believed it not possible that we should succeed ; still there appeared to lurk some danger even in certainty. I went : I saw her, she came to me. Yet one quarter of an hour remained. Still some arrangement must be made and she left me for a short time.'

19. For Shelley buying bread, see letter 4, Appendix D.

22. For conditions at French Inns see unpublished Journal of Maria Gisborne (Ashley) and cf. also Mary Shelley's *Rambles*, published in 1844.

22. Mrs. Godwin made out that it was not she but Mr. Marshall who followed them, Appendix D. That this was not the case can be shown from the entries in the Shelley Journal.

25. For description of each Journal, see Appendix A.

26. Unpublished extract from Claire's Journal.

Notes to the Text

27. Extract from Journal quoted by Dowden, Vol. I, p. 451.

28. Noë in the Journals should be Nouailles (Koszul, *Jeunesse de Shelley*).

28. Unpublished entries from Claire's Journal.

31. The Faucon Inn is still in existence.

32 *seqq*. Unpublished entries from Claire's Journal, with exception of first paragraph of entry for August 27th, which is quoted by Dowden, Vol. I, p. 456.

35. Claire's story was afterwards sent to Byron. See Vol. III, Appendix VII, Letter 7, Prothero.

38. Quotation from letter to Harriet from *Shelley's Lost Letters to Harriet* (ed. Leslie Hotson, 1930).

38. Unpublished entry from Claire's Journal.

38. Extract from Mrs. Godwin's letter 3, Appendix D.

42. Extract from Claire's Journal quoted by Dowden, Vol. I, p. 484.

43. Entry for October 24th from Dowden, Vol. I, p. 492, note.

44 *seqq*. Unpublished entries from Claire's Journal.

46. For Mary's relations with Hogg at this time see *Mary Shelley*, pp. 47–8, and Note I, where reference is made to forthcoming disclosures.

48. Unpublished extract from Claire's Journal. On the other hand, the day had been happy for Mary ! Her Journal entry records : ' Talk to Shelley. He writes a heap of letters. Read part of *St. Leon*. Talk with him all evening ; this is a day devoted to Love in idleness. Go to sleep early in the evening. Shelley goes a little before 10.'

  Claire's Journal ends on November 9th, 1814, and the next volume does not begin until January 18th, 1818. Letters and the Shelley Journals supply the available information for the period between.

49. Mrs. Godwin claimed to have arranged for Claire to stay at Lynmouth with a Mrs. Bicknell (see Letter 6,

Appendix D.), but Claire's letter to Fanny shows that she did not want Skinner Street to know her plans.

50–2. Letter quoted from Dowden, Vol. I, p. 519.

53. The date of Jane's change of name is not certain. She is referred to as Clare, Clara, and Cleary in the Shelleys' Journal before this time. To the Godwins she always remained Jane.

54–6. The letters from Claire to Byron and his note are published in *Byron's Works*, Prothero, Vol. III, Appendix VII ; partly republished in *The Cornhill* (August and September, 1934). Collated with originals.

57. For Byron on the Seraglio, see *Childe Harold*, Canto II, Verse LXI :

> She yields to one her person and her heart,
> Tamed to her cage, nor feels a wish to rove.

59. (1) Letter No. 8 from Prothero, Vol. III, Appendix VII.

60. (2) Unpublished letter. (J.M.)

61. (3) Letter published *Cornhill*, August 1934.

61. (4) Unpublished letter. (J.M.)

62. Couplet by Charles Armitage Brown, the friend of Keats. *Some Letters*, etc., M. Buxton Forman, 1937.

63. It has been stated that Byron and Shelley had met at Marlow (William Graham's *Last Links*), but in a letter from Mary to Byron on January 13th, 1817, she says : ' . . . Where we had hope [sic] to have the pleasure of your society on your return to England. The town of Marlow is about 30 miles from London.' (J.M.)

63. Extract from Claire's letter. *Cornhill*, August 1934.

64. Description of coach from the *Diary of Polidori*, ed. W. M. Rossetti. From Polidori's diary it appears that Dowden's assumption that Byron and the Shelleys were at the same hotel had no foundation.

64. Extract from unpublished letter. (J.M.)

64. Extract from unpublished letter. (J.M.)

Notes to the Text

67. The anecdotes of Byron and the incident of Augusta Leigh's letter are from Claire's letters to Trelawny. (C.P.) This passage was written some fifty years after the events alluded to. ' *Childe Harold* ' is probably a lapse of memory for *The Prisoner of Chillon*. See Appendix C.

68. Cf. Claire later on Shelley's idealizing of Byron's genius. Appendix C.

68. For Byron's promises see Claire's letters. Appendix C.

68. ' Love caused our first imprudence.' Quotation from Mary Shelley's letter to Mrs. Hoppner, August 11th, 1821. *Lord Byron's Correspondence*, Murray, Vol. II, p. 185.

69. Letter partly quoted in *Cornhill*, August 1934.

PART TWO

73. Lines from *Othello*.

73–5. Passage from Claire's letter, published *Cornhill*, August 1934. Final paragraph unpublished. (J.M.)

76. Passage from Claire's letter, published *Cornhill*, August 1934.

77. Unpublished passage from letter. (J.M.)

78. Passage from Claire's letter, published *Cornhill*, August 1934.

79. Mrs. Godwin's opinion from Letter 6, Appendix D.

81. For the story of Shelley and the baby on Magdalen Bridge, see Hogg's *Life*, p. 239, (Moxon, 1858).

82. Unpublished passage from Claire's Journal. It was probably on this visit that Godwin was told of Claire's relationship to Allegra. That Mrs. Godwin was reluctant to believe that anybody but Shelley ' was the real author of her misfortunes ' is shown from a passage of Maria Gisborne's Journal (unpublished, Ashley) when she and her husband visited the Godwins in 1820.

233

83. Passage from Mary Wollstonecraft's letter quoted from *New letters of Mary Wollstonecraft and Helen M. Williams*, ed. P. Kurtz and Carrie C. Autry, Cambridge University Press, 1937.

84. ' *absentia Claria*.' For this emendation I am indebted to Miss Nitchie, whose re-reading of the original letter in the Bodleian MSS. shows that the form usually quoted, ' *absentia Claire*,' is incorrect.

85. Unpublished passage from Claire's memoranda. (C.P.)

87. Unpublished passages from Claire's Journal.

87. The Apollonicon was a ' chamber organ of vast power, supplied with both keys and barrels . . . the keyboards are 5 in number ; the central and largest comprising 5 octaves and the smaller ones of which 2 are placed on each side the larger, two octaves each . . . This magnificent instrument performs Mozart's Overture to the *Zauberflöte*, *Figaro* and *Idomeneo*.' (From *Curiosities of London*, Timbs.)

87. The description of Stella's mentality certainly fits Claire, as Scythrop has also much in common with Shelley. Dowden states (Vol. II, p. 396, note) that Claire wrote in a note-book about herself : ' in 1818 she refused an offer of marriage from P— : he knew her whole history.' I have not been able to trace the note-book with this reference, but, like other statements she made in later life in preparation for writing her Memoirs, it cannot be accepted without a *caveat*.

88. Mrs. Gisborne's remark quoted from unpublished letter used in *Mary Shelley*. (Boscombe MSS.A.)

88. Unpublished passage from Claire's Journal. The Shelley children and Allegra were baptized at St Giles-in-the-Fields, see certificate opposite.

89–94. Passages from Claire's letter, published *Cornhill*, Sept., 1934.

94–5. Passage from Claire's Journal, quoted by Dowden, Vol. II, pp. 203–4.

Notes to the Text

ALLEGRA'S BAPTISMAL CERTIFICATE *

Date of Baptism	Christian Name	Parents' Christian Names	Surname	Date of Birth	Father's Residence	Father's Rank	By Whom
1818 March 9th	Clara Allegra Byron born of	Rt. Hon. George Gordon Lord Byron ye reputed Father by Clara Mary Jane	Clairmont	12th Jan. 1817	No fixed residence, travelling on the Continent	Peer	Charles Macarthy

* From *Allegra*, by Iris Origo (The Hogarth Press, 1935).

PAGE

95–6. Passages from Claire's letter, May 20th, 1818, published *Cornhill*, 1934.

104. Some newly discovered documents about this child are to be published in a biography of Shelley now nearing completion by Professor Newman I. White of Duke University, North Carolina. Professor White offers some new arguments for believing the child to be neither Shelley's nor Claire's, but an adopted child of unknown parentage.

Although the new documents point at first sight to some astonishing conclusions, I subscribe to the view put forward by Professor White, bearing in mind Shelley's known predilection for adopting children, e.g. Polly Rose at Marlow (Dowden) and Marguerite Pascal on the first Tour in France (Koszul).

105. The original of Mrs. Hoppner's letter quoted in part by Dowden and Mrs. Marshall is given in full in *Mary Shelley*, Appendix C.

105. Shelley's verse from *Julian and Maddalo*.

107–8. Claire's Journal entry for March 28th, quoted by Dowden, Vol. II, p. 258. Entry for March 29th, unpublished.

108. Unpublished passage from Claire's Journal.

Notes to the Text

236

Notes to the Text

125–7. Unpublished entries from Claire's Journal. Cf. Dowden, Vol. II, p. 357. The " Claire and the Ma " lines are quoted by Dowden, Vol. II, p. 331.

128. Passage on Emilia quoted by Dowden, Vol. II, p. 372.

129. Description of Claire from Medwin's *Angler in Wales*.

129–31. Entry for March 15th partly quoted by Dowden, Vol. II, p. 402. ╱

132. For La Guiccioli's jealousy, see Letter 4, Appendix C.

133. For Mary Shelley's letter to Mrs. Hoppner in full and the editor's attempt at a defence of Byron, see *Lord Byron's Correspondence*, Murray, Vol. III, p. 185 *seq.*

133. Quotation from Claire's letter published Prothero, Vol. III, Appendix VII.

134. Passage from Claire's Journal quoted Dowden, Vol. II, p. 420.

135. Passage from unpublished letter to Trelawny. See Appendix C.

138–9. Passage from Claire's letter, March 24th, 1821, published *Cornhill*, Sept., 1934, partly quoted Dowden, Vol. II, p. 403.

140. Elise's story from Claire's memoranda. See Appendix B.

141. This seems to me the only possible interpretation of the passage in the memoranda kept with Claire's Journals, Appendix B.

141. Passage from unpublished letters to Trelawny. See Appendix C.

143. Passage from unpublished letter to Mary Shelley. (Boscombe MSS.A.)

145. Mary and Shelley on Byron from Trelawny's *Records of Shelley, Byron and the Author*, 1878.

151. Passage from Claire's letter, published *Cornhill*, Sept., 1934.

152. " Quick Natures " . . . George Eliot.

Notes to the Text

153. From unpublished memoranda. See Appendix B.

155. Claire's letter (Ashley), quoted by Mrs. Marshall, Vol. II, p. 3.

157. Description of the burial and Byron's words from Trelawny's *Last Days of Shelley and Byron*, 1858.

160. Passage from Claire's letter, *Shelley and Mary*.

160-1. Unpublished passage from Claire's Journal.

PART THREE

165-6. Extract from unpublished letter to Mrs. Mason, September 14th, 1822, from 37 Biber Bastei, Wien. C.P.

166. The particulars of where Claire lived and details of the *Kaffee Haus* are from the Police *dossier*.

167. For the position of the Biber Bastion I am indebted to Frau Alma Crüwell, who also sent me a contemporary print of it.

173. There is no evidence that Claire consented to become Trelawny's mistress, and from the few minor passages suppressed in his *Letters* (ed. H. Buxton Forman) nothing more appears than that, as he had probably embraced her with a platonic ardour proper to the period, his highly individual style could also lapse into conventional amorousness.

177. *Kamelavke* = the black upstanding head-dress of Russian priests.

177. The Square has always had the same name and has not changed colour with the addition of Lenin's mausoleum in front of the Kremlin.

177. Sometimes the priests showed themselves fully alive to their penitents' motives. Claire's Journal has the following entry : ' October 26th–November 7th . . . When they were all gone sat with Marie Ivanovna who related an interview she had with the Bishop Porphyry. She was remarkably pious and always running after holy men, hoping to benefit her soul

thereby. No sooner did she hear of Porphyry's arrival, than she ran to see him at the monastery where he was lodged with her niece Miss Olga. Porphyry a man of about thirty and very handsome, seemed very little flattered by her hurry to seek his society ; but began to grumble rather uncourteously after listening to her apology for intruding upon his solitude upon the score of the benefit his pious counsels would be of to her soul ; " this is the way," replied he, " this is just the way with the women, you only run after us because it is the fashion, just as it is at the Smith's Bridge, one day pink is the fashion, the next blue is, one day the Bishop Eugene is all the rage and the next Porphyry. We are truly much obliged to you. You come here pretending to seek the salvation of your souls ; all I know of the affair is that you make us lose ours—such a crowd of women, pretty, ugly, old and young, good ones, bad ones, prudes, coquettes, and we must hear all they have to confess, and I would like to know how it is possible for us to be pious with all the folly of the beau monde pouring at every instant into our ears. Be pleased when you come, not to bring your pretty young niece with you at least." After this exordium he allowed her to explain the doubtful state of her soul, its wavering state between her love of religion and its perpetual yielding to worldly vanities and pleasures. " Above all," said she, " what most distresses me, is the pleasure, the transport I feel when the Emperor honours us with a visit." " Bah ! " said Porphyry, interrupting her. " Do you think I don't perceive you tell me all this in order to find opportunity of letting me know the Emperor comes sometimes to see you." '

179 *seqq.* Unpublished entries from Journal.

180–2. Unpublished letter to Mary Shelley. (Boscombe MSS.A.)

185. For Mary's mention of Fletcher, see Mrs. Marshall, Vol. II, p. 118.

185-6. There are discrepancies in the several accounts that Trelawny gave of the actual structure of Byron's deformity. I have quoted his account of the treasures he found from his *Records.*

188. Verse from *Letter to Maria Gisborne.*

189. Letter to Jane Williams. Mrs. Marshall, Vol. II, p. 161.

190. *Linieke* are wagons made of a single plank of wood on which it is necessary to ride astride.

190. Letter to Jane Williams. Mrs. Marshall, Vol. II, p. 161.

191. For Claire on Madame Kaisaroff and Natalie, see Appendix B.

192. For description of Godwin's manner of speech see extract from Mrs. Gisborne's Diary, 1820, unpublished (Ashley). ' When I happen to be alone with Mr. Godwin he takes the opportunity of asking me as many questions as the time will allow of, respecting Miss C., but he lengthens out his sentences very much in order to speak with perfect correctness and often uses the parenthesis, so that he gets on very slowly.'

193. Claire's letter quoted by Mrs. Marshall, Vol. II, p. 248.

193. Letters in *Shelley and Mary* show that Sir Timothy visited his grandson at school, but not as frequently as Mary would have liked.

194. An importunate letter from Everina Wollstonecraft (unpublished) is among the Bodleian MSS.

195. " Blue Bag " from his barrister's bag. It seems as if Jane had not divulged his identity at first when she announced her ' union ' to Claire.

195. Lines from *The Wife Speaks,* Cecil Day Lewis.

196. Passage from Claire's letter, Mrs. Marshall, Vol. II, p. 202.

196. On Moore from unpublished letter. (Boscombe MSS.A.)

197. Passage from unpublished letter of Mary Shelley. (Ashley.)

198. Passage from Claire's letter. (*Shelley and Mary.*)

198. There has been controversy as to whether the legacy of £12,000 was a mistake from £6,000 being written twice over. For full discussion see Ingpen, *Shelley in England*, p. 473.

198. Extract from Claire's letter to Byron, published *Cornhill*, Sept., 1934.

198. Lines from *Biography*, John Masefield.

199. Extract from letter, March 24th, 1832. (*Shelley and Mary*.)

199. Passage from letter, February 1st, 1833. (*Shelley and Mary*.)

201. Passage from unpublished letter. (*Shelley and Mary*.)

201. Passage from letter in Mrs. Marshall, Vol. II, p. 252.

201. For this and other particulars about the Cini family and for permission to use extracts from Claire's letter to Bartolomeo Cini, I am indebted to Signora Farina-Cini and her husband, a grandson of Nerina Mason who married Bartolomeo Cini.

202. Unpublished extract from letter to Jane Williams, 1833. February 1st. Part in Mrs. Marshall. (*Shelley and Mary*.)

202. Extract from letter in *Shelley and Mary*.

202. For fuller particulars about *The Pole* see a paper by Professor Bradford A. Booth in *A Journal of English Literary History*, Vol. V, No. 1, March, 1838.

203. Extract from Claire's letter, *Mary Shelley*. (Boscombe MSS.A.)

204. Extract from Claire's letter, *Mary Shelley*. (Boscombe MSS.A.)

204. Passage from unpublished letter. (Boscombe MSS.A.)

205. ' In the Portfolio of the Vienna University, Clairmont is designated as teacher of the English language and literature at the University and the Theresianische Ritter-Akademie, proprietor of a private English language school, and residing in Landhausgasse No. 31.' Extract from a letter the author received in

Notes to the Text

confirmation of a personal call in September 1937 to the State Archives (*Haus-Hof-und Staatsarchiv*) in Vienna.

206. Extracts from Claire's letter, *Mary Shelley*.

207. Extract from Claire's letter, *Mary Shelley*. For a further note on Mrs. Boinville, see Mrs. Godwin's letter 6, Appendix D.

207. Passage from unpublished letter. (Boscombe MSS.A.)

208. Passage from unpublished letter. (Boscombe MSS.A.)

209. For further reference to Georgina and to Claire's financial affairs see letter to Bartolomeo Cini. Appendix E.

209. Unpublished letter from Jane Williams. (Ashley.)

210. Extracts from Claire's letters, *Mary Shelley*. (Boscombe MSS.A.)

211. Letter from Sir Percy Florence Shelley sent to Browning for forwarding is quoted in full, *Mary Shelley*. (Boscombe MSS.A.)

211. Passage from Claire's letter quoted in *Mary Shelley*. (Boscombe MSS.A.)

212. Description of Claire from letter of one of Charles Clairmont's sons. (By permission of Frau Alma Crüwell.)

212-13. Extract from unpublished letter. (C.P.)

213. Her niece writes of Paula : ' We used to call her Aunt Plin ; she was a gifted, original, high-tempered, somewhat eccentric person, and if tempers clashed between Claire and the gentle Mary Shelley they certainly clashed between Aunt and Niece . . .' [She was anxious that money should not be left away from the family.]. ' She was perfectly and utterly unselfish in her devoted love to her brother.'

In *Last Links* W. Graham says that Paula died from a fall into a glacier. Her niece writes : ' She did perish in the mountains but on an almost harmless walk, and she fell into a river from a certain height. It never was ascertained whether she merely slipped or whether the slip happened by her turning dizzy or by some heart attack.'

242

Notes to the Text

In *Notes and Queries*, October 8th, 1804, there is the following description of the grave from a correspondent, A Francis Steuart. ' It is at Campo Santo della Misericordia de Ste. Maria d'Antella about 3 miles to the south-east of Florence. . . . The inscription (below a cross) upon her tomb reads thus :

In Memory of
Clara Mary Constantia Jane Clairmont
born April 27th 1798, died March 19th, 1879.
She passed her life in sufferings, expiating not only her faults but also her virtues.'

The tomb has now been removed and Claire's name is only commemorated on a small slab of white marble in the black and white pavement under one of the arcades opposite the chapel of the S. Annunziata.

✠

JANE CLAIRMONT
CLARA MARY
DI ANNI 81
M. IL 19 MARZO 1879

Signora Farina-Cini, who has sent me a description of the cemetery and very kindly taken photographs, writes : ' It looked to me as if the cemetery, a large place with several squares of burying ground each surrounded by porticoes running round all 4 sides, still being enlarged and improved, must have much changed within the 60 years since Claire was buried there ; and it seems likely that coffins may have been removed or tombstones tidily rearranged and a short inscription substituted to original more lengthy one. There are many little inscriptions like Claire's here and there on the regular tiles of the marble floor of the portico.'

215. Verse from Shelley's poem.

215. Two French lines quoted from *Melloney Holtspur*, by John Masefield.

215–16. Extract from letter to Jane Williams, quoted by Mrs. Marshall, p. 160.

216. ' Passion the high tide of the mind,' from an entry in Journal VI.

217. Mary Shelley died in Chester Square, London, on February 1st, 1851. Her letter from which extracts are given is quoted in full, Appendix E. Lady Shelley wrote on her death to Alexander Berry, (unpublished) ' . . . our sorrow is a terrible one, no Mother and Son were ever bound together by such ties of love as my husband and such a mother as she had been to him and to myself, the loss is indeed a fearful one. For 3 years she has been to me more than a Mother, Sister, Friend—my daily and hourly companion—it was impossible for any living thing to approach her and not love her and heaven knows no words can express what my love for her was . . . It was her desire to be buried by her Father and Mother who were laid in St. Pancras Churchyard, however it would have broken my heart to let her loveliness wither in such a dreadful place. We have therefore

removed them to a vault in the churchyard at Bournemouth, a lovely spot in Hampshire and about a mile from a little place we have taken and which we intend to make our future residence—there she rests with her Father on one side of her and her Mother on the other and in a year or two should we be spared we intend to make a pilgrimage to Rome to bring home the urn containing the ashes of her beloved husband which we shall place in her grave . . .' Lady Shelley wished to raise a new monument on Shelley's grave in Rome. Trelawny forbade it as the ground was his property.

217. For further descriptions of Jane Williams and her life with Hogg, see *After Shelley*, by Sylva Norman.

218. For Hogg's letters to Lady Shelley while engaged on his biography of the poet, see Appendix C, *Mary Shelley*.

218. Peacock died on January 23rd, 1866. Extract from Jane Williams' letter, unpublished. (Ashley.)

218–19. Extract from letter, to Mary, Sept. 1st, 1835. (*Shelley and Mary*.)

219. Extract from letter quoted by Mrs. Marshall, Vol. II, p. 265.

220. For this and other letters to Trelawny, see Appendix C.

222. ' Love's proved. . . .' *From Feathers to Iron*, Cecil Day Lewis.

APPENDICES

A. Description of the Journals. (Ashley.)

B. Extracts from memoranda with Claire's Journals. (Ashley.)

C. Extracts from unpublished letters to Trelawny. (C.P.)

D. Extracts from Mrs. Godwin's letters copied by Claire. (C.P.)

E. Two unpublished letters from Claire to Bartolomeo Cini ; an unpublished letter from Mary Shelley to Alexander Berry, and a published letter from E. J. Trelawny to his daughter, Laetitia Call.

Many of the statements made by Claire Clairmont in her letters to Trelawny and in other memoranda quoted below can only be accepted with a caveat. *This is particularly the case in the copies of the letters she made from Mrs. Godwin to Lady Mountcashell which were quoted with notes on their inaccuracies by Dowden,* Life *of Shelley, Vol. II, Appendix B.*

In my text I have only used Claire's statements and those of Mrs. Godwin where they ring true to character and involve no perversion of facts.

I. *August 14th to November, 1814.* (*Ashley.*)

' Oblong pocket book, size $5\frac{1}{2} \times 4\frac{1}{4}$, bound in red roan, with metal clasp broken and the sheath for the pencil torn. 94 leaves remain, but some pages have been torn out. The front edges damaged by fire, but only a few words have been destroyed. In many cases portions of words remain—enough to provide a clue.

The writing on the fly leaves of this book is very interesting as it is mostly in Shelley's hand and it is highly probable that it may originally have belonged to him. However, it passed into the hands of Mary Jane Clairmont, as she has written her name thus on the inside front cover (and afterwards obliterated it), with the date " August 13 1814." The 5 pages at the end of the book are all in Shelley's handwriting. Page 1 begins with a Latin phrase expressing a hope that the French Encyclopædia may never be forgotten. Then the line from Dante's Inferno III, 9, *Lasciate ogni speranza, voi che intrate.* This is followed by a piece of erotic Latin prose (continued for two lines on page 2)—unidentified. On page 2 Shelley has also written the phrase " *Nondum amabam &c.*" (from St. August. Confess., Bk. III, Cap. I) which he used as a motto for " Alastor." Then there is the short piece of prose " True Knowledge " &c., which Forman printed in his edition of Shelley, Vol. 3, p. 79. On pages 3 and 4 Shelley has copied out another passage from Dante's Inferno Canto V. This is carried on for two lines on page 4. On this and the next page 5 there is a poem possibly by Shelley on Moonlight. But if by him it is strange that Forman did not print it. On the end cover Jane Clairmont has written " I have nothing left to do but to fry in the sun for your amusement." '

I have quoted this description from the transcript made by the late Roger Ingpen. It should be added that on the inside cover there is one of Shelley's drawings of trees in pencil resembling those scribbled on the covers of his own Journals.—Author.

II. *January 17th to Wednesday, April 22nd, 1818.* (*Ashley.*)

8vo. Two quires of 8 loose leaves ($4\frac{3}{4} \times 7\frac{1}{4}$) totalling 32 pages. The Journal begins in the middle of a sentence : " like a savage."

III. *Portion of January 17th, January 18th, 1818 ; then from April 23rd to June 1818 (Carl Pforzheimer).*

I have not seen the original, but the following story told by Hogg which fits in to the entry for January 17th in Volume II was quoted in the Sales Catalogue of the Harry B. Smith collection, and I therefore give it here. It has interest for Claire's reaction to its " moral " and for Hogg's, relation of it which was probably not without *arrière pensée*.

'*January, 1818.* Hogg tell us a curious story very descriptive of the Christian virtues. A gentleman of fortune lived very happily with his wife. Her sister fell in love with him and as the Sisters loved each other this made no difference in their happiness. Unhappily, both the love and the consequences came to the knowledge of the family of the Sisters and then began the persecution. The Husband though a man of immense wealth possessed his estates only for life ; he was therefore very averse to accept the Challenge of the irritated Brother as they were pleased to call him. These three people went abroad ; they tried every means to avoid a meeting but the Brother followed thirsting (continued in first entry for Journal II) like a savage beast for blood ; he had blood and may it lie like lead on his soul ! The poor husband was shot dead in the mutiny ! The wife was left with her children starving and desolate, and the poor Sister went instantly mad and has been ever since confined. But their miseries are nothing. Do we not know that the Brother had blood ? Shortly after this " blood hunter " was canvassing for some office or other at one of the Universities and he won it because so many, people admired this " noble generous action " of his.'

IV. *March 7th, 1819 to August 1st, 1820. (Ashley.)*

A small volume ($4\frac{1}{2} \times 5\frac{3}{4}$) with red marbled paper cover of Italian origin. 86 leaves.

On the inside cover there are notes of Italian words and a series of headings :

'On the country of Italy.
On the manners and customs, including those of the country and those of the town.
On the pictures and statuary.

On Music and the State of the Opera.
Letter for Bolgona.
Passport.
Blk. silk stockings and shoes.
Ivy leaves.'

After half a dozen pages there is a page for accounts, and on the pages at the end translations of Greek epigrams and one written in Greek.

V. *Saturday, August 5th, 1820, to Friday, September 20th, 1822. (Ashley.)*

240 small quarto pages in white vellum binding. The inside cover has odd addresses, there follow seven blank pages and then on the left-hand page is an Indian Song transliterated, next page has translation, ' Songster sweet begin the lay.' Then a recipe for an Ague.

' *For an Ague . . . Dr. Warren.*
1 Oz. of the best red Bark.
1 Nutmeg grated.
1 Table spoonful of beaten blk. pepper.
1 —— —— of coarse sugar.
To be mixed with Syrup of Poppies into an Electuary.
A large Tea Spoonful to be taken as soon as the Fit is quite off and to be repeated every half hour that the whole quantity may be tekn in 24 Hours—
An Emetic is to be taken the Evening before the Fit is expected—
Half the quantity for a Child—'

Description of the Journals *Description of the Journals*

On the inside of the end cover there are lines in Russian and written over is ' Sunday, May 27th at three or four o'clock.'

VI. *May 12th–24th, 1825, to January 2nd–13th, 1826. (Ashley.)*

A small quarto volume bound in brown leather or hide, apparently of Russian make, 69 leaves. On the last page before the cover are written notes ;

' The Thaumatrope, being rounds of Amusements or how to please and surprise by turns at 10s. and 6d. By Boosey & Sons, Bond Street. Papyro plastics, or the art of modelling in Paper, an instructive amusement for young people. 5s.'

Some lines of Russian and Mary Shelley's addresses at Mortimer Terrace and Bartholomew Place.

VII. *Sunday, December 21st. 1826 to September 7th, 1827. (In possession of Frau Alma Crüwell who has sent me the following particulars) :*

' The diary opens with the words, " My Journal has been a long while interrupted, every day I have put off writing it, tired of having nothing to say and because I was overwhelmed with work. Now I am a little quieter. I am at the Princess Galizin's in Dmitrieff's house opposite the Strathnova monastery on the Doerska Boulevard. The Prince and Princess, Helen and Miss Harriet are all in the country. So I am as quiet as a bird roosting for the night." It goes on till February—then a pause—and starts again, written rather badly, on August 14th, and is continued till September 7th, 1827.'

I have not been able to see the originals of these memoranda kept with Claire's Journals, but have used extracts from the transcripts made by the late Roger Ingpen. Vagaries of grammar and punctuation (with which I have not interfered) are no doubt accounted for by the fact that Claire wrote the passages roughly with a view to incorporating them later in Memoirs.

On Mary Shelley

Mary's hair is light brown, of a sunny and burnished brightness like the autumnal foliage when played upon by the rays of the setting sun ; it sets in round her face and falls upon her shoulders in gauzy wavings and is so fine it looks as if the wind had tangled it together into golden network/she wore it in its natural state, flowing in gauzy wavings round her face and throat, and upon her shoulders, and it was so fine the slightest wind or motion tangled it into a golden network,/it was rather short and she let it fall into its natural state like golden network round her face and throat, and half way down her shoulders, and it was so fine one feared/to disturb the beauty of its gauzy wavings with a breath/lest the slightest breath should disturb the beauty of its gauzy wavings.

She has given up every hope of imaginary excellence, and has compromised all the nobler parts of her nature and has sneaked in upon any terms she could get into society although she full well knew she could meet with nothing there but depravity. Others still cling round the image and memory of Shelley —with her it ought to be the sole thought of her being, his ardent youth, his exalted being, his simplicity and enthusiasm are the sole thoughts of their being, but she has forsaken even their memory for the pitiful pleasure of trifling with trifles, and has exchanged the sole thought of his being for a share in the corruptions of society. Would to God she could perish without note or remembrance, so the brightness of his name might not be darkened by the corruptions she sheds upon it. What low ambition is that, that seeks for tinsel and gaudiness when the reality of all that is noble and worthy has passed away. It will perhaps be objected to these. The only other palliation I have to offer to these meannesses of conduct and heart, is the surpassing beauty of her mind ; every sentiment of hers is so glowing and beautiful, it is worth the actions of another person.

She is a mixture of vanity and good nature. Recollecting her conduct at Pisa I can never help feeling horror even in only looking at her—the instant she appears I feel not as if I had blood in my veins but in its stead the sickening crawling motion of the Death Worm.

What should one say of a Woman who should go/how would feel towards her who should go/and gaze upon the spectacle of a Child led to the scaffold—one would turn from her with horror—yet she did so, she looked coolly on, rejoiced in the comfortable place she had got in the show, chatted with her neighbours, and after all never winced once during the exhibition and after all was over, went up and claimed acquaintance with the executioner and shook hands with him.

I never saw her afterwards without feeling as if the sickening crawling motion of a Deathworm had replaced the usual flow of my Blood in my veins.

Shelley on the contrary acted like himself—it was his principle never to refuse his countenance even to the most guilty ; he could not therefore now that he was touched withdraw ; but his sad countenance betrayed how painful was the duty imposed upon him.

Excerpta

At Lerici I know not how it was I had a stern tranquility in me united to the time—the flame of a deep sullen resentment for unmerited misfortunes burned within me and I bid defiance to the dark visitings of misfortune and to the disastrous hauntings of hate. I said. You cannot inflict more than I will proudly bear.

I went to Russia that I might forget the visitings of my dark and wayward fate, the disastrous hauntings that seemed inseparable with my name.

I have trodden life alone without a guide and without a companion and before I depart for ever I would willingly leave with another what my tongue has never yet ventured to tell. I would willingly think that my memory may not be lost in oblivion as my life has been.

Amid the thousand thousand lines of human life, branching and intersecting in endless and infinite directions, there was not one I could choose that would lead to safety.

Claire's Memoranda

All is love in the universe—the silver showers of the fountain, the quiet life of the leaves, the flowery path in May even the deep night of Heaven is strewn with golden blossoms drawn alone as a disastrous and discordant atom amid these elements of harmony and love.

On friendship with Madame Kaisaroff

To hope against hope—this is the key of the secret intelligence that reigns between me and Mrs. Kaisaroff. She met with me when I was a solitary and uncertain wanderer upon the face of the earth ; a branch cut off from the plantation where it had grown and abandoned amid strangers ; my mind was in that state of destitution and misery which are the surest roads to vice. I met her in the lucky hour ; she gave me a home, she gave me consideration and kindness, and beyond all these, sympathy in my thoughts and feelings. I was cut off for ever, as I considered, from the list of human beings ; I might exist, but the joys, the honours, the pleasures of existence were not to be allowed to me in the least portion. I belonged to an outcast race ; our name was one of utter reprobation ; it lived in my heart, but was never in those many long years pronounced by my lips. The most unworthy conduct, the most unworthy principles were attributed to the beings whom I belonged to, and whom I looked upon as sacred ; the principles that I looked upon as sacred were objects of execration to the rest of mankind ; the persons whom I cherished and revered were the objects of scorn and blame whenever they were mentioned. Every quality that can disgrace the human nature was attributed to them ; how unjustly I well knew, though none beside did know ; their race was cursed, their name one of utter reprobation ; and so forbidden that though deeply graven in my heart it never passed my lips. In this state of destitution and misery Mrs. K. found me ; an outcast from society, an uncertain and solitary wanderer, sullen from the sense of unmerited sufferings, in hatred with all mankind ; /except these one or two individuals who yet survived the destruction that has been made of us, but these were too far/ who had known human nature but knows that this state of mental solitude, this state of insensibility to all social claims, is the surest forerunner of Vice. In this state I was. One or two individuals yet there were, who still lived, having survived the destruction that had been heaped upon us, but these were too far from me to afford me succour. I looked upon them with suppliant eyes, as the drowning mariner may look upon the distant clouds that are congregated in the horizon. But whilst I admired and adored, I expected no help. In this state, I met Mrs. K.[1] She selected me from the crowd where I was lost and overlooked ; raised me from the state of despondency into which I had fallen, gave me a home and a sister in herself, and far more than these, restored to me that which I had been accustomed to and which of all my losses seemed the heaviest, sympathy for my thoughts and opinions. Once more they breathed the light of day ; once more my lips revealed the workings of my mind ; once more I received and gave noble aspirations. By how many pledges therefore am I

[1] Her enthusiasm for Mrs. Kaisaroff did not long survive (see letter in Mrs. Marshall, Vol. II, p. 238).

not bound to her. By the honour of the sect to whom I belong, by my duty to prove by my actions that these calumniated persons are worthy of a better name and better fate. My whole soul is bent upon preserving this friendship ; my first thought when I rise in the morning, my last at night, is how shall I guard our affection from these blights of coldness, distrust, or misunderstanding, which are the reproach of commoner affections ; how may I preserve it as it now is inviolate, untouched by time, or the world's abuse, that to the end it may last in all its present perfection. To this my being is dedicated.

Natalie Kaisaroff

She neglects no opportunity of saying everything she conceives to be most disagreeable to me. I was regretting not hearing from M. Miltez because I had written requesting him to furnish me with letters of introduction—she instantly thrust herself into the discourse with a toss of the head. " I wonder you are always writing for letters of introduction, you who pretend to be so fond of solitude have no need for letters in order to make acquaintances ". This is one of a hundred instances—in future I shall note them down. But I remark with the greatest pain the excessive malice of her disposition. This is the principle upon which she proceeds ; as I am not loved so I am determined to make myself hated. This is the object of her solitude, the object which employs her thoughts night and day. Every preparative that I make for the journey she blames : I cannot stir a step but she throws ridicule and scorn and ineffable contempt upon my proceedings. There is

259

no end to the predictions she makes as to the accidents we are to meet with in the journey. We are to roll down the hill, or fall over the precipice, or be blown over by the wind or be struck dead by a flash of lightning and assassinated by robbers : these are the great evils ; when her tongue is tired of expatiating upon these, then she sinks into an enumeration of all the evils which are to befall us ; we shall find no bed, or if we do, such as cannot be slept upon, we shall have nothing to eat, or only *Schwein's Caire*. What their *Schwein's Caire* are I know not, nor how they got into her head, unless by that peculiar sympathy which attracts noble thoughts to noble minds, and mean thoughts to mean minds. She pays not the slightest attention to my representations. They assist to think that the roads we go over are, at the moment we speak, being traversed by hundreds of individuals, some sick, most of them poor, and that of these hundreds and hundreds, it is rare that a slight accident should happen, and a mortal one almost impossible. I point out to her Major Milner who has travelled like fifty thousand other people, all over Europe alone, Mr. and Mrs. Carlen who have been wandering in every country except Russia and Poland for these many years, quite unattended and nothing ever happened to them ; finally Miss de Lally and Miss Sabine who though of high birth travel quite alone. She has seen all these people and has heard their accounts and must know that what they say is true. It has all no effect upon her ; her mind too narrow to take it all in ; there is one idea there and that is *Schwein's Caire* and that is all it will hold. Or perhaps she does not choose to give up her position, because if she did, she must give up at the same time, her pretext for tormenting me.   So now she goes on in this way for three weeks, the same stupid arguments repeated every moment, till at length I am as wearied of them as of the clack of a watermill. . . .

1. *Letter* circa *1870*

. . . Before we parted at Geneva he [Byron] talked over with me our situation—he proposed to place the Child when born in Mrs. Leigh's care. To this I objected on the ground that a Child always wanted a parent's care at least till seven years old. . . . He yielded and said it was best it should live with him —he promised faithfully never to give it until seven years of age into a stranger's care. I was to be called the Child's Aunt and in that character I could see it and watch over it without injury to anyone's reputation. Believing in these promises in the spring of 1818 I sent my little darling to him. She was the only thing I had to love—the only object in the world I could call my very own : and I had never parted with her from her birth not for an hour even and I had provided as her nurse a very superior Swiss woman of about thirty, a mother herself ; this person I had kept with me many months in order to ascertain her real disposition. I found it to be good and gentle ; and she was the person who took the Child from Milan to Venice. I did not go myself for I feared he might put a bad interpretation upon my coming into the city he inhabited. I will say nothing as to what the parting cost me—but I felt that I ought not

262

for the sake of gratifying my own affections deprive her of a brilliant position in life. From Milan we went into Tuscany. The nurse I mentioned wrote to me every week to state how the Child was. About three months afterwards I got a letter from her in which she told me that the day before, Lord Byron had been in the nursery and sat some time observing Allegrina at play. Of a sudden he said to the nurse, ' She will grow up a very pretty woman and then I will take her for my mistress.' Elise was shocked and said, ' I suppose My Lord you are joking, but even as a joke, it is a very improper one.' He answered he was not joking at all. ' I'll do it.' She seemed still further shocked. He then said—' I can very well do it—she is no child of mine—She is Mr. Shelley's child.' Next day she wrote me what had passed. On reading her letter I felt extreme indignation and extreme alarm. For the first time there rushed into my mind the idea that he was a most wicked man. I shewed Elise's letter to Lady M.[1] and asked her advice—and she was of opinion I must go to Venice directly, withdraw Allegra from his protection and drop all intercourse with him. She promised to give me the means to emigrate with my Child to Australia—and there I would set up a school and earn our breads and far from the wicked live a peaceful life. I must tell you Lady M. on two accounts had ever had a bad opinion of Lord Byron ; first from his writings she thought them the greater part of them calculated to demoralize rather than elevate. Everywhere he

[1] This is supposed to be in August, 1818, when Claire went with Shelley to Venice, but she did not meet Lady Mountcashell (Mrs. Mason) until January, 1820.

sneers at Truth, Virtue, Justice, Benevolence and considers them as Utopias—He describes fatal impulses in Love, fatal impulses in Hatred with great strength and idealized them by poetry as far as ugly deformed things can be idealized, and it was this constant inclination in him to treat only painful subjects which made her distrust him. She constantly said the soul becomes like what it contemplates and no man who invariably recreates his intellect with subjects full of vicious disorder can be anything but a bad man. His writings gave her the impression that Fury was his wisdom, revenge his religion . . . She was a passionate admirer of Shelley's writings, not that her mode of belief agreed on many subjects with his, but she said every line of his inspired the reader with a holy enthusiasm for good.

2. *Extract from another Letter*

. . . Shelley as you know adored Genius—Lord Byron possessed it undoubtedly—at that period this was sufficient to decide Shelley to think no ill of him. Three years later he altered his opinion and became convinced that Lord Byron's genius was a fatal gift that developed in him inordinate pride and a dryness of heart and fierceness of feeling most dangerous in theory as in practice.

3. *Letter written from 83, Via Valfonda, Florence* circa *March 1870, evidently in answer to Trelawny's letter of February 1st, 1870* (Letters, *ed. M. Buxton Forman*).

. . . I have read two articles in the Saturday Review upon the History of Medora Leigh. You say it is all true—in that case the likeness in character Georgiana and Medora Leigh bore their Uncle is very striking. Same love of doing wrong, same hatred of those who had once been dear to them, same irrepressible instinct of defaming those who offended them. It really would half justify one in supposing they were his children. However that may have been, there are few daughters who would not rather have died than breathe one word of a tale so ruinous to their Mother's reputation and happiness. Poor Mrs. Leigh! What with her Brother, and what with her two daughters, she must have undergone torture. There is no positive proof that the connexion between L.B. and Mrs. Leigh existed ; but his verses to Augusta, are far more passionate and tender than were ever before written by a Brother to a Sister—then his fit of hysterics at Bologna when he witnessed the performance of Myrrha—then Manfred and Cain—all form presumptive evidence against him. It is also so odd that he never went to England to see Ada though he was so fond of her ; was it because he knew that Lady Byron had full power to forbid his seeing her ?

[She admires Trelawny's magnanimity in granting Whitcomb his life (" I took the rope off a man's neck —as my men were about to hang him for assassinating me—so you may leave Byron alone ") and pleading in excuse for Byron, but goes on :]

But never, never, neither here nor in Eternity can I, nor will I, forgive the injuries he inflicted upon my defenceless Child. I should be the vilest of traitors if I did not remain faithful to her memory and the eternal foe to her destroyer. I am pretty sure you do not know the real history concerning her. If you did you also would judge L.B. with the severity he deserves. It seems difficult to believe, but nevertheless, you at least know that it is true, that for fifty years I have kept a profound silence with every one on the subject of her wrongs : for all that long space I never mentioned his name, never read his works nor any that were published concerning him. This ought not to cause wonder—so dreadfully had he made me suffer, the chill of Death fell upon my heart if anything recalled him in the most remote degree to my mind and of a necessity I shrouded myself in silence. But now that in spite of my resolution I have been forced by that strange report about Allegrina,[1] to recall the past, I will relate to you all that which I feel pretty sure you have ever been ignorant of—not all for I have not room—but at least some part. When you hear all about the Convent he shut her up in, I think you will conceive some suspicions that he did not mean fair play by his poor Child. Bagnacavallo is situated in a very slight eminence. On the side that looks towards Ravenna it is tolerably healthy. On all its other sides at some distance however, the country is one immense swamp which extends for miles to Argenta on the road to Bologna. When the wind blows from that quarter, Bagnacavallo is infested

[1] A report that Allegra had not died. On this Trelawny had written (*Letters*, Nov. 27th, 1869) : ' If I was in Italy I would cure you of your wild fancy regarding Allegra . . . I cannot conceive a greater horror than an old man or woman that I had never seen for forty-three years claiming me as Father.'

with Malaria fever and is considered an unhealthy spot. The fever that prevails they call there " wandering typhus ", it attacks the townspeople but especially strangers and it was of this fever my poor child died. . . .

The convent was inhabited by Capuchin nuns, the most ascetic of all the religious orders : they are professed mendicants, can never possess so much as sixpence of their own, and *must live on alms.* Ask any Catholic, or consult any book that treats of the subject, and you will find that the order of Capuchins (men or women) renounce every comfort and devote themselves to the practice of the most terrible austerities. Once a week at midnight, in their Chapel they scourge themselves with an iron chain, they never touch meat, the winters in Romagna are extremely severe, but no fire is ever allowed in that Convent, except what is just necessary to make sometimes a little soup. And the building is of course in keeping with the severity of the order, and is dark as a prison, gloomy, damp walls and almost bare of furniture. You may think what pangs of anguish I suffered in the winter of 21 when I saw a bright fire, and people and children warming themselves by it, and knew my darling never saw or felt a cheerful blaze and was more starved with cold than an English pauper Child in our Unions. And how I trembled for the consequences and lived every day and every hour in fear of bad news, and went about wildly from one to another, imploring them to help me to get her out, and received everywhere a refusal to do anything, and the advice to be patient and wait more favorable events. In this life, one dies of anguish many times before one really dies. And not the promise of cycles and cycles of unbroken felicity could bribe or win me to live over again that period and re-suffer what I then suffered. . . . Countess Ginnani told me last Autumn when I saw her in Ravenna, that no well-to-do person (she used the expression of *Benestante*) would think of sending their child to that Convent of Bagnacavallo.

4. *Extract from another Letter* (circa *1870*) *with reference to the Convent*

Bagnacavallo did not depend upon the Bishop of Faenza but upon the Bishop of Ravenna—moreover the child was not placed in the Convent by Lord Byron, but by the Countess Guiccioli and every notice that was sent concerning her, was addressed to the Countess G. and not to her father. . . . Mr. Tighe saw Countess Benzoni who gave him letters for Ravenna where he heard that La G. was jealous of Allegra and disappointed that she had no children. " Abbiamo fatto il nostro possibile, ma non abbiamo figli e questo è una gran croce per Milordi e me, segnatamente quando penso che quella giovane inglese di buona nascita gli ha fatto una Bambina."

5. *Extract from Letter* (circa *1870*)

One of Byron's principles was that in this world you must either inflict misery on others or they would inflict it on you—and he would rather be an inflicter than be inflicted upon. [Story that in Constantinople he had had a woman thrown in the Bosphorus and that Thirza] was a young girl whom he had seduced and had two children by ; that she wanted him to marry her, but he would not and went to the East and she committed suicide and was buried in a cross row which was the reason he could not erect a stone to her memory—he said he fretted very much about her death, but nothing, not even that would have made him marry her because she was of mean birth.

[There follows the story of her visit to Diodati quoted in Part I, p. 67.]

6. *Extract from another Letter with reference to Diodati incident, with following addition :*

. . . none knew that secret besides us, Lady Byron and Lady Caroline Lamb. Lady Byron had obtained it by breaking open his secretaire, and he himself had told it to Lady Caroline. When he quarrelled with the latter, she was very wroth, and he understood she had talked of what he had confided to her : in order to render her treachery innocuous, he said he was compelled in his own and his sister's defence, to discredit her by asserting that she used to visit him disguised as a waggoner and also that she had hired two men to waylay and assassinate him . . . I considered these ebullitions as temper . . . what wretchedness it is to be young and to believe that human beings are incapable of harbouring bad passions in their breasts.

7. *Extract from Letter* (circa *1870*)

. . . You state that the elopement of Shelley and Mary was effected without concealment—this is incorrect—Mary had given her solemn promise to her father not to do so and went at the end of June with me to see Harriet in Chapel Street at her father's house. I was present at the whole interview and heard Mary assure Harriet that she would not think

of Shelley's love for her.[1] At this time Mary did
not see Shelley that I am aware of, before his declaration of love we both used to walk with him in the
Wilderness of the Charterhouse and also to Mary
Wollstonecraft's tomb—they always sent me to walk
at some distance from them, alleging that they wished
to talk on philosophical subjects and that I did not
like or know anything about those subjects I willingly
left. I did not hear what they talked about. After
Mary had seen Harriet with me in Chapel Street at
the latter part of June 1814 and given her the assur-
ance that she would not yield to Shelley's entreaties
which was certainly her sincere intention at this time
—Shelley bribed the porter of our shop to deliver
letters to Mary—in these he declared unless she joined
him as Partner of his Life—he would destroy himself
—Poor Mary was agitated by these letters and by the
recollection of an attempt at suicide which he had
made a few weeks before—she knew not what to do
—if she shewed these letters to her Father and he
took measures to prevent the correspondence she
believed firmly Shelley would destroy himself—thus
much she told me and wept bitterly—apparently overcome with apprehension she wrote her consent to
fly with him. She never told me of it—I only knew
it at the Corner of Hatton Garden as we walked out
early up Holborn Hill on the 28th of July, in order,

[1] Harriet Shelley refers to Mary's threat of suicide in *Letters
to Catherine Nugent* (1889), but does not mention that she was
visited by Claire. In view of Claire's other inaccuracies it is
not possible to accept her version of the elopement ; e.g. Shelley
refers to fetching trunks and Claire could hardly have been
unaware of this.

Extracts from Unpublished Letters to Trelawny

as she said, to breathe a little morning air in Marylebone fields . . .

8. *Extract from Letter, December 26th, 1870. In reply to Trelawny's letter, April 3rd, 1870, where he says : 'Mary was the most conventional slave I ever met—she even affected the pious dodge . . .'*

I can at least tell you what I know with regard to Mary Shelley's religious beliefs. We often talked on the subject ; I never saw the smallest appearance of hypocrisy in her on this point, and I believe in her attendance at Church she followed the impulse of her convictions and feelings. What is more natural when one's happiness lies in ruins around one than to hope there is a better world ? Had not Mary sense enough to perceive that on Earth no Joy may ripen and that the human heart must not dare to cling to any felicity ? Have you not yourself known that Happiness, when we most worship her, repulses us with cruel severity ? And why should it seem strange that Mary drew from this experience the deduction that we do not belong entirely to this world, else there had been no such thing as Death, nor any such thing as a deep, life-long sorrow for those we have loved and lost. My own firm conviction after years and years of reflection is that our Home is beyond the Stars, not beneath them. Life is only the prologue to an Eternal Drama as a Cathedral is the vestibule of Heaven. . . .[1] My

[1] Trelawny replied to this in letter, January 17th, 1871 : ' Dissatisfied with this world, you have faith in another—I have not,' and, ' as to Mary Shelley, you are welcome to her ; she is nothing but the weakest of her sex.'

271

life has been most desolate ; no one cared for me no one helped me.

9. *Note to Trelawny on Shelley's letter of December 30th, 1816*

As you will.perceive he wrote this letter on his marriage day with Mary about a month after Harriet had drowned herself. As soon as Mr. Godwin heard of that dismal event he wrote to Mary to come to London immediately for he would insist upon S's marrying her.[1] Shelley as you see in the first paragraph of this letter considered this precaution unnecessary.

My Mother in a letter related to Lady Mount-cashell that Mary came at her father's call and they both went to Skinner Street and Mr. Godwin and Shelley had an argument as to whether the latter should marry Mary. Mr. Shelley repeated all his reasons against marriage and seemed determined not to perform the ceremony. Mary was sitting at another part of the room listening attentively—when there seemed no likelihood of either party agreeing, she rose and coming up to Shelley, put her hand on

[1] That Shelley did not need this persuasion to marry Mary is clear from his letter of December 16th, 1816, written the day after he received the news of Harriet's death and referring to his ' nominal union.' See p. 77.

The paragraph referred to reads : ' Dearest Clare, Your letter to-day relieved me from a weight of painful anxiety. Thank you, too, my kind girl for not expressing much of what you must feel, the loneliness and the low spirits which arise from being entirely left. Nothing could be more provoking than to find all this unnecessary. However, they will now be satisfied and quiet.'

his shoulder and said—" Of course you are free to do what you please—and I am free to act as I like and I have to tell you, dear Shelley, if you do not marry me, I will not live—I will destroy myself and my child with me." Shelley turned a little pale, looked at her steadily and reading determination in her countenance, said " If such are your intentions of course I will marry you, but allow me to say, that your mode of action leaves me no liberty whatever." The next morning Mr. Godwin asked when the ceremony was to be performed. Shelley said he had given his word and he would keep it, but out of respect to Harriet he would like to postpone it for a year. Mr. Godwin objected and at last it was settled to ask Sir Lumley Skeffington's opinion whether it was proper to marry immediately after the first wife's death. Sir Lumley was asked—all the circumstances were placed before him, only the names of the parties were not mentioned. He gave his dictum in favour of an immediate marriage, saying where the greater etiquette had been violated, the smaller one must give way. And they were married.

All this part I transcribe from my Mother's letter.[1] She makes some remarks about Mary's conduct being worthy of the Authoress of Frankenstein, which she had read in Manuscript, also of the sagacity she shewed in threatening him with a third suicide on his account in the very room in which he had lived so familiarly both with Harriet and Frances and she thinks their two shades must have risen to his mind, and forced him to the conclusion he came to. His letter to me

[1] Unfortunately there is no copy of this letter of Mrs. Godwin's.

confirms this idea. He says how dreadfully melancholy Skinner Street appears to him with all its associations. " The most horrid thought is how people can be merry there ! " " But I am determined to overcome such sensations," he goes on to say—" if I do not destroy them, I may be myself destroyed." These words alone would prove I think that he suffered much bitter feeling in recollecting these two lost ones, lost, destroyed by their own hands, when neither were much past twenty years. Skinner Street was dull to him, but to all others it was a lively and cheerful life that had been led there till he entered it. All the family worked hard, learning and studying : we all took the liveliest interest in the great questions of the day—common topics, gossiping, scandal, found no entrance in our circle for we had been brought up by Mr. Godwin to think it was the greatest misfortune to be fond of the world, or worldly pleasures or of luxury or money ; and that there was no greater happiness than to think well of those around us, to love them, and to delight in being useful or pleasing to them. But after he carried off Mary and me— there came a change—the parents were unhappy, Frances suffered deeply—and when she died, my brother Charles was so affected by the sad catastrophe, that he fell ill and spit blood and fell into such melancholy that he was sent to Bordeaux and entered a merchant's house there.[1] It was thought complete change of scene would banish the sad remembrances associated with his home ; but he was an extremely

[1] That this is untrue and that he was kept in ignorance of Fanny's death while abroad is shown from a letter Charles Clairmont wrote on August 9th, 1817, referring to her.

sensitive person, far worse even than I was, and he remained for the rest of his life of a disponding, apprehensive disposition. My Mother does not meet with gentle treatment from Shelley. He did not understand her character and her commonplace prosy way of viewing all things disgusted him—she was cold in her manner to him, because he had withdrawn me from her protection and care, this he called heartless pride. Her affection and devotion to Godwin were admirable and remained unalterable from the day of their marriage till his death.

APPENDIX D

LETTERS FROM MRS. GODWIN TO MRS. MASON
(LADY MOUNTCASHELL). (C.P.)

These letters, copied by Claire, were also seen by
Professor Dowden, who quotes them with notes in
Appendix B to his *Life of Shelley*. In each case
Claire made several copies, with additions and deletions
of words and sentences. Typical of her " editing "
is a passage about the girls' education where ' taking
a lesson with a French mistress ' is changed to ' preparing their French exercises at the same table ' and
finally ' French ' is changed for ' Italian.'

Without further *caveats* as to their accuracy than
are given in the text and notes, I have quoted passages
here which are omitted or only paraphrased by
Dowden.

Letter 2. [The Postillions had said that they were
going to Dover] . . . Still as yet I hope she [Claire]
is safe—she is only sixteen—and as childlike in her
manners and thoughts and tastes as if she were only
twelve—no young man would feel much interest in
her I think at present, though she is clever and
interesting from her affectionate heart and cheerful
docility—and then I imagine he is thoroughly taken
up with Mary for he certainly was desperately in love
with her. Poor Mary—one must feel for her—she
shewed so much serious intention of not encouraging

276

him. . . . I have ascertained that the two girls walked every day in the Wilderness of the Charterhouse, a nice garden with old trees not far from us and the gardener's wife tells me they were always joined by a young gentleman—that must have been Mr. Shelley—she says the fair young lady and the young gentleman always retired to sit in the arbour and the little young lady used to walk up and. down by herself—in these meetings he must have persuaded Mary to elope—and have probably menaced to take his own life if she refused. . . .

Letter 3.' [Mrs. Godwin's efforts " to maintain the family in tolerable comfort and to give them an excellent education and many accomplishments."] . . . Charles knows Latin, Greek and French, mathematics and draws well. The girls have been taught by Mr. Godwin, Roman, Greek and English History, French and Italian from masters—Frances and Mary draw very well—Jane could never draw and therefore she had learnt music and singing. And Mrs. B.[oinville] observed what a terrible drawback it would be to Willy if he knew only reading writing and arithmetic which is all the learning we could give him without being helped in some way.

Letter 4. . . . Perhaps you will be vexed with me, but I mentioned you to him, as our friend, and being distinguished for your genius, your liberal opinions and every virtue and yet how different you were from him, for let a woman be as poor or ignorant as possible I was certain you would consider her maternal feelings as worthy of as much care, consideration and respect as those of the most refined and

277

educated lady. I implored him to let me see my daughter . . .

[Shelley bought them bread at Dover. Mrs. Godwin, when she saw Jane, said to her :] " you have lost your bright colour a good deal, how is that ? " She said she had had an inflammation in her side in Switzerland from walking so much and had been much bled, and also Mr. Shelley would not let them eat any meat and both she and Mary felt weak on this diet and had grown very pale . . . C.[1] always walks with him and gets into trouble because she has not time to do all the lessons he sets her. Mary is often very cross with C. The latter asked the reason of it but Mary denied being so except when C. was stupid. She then asked Mr. Shelley the same question and he replied that he thought Mary was jealous of his giving her instructions. I asked C. if she liked Mr. Shelley and she answered with her usual enthusiasm that she thought him absolutely perfect. On leaving her I had much to think of. I am grieved she has abandoned her musical studies. I am uneasy at Mary's being jealous of her ; stupid she always thought and called C.—because she has not such first rate abilities as her own. . . .

Letter 6. . . . In the bitterness of my heart I wrote to Mr. Shelley and enclosed Mrs. Bishop's [2] letter and I reproached him with having deprived my poor Child of her home and made her an outcast in the world. He wrote back to say he should never

---

[1] " C." is written as an abbreviation for " Claire," but in fact Mrs. Godwin never called her anything but " Jane."
[2] Mrs. Bishop was Fanny's aunt.

regret having rescued one victim from the tyranny of prejudice and then a long discourse on the evils of society, very fine, very eloquent, but too long for me to insert here. He at the close of his epistle acknowledged that very likely she was injured by his conduct in the opinion of the world and as a compensation and being anxious for her welfare as she was a nice dispositioned girl, he had come to the resolution of leaving her an independence in his Will. This of course calmed my anxieties as to her ever coming to want bread and I feel grateful, most grateful, to him that he is so careful of her future welfare. I never could have believed that such a harum-scarum man could be so thoughtful.

Three years ago I visited my sister at a little village called Lymouth on the sea coast of Devon and there made acquaintance with Mrs. Bicknell the widow of an Indian Officer. . . . You may think my dear friend, how I rejoiced to get her out of Mr. Shelley's clutches and what hopes I now entertain that a respectable career may open for the poor girl who has incurred such a stain without any fault of her own. My satisfaction would be complete if down there she meets with a good husband and gets settled for life.

[Mrs. de Boinville on Shelley] . . . as regards genius Mr. Shelley has more of it than anyone that has ever existed but she says it is marred by his intense self conceit which makes him despise every one who does not think like him. She thinks this defect arises from his having been born a Protestant and having been bred in a Protestant country. I do not see what that can have to do with it but I am no judge of these sort of things. I remember Mr. Godwin telling him once that he was too young to be so certain he was in the right—that he ought to have more experience before being so dogmatic and then he said some Saint, St. Cyril I think, but I know the name began with a C., had spoken most wisely that Humility was Truth. Mr. Shelley laughed and said he would listen to Socrates or Plato but not to a Saint as he could not see any merit in Past ages except in the Pagan republic of Athens. I could tell you much more if I was not at the end of my paper.

APPENDIX E

1. *Unpublished letter from Mary Shelley to Alexander Berry, brother-in-law of Edward Wollstonecraft, who was brother of Mary Godwin.*

The meeting between Alexander Berry and Edward Wollstonecraft is described in an article from *The Scottish Australasian*, April 5th, 1919.

' When he [Berry] embarked on the Spanish ship at Lisbon (1810) there was an English passenger on board, who had come from England on the vessel. This gentleman made no overtures to speak to a fellow countryman, but rather the reverse. Berry found his name was Wollstonecraft and that he was connected with the business firm that he corresponded with, so Mr. Berry introduced himself to the " tall, formal-looking young man dressed in black," who was destined to become his partner in business and whose sister he was to marry and whose names would be associated together as long as Wollstonecraft and the Berry Estate are residential suburbs of North Sydney. . . .'

[Envelope dated
SYDNEY, *July 19th, 1848.*]

24 CHESTER SQ.
28 March.

MY DEAR MR. BERRY,

You are very kind to write to me. It always gives me great pleasure to hear from you. It is pleasant to

281

know that I have a connection so far off who takes
interest in my fortunes. Sometimes I have thought
that the feeling solitude with which you felt assailed
after losing your dear wife might impel you to revisit
this country—& should have been delighted to give
you a cordial welcome. This feeling has probably
worn off by this time, & you are too great a man in
Australia—& your interests & influence there are too
great to allow of your coming home, is it so ? or is it
possible that I may see you ? Percy & I are the
nearest relatives of Elizabeth—indeed I believe her
only ones left (for I think our Uncle Charles, who
went to America left no family) & we should be most
happy to welcome you under our roof—if the epidemic
of revolutions leave us one. It is terrible to write
such words half in jest—but these are awful times,
the total overthrow of law, the dislocation of the social
system in France presents a fearful aspect. In Italy
& in Germany the people aim at political rather than
social change—but the French will spare no pains to
inculcate their wicked & desolating principles—& to
extend the power of their nefarious Provisional
Government all over Europe. At first indeed the
P. G. was looked on with favour—as standing in the
gaps to prevent worse anarchy—but their measures
are so tyrannical—so ruinous that they must be
looked upon as the worst engines of a bad system.
There is no doubt that a French propoganda is spread
amongst all the nations—they are rousing the Irish &
even exciting the English Chartists. Ireland is fortunate in having Lord Clarendon, a man of courage &
wisdom—but will he be able to repress all the risings
with which that country is menaced—who can tell ?

One half of Ireland detests the other half—nor have
the Irish any political grievance (for they have not
the burthen of our taxes) except that the Catholics
are forced to support the Protestant Church—with us
—the Chartists are full of menace—covert & secret
—but not the less to be guarded again—I do believe
that in England law & the orderly portion of the community will prevail, God grant it—God preserve us
from the tyranny & lawlessness now oppressing
France. I write seriously—perhaps too much so—
I perpetually see & hear of people ruined by this
late French revolution. Many English have invested
funds in the French railways & funds—& London is
also crowded with runaway French—Suppose here
also we should be runaways—We would make fight
first but if Percy & I ran to Australia would you allow
us to squat on your land ? he would pay you a fair rent,
as soon as we could raise crops & sell them. Public
matters are thrusting private ones from this letter
but I must say something of what *is* with regard to us
—Percy is just now candidate for a seat in Parliament
—the bribery & corruption practised in the last
election for Horsham has caused the Parliament to
declare it void—& Percy was entreated to come forward & to try purity of election—he has a fair chance
—of course I am anxious for his success—He is at
present at Horsham canvassing—it will be decided
next week—but I believe letters for Australia must
be posted before the 1st of the month. It will cost
a little money & that we can ill afford—but it is right
that Percy should enter into active life—& tho' I
do not expect that he will make a brilliant figure—
I am sure that his good understanding, his stainless

integrity & uprightness will command for him respect from all. Our friend Charles Robinson I am sorry to say has failed in procuring employment in this country. He has relations who could have served him —but they are inconceivably selfish—& have done nothing. He talks of taking Sidney in his way back to New Zealand. I shall send my book for you which I published a few years ago—He tells us that you smoke & find difficulty in getting cigars to your liking —Percy intends to ask your acceptance of a few which he hopes will please you. Charles deserves a better fate—I hope he will have better success in this his second emigration.

> Believe me dear Mr. Berry,
> MARY W. SHELLEY.

March 30th.

Percy is still canvassing he has a fair chance—we are all quiet here—but sad tidings are expected sooner or later from Ireland—It is the fashion here for gentlemen of London to swear in as special constables—& enrol themselves under the Commander of their district but this is all done quietly & I trust there will be no active need for them.

> I am dear Mr. Berry,
> Yrs very truly
> MARY W. SHELLEY.

2. *Letter from Claire to Bartolomeo Cini, husband of Nerina Mason, written in 1835 after the death of Mrs. Mason (Lady Mountcashell)*

DEAR CINI,

I thank you from my heart for your letter, which has greatly relieved my mind with regard to Nerina and yourself. I have been constantly and terribly worried about you ; this may surprise you, but not so much when you remember that I have very little reason to expect much of life, which has gone so very hard with me, that I cannot help always fearing for those dear to me. So you are all well ! It is a great comfort to know that. I only wish I could see Nerina, you, and the dear little girl ; but it is perhaps better to let a little more time pass before I see Nerina ; her bereavement is still too recent, and I could not help talking about it, which would renew her grief. I do not wish to write to you at length, dear Cini, because you are so very busy ; I only wish to say two or three things, before closing : firstly, I wish to tell Nerina how deeply I appreciated the beautiful and firm spirit which she showed in her sorrow ; thus she proved greater love for her dear mother, and has honoured her memory more greatly than with useless tears ; surely she who loved everything that was magnanimous and great, would have taken pride in the resignation of her daughter, had she been here to see it. Further, I should like to say to our Nerina that she is not to write to me until she feels that she can do so without upsetting herself, and further, that I rejoice to know her with you, dear Cini, and in your care : it is impossible to say what peace of mind and relief on her account this thought brings me. You are and always will be her guardian angel. Nerina is indeed happy to have found you, whilst she fully deserved to do so. I should like to ask you both to think of me sometimes with the same very affectionate friendship which I bear towards you. Heaven only knows where fate will lead me, but be it where it will, Laura, Nerina and Cini are from now onwards (with the exception of my little nephew) the beings most dear to me in the whole world. Poor Laura seems to be heartbroken and in view of her happiness not being as complete as that of Nerina, it is only natural that she should be. She and Signor Tighe have lost everything—on this last score I cannot say how much I sympathize with her, but I hope that time, and seeing the happiness of Nerina, will bring him to a reconciliation with life. Goodbye, dear Cini—give my fondest love to your Nerina for me and believe me to be always

Your most affectionate friend

CHIARA.

CASINO NERLI
VIA DELL'ORTO—*22nd February, 1835.*

3. *Letter from Claire to Bartolomeo Cini written at the age of eighty, 11th August, 1876*

MY DEAR CINI,

I am so sorry to have given you the trouble of writing twice to me about the Books, for I know that you have always far too much to do. Illness was the cause of my delay in answering and thanking you for the Books all of which I duly received but was confined to my Bed by the heat and so weak I could think of nothing. Parigi [?] was at Poretta— another doctor came and bid me go without delay to Fiesole. I was put in a carriage and threw myself on the kindness of two old maiden ladies, whom I know at Fiesole, and I am very happy with them and am recovering some strength—the air here is so fresh and pure. Still I am very shaky—Paola is in Casentino—so I was obliged to wait till my hand got a little stronger ere I could thank you, which I do most sincerely for the Books. One, your prize book at the University, gave me on that account the greatest pleasure to look at only, and recalled so pleasantly to my mind Auld Lang Syne, when Bartolomeo Cini was la Crême de la Crême of young men, in instruction in beautiful feelings and delightful manners. I find a great consolation how many distinguished and excellent and virtuous friends I have had. *Nudrirmi di memoria più che di speme* is my daily occupation. And in this way I banish from my old age that stupid Melancholy which generally accompanies that stage of life. So many loves I send to you and Margaret and Helen—also to Gianni—I do hope to see a good deal of dear Margaret next winter—if I live so long. A thousand thanks for writing to Panizzi—I hope he will sell the letters, for I want if I can get it, an addition to my Income ; it is enough for me as it is —but I want so much to give a tolerable education to dear Georgina—and that I cannot do on my present resources. And you know that now it is absolutely necessary for a young girl who probably will have to do something towards earning her livelihood to be well educated. For myself I would not sell my letters —but to benefit Georgina, but when your wound will be somewhat healed, I do hope you will do justice to your children and friends, and preserve yourself for them by retiring from affairs altogether or only doing as much as not to encroach too much on your strength. I had a letter from Marianna the other day—she has been attending the death-bed of her sister-in-law and

287

taking care of her brother Henry, who felt his loss deeply—and she bid me say how much she regrets not having yet been able to answer a charming letter which Margaret wrote her. But she will do so, as soon as she possibly can. Farewell, dear good kind Cini—you can scarcely tell how deeply grateful I am to you for your kind friendship to me. My niece joins with me in the best remembrances to you and your dear children.

Your obliged and old friend,

CL. CLAIRMONT.

I began this on the 27th Feby.—but my eyes got weak and I could not finish it until now 2nd March.

4. *Letter from E. J. Trelawny to his daughter, Laetitia, wife of Colonel Charles Call.*[1]

MY DEAR LAETITIA,

After 6 months dreary wr. it has relented and the sun shines—and after 3 months' silence I have a letter from E. Detmold not very cheerful if he is still at Rome he must pay me his promised visit—and stay in my custody—my age won't admit of delay.

Mr. John Millais our best painter asked me to sit for a great picture he was compassing—of strenth [sic] and meekness he wanted a resolute man and gentle girl he had sought in vain over Town and could not find one—I was the only one that would do—it's a £2000-er and he has done it the likeness is perfect— 2 years ago you remember Mrs. Burley[2] sent her

---

[1] Mrs. Call died on January 20th, 1938. She was Trelawny's daughter by Augusta Goring, (*née* Harvey) whom he married after her divorce.

[2] Mrs. Burley was his daughter by his first English wife.

daughter anticipating to find me bedridden, &c., &c., &c., so you see the different views the interested and disinterested take that's why I mention it—you should go on portrait painting its the most difficult—but you are inclined that way—here things are much as they were I have seen Lady Hillary—Kirkup has written he seems breaking—his brother Alfred died in the winter he married an old woman to get her money but she has outlived and got his.

If the Detmolds have left Rome—and you have his address write and tell him how anxious I am to see him here. Miss Mary sends her Love.

Your affte. Father,
E. J. TRELAWNY.

INDEX

291

Clairmont, Claire (Mary Jane) : at Skinner Street, 3–18 ; described, 11, 12 ; admiration for Mary, 12, 13 ; walks with Shelley and Mary, 15 ; invited to join elopement, 16; leaves Skinner Street, 18 ; crosses to Calais, 19, 20 ; description of Shelley, 20, 21 ; Mrs. Godwin's pursuit, 22, 23 ; in Paris, 23, 24 ; begins Journal, 25 ; walking tour to Switzerland, 25, 26 ; Journal description of French towns, 26 ; a bad night, 27, 28 ; Journal description of Switzerland, 29–31 ; decision to return, 32 ; Journal reflections and description of journey, 32–7 ; writing a book, *The Ideot*, 35 ; arrival in London, 37 ; the Godwins' boycott, 37, 38 ; Shelley's plans for education, 39 ; plans for pantisocracy, 40, 41 ; becoming discontented, 41, 42 ; Journal descriptions of Shelley's escape from duns, 43–6 ; walks with Shelley, 46 ; Journal criticism of Hogg, 47 ; discontent at seventeen, 48 ; her prevailing *accidie*, 47, 48 ; goes to Lynmouth, 49 ; letter to Fanny, 50–2 ; alters name and writes to Byron, 53 ; two letters to Byron, 54–6 ;

association with Byron, 56, 57, 58, 59 ; letters to Byron, 59–62 ; persuades Shelley to go to Geneva, 62, 63 ; wants the Shelleys to be friendly with Byron, 63 ; disappointed at Byron's slowness, 64 ; Byron's restiveness, 66 ; incident over Mrs. Leigh, 67–8 ; departure, 68, 69 ; self-confidence ebbing, 73, 75 ; at Bath, 76–80 ; extracts from letters to Byron, 76, 77, 78 ; on Fanny's suicide, 77 ; Shelley's marriage, 79, 80 ; Allegra born, 81 ; at Marlow, 82–6 ; friction with Mary, 84 ; relations with Shelley, 85 ; devotion to Allegra, 85 ; plans for Allegra to go to Byron, 86 ; Journal accounts of visit to London, 86–8 ; relations with Peacock, 87, 88 ; describes Allegra to Byron, 89, 90 ; hesitates at sending her, 92 ; final decision, 93 ; Journal account of journey south, 94–5 ; a tactless letter to Byron, 95–6 ; anxiety for Allegra, 98, 99 ; goes to Venice, 99 ; at the Hoppners', 100, 101 ; allowed to have Allegra, 101, 102 ; illness, 102 ; Allegra returned to Venice, 103 ; at Naples, 104 ; Journal account of Rome, 107–8 ;

293

portrait painted by Miss
Curran, 108 ; death of William Shelley, 109 ; Journal
records journey from Rome,
110 ; Journal records move
to Pisa, 113–14 ; the Mason
family, 114, 115 ; Mrs.
Mason's influence, 116 ;
Journal records anecdotes,
116–19 ; an adventure
with Finch, 120 ; anxiety
for news of Allegra, 121,
122 ; answers atheistic
charges, 123 ; Journal *Caricatures for Albé*, 125–6, on
Shelley, 126–7 ; goes to
stay in Florence, 127 ; Pisan
acquaintances, 127, 128 ;
meets Emilia Viviani, 128 ;
social interests in Florence,
129 ; described by Medwin,
129 ; Journal references to
Allegra, 129, 131 ; news of
convent, 131, 132 ; tribute
from Mary, 133 ; low
spirits, 133 ; an offer of
marriage, 133 ; Shelley's
visit to Leghorn, 134 ; on
the convent, 135 ; dis-
appointment at no visit from
Allegra, 136 ; plans to
travel as *dame de compagnie*,
137 ; passes Byron's coach
at Empoli, 137 ; translation
of Goethe, 137, 159 ; plans
for Vienna, 138 ; final
appeal to Byron, 138–9 ;
rash advice from friends,
139, 140, 141 ; stories from

Elise, 140 ; stays at Tre
Palazzi, 141, 142, 143 ;
meets the Williamses, 141,
143 ; on Trelawny, 143 ;
his admiration for her, 145,
146 ; death of Allegra, 147 ;
letter of reproach to Byron,
149 ; development of character, 150, 151 ; farewell
visit, 151 ; bad news, 155–
6 ; keeps to Vienna resolution, 159, 160 ; Journal
account of journey, 160–1 ;
letter on journey, 165, 166 ;
Charles' welcome, 166 ;
police investigations, 168–
71 ; dislike of Vienna, 171,
172, 173 ; plans for Moscow,
173 ; Trelawny's entreaties,
173, 175 ; in Russian
family, 178 ; Journal ac-
count of a day, 179–80 ; a
letter describing a " scene,"
180–2 ; Journal account
of a pupil's death, 183–4 ;
thoughts of Trelawny, 185,
186, 187 ; news of Byron's
death, 185 ; need for cir-
cumspection, 188 ; congenial
friends, 188, 189 ; stric-
tures on the Russians, 189,
190, 191 ; companion to
the Kaisaroffs, 191 ; leaves
Russia, 191, 192 ; visits
London, 192–8 ; estimates
of friends : William God-
win, 193, Mary, 193, 194,
Percy Florence, 193, Jane
Williams, 194–5, Hogg, 195,

Index

Date Due

CAT. NO. 23 233   PRINTED IN U.S.A.

CPSIA information can be obtained
at www.ICGtesting.com
Printed in the USA
BVHW052234130223
658470BV00009B/103

9 781013 663